HUMAN EXCELLENCE
AND AN ECOLOGICAL CONCEPTION
OF THE PSYCHE

HUMAN EXCELLENCE
AND AN ECOLOGICAL CONCEPTION
OF THE PSYCHE

JOHN H. RIKER

STATE UNIVERSITY OF NEW YORK PRESS

Published by
State University of New York Press, Albany

For information, address State University of New York
Press, State University Plaza, Albany, N.Y., 12246

Production by Diane Ganeles
Marketing by Fran Keneston

Library of Congress Cataloging-in-Publication Data

Riker, John, 1943-
    Human excellence and an ecological conception of the psyche / John
Riker.
        p.   cm.
    ISBN 0-7914-0518-4 (alk. paper). — ISBN 0-7914-0519-2 (pbk. :
alk. paper)
    1. Ethics, Greek. 2. Philosophical anthropology—History.
I. Title.
BJ161.R55 1991
170—dc20   90-34437
                                                                CIP

10 9 8 7 6 5 4 3 2 1

To Marcia
colleague, wife, soulmate

CONTENTS

PREFACE

Recently, the achievement of excellence has become a preeminent concern for our culture, as attested to by the popularity of such books as Peters and Waterman, *In Search of Excellence;* Peters and Austin, *A Passion for Excellence;* and John Gardner, *Excellence.* These contemporary discussions of excellence invariably attempt to define what excellence means for a particular kind of institution, activity, profession, or task. For instance, Peters and Waterman and Peters and Austin focus on what constitutes excellence in business practices, and Gardner identifies excellence in general with the development of a special talent for doing some specific activity or task extraordinarily well. But in the midst of developing excellent corporations and particular talents, the fundamental question of excellence remains unasked and unexplored: "What constitutes human excellence?" "What does it mean to live well as a human being?" Our culture abounds with examples of persons who develop extraordinary talents or achieve great professional success, but, who, in so doing, lose a vital part of their humanness. Professional success does not necessarily reap happiness; attaining excellence in a specialty does not mean that one has attained excellence in human living.

The aim of this book is to explore the question "What does it mean to live well as a human being?" The intended audience is everyone who is concerned with this question, whether or not they have been philosophically trained. I wrote the book in order to answer the question for myself, for although I have been professionally educated in philosophy and have been teaching the great moral thinkers for two decades, I found that I had not fully come to terms in my own life with the question of what constitutes excellence in human living. Hence, I author this book both as a philosopher and as a person raising for himself the most important question we face: "How ought I to live?"

This book is a journey into that question. I did not know what I would find when I began this exploration, or whether I would find anything. There are many signs in contemporary philosophy that it should not be asked what constitutes human nature or human excellence, either because such questions are meaningless or because there are no philosophically compelling answers available. But the question of excellence would not leave, and I found myself traveling not only to some odd places in philosophy to explore this question, but also to such foreign lands (for a philosopher) as psychoanalytic theory, ethogenic sociology, cultural anthropology, sociobiology, and emotion theory. My journey has been long. It has taken over a decade for me to research and write this book—about as long as it took Odysseus to travel from Troy to Ithaca. Its trials and pains have been many, but its discoveries and transformations have been of immeasurable worth.

Thinking is, in essence, a communal activity. The thoughts in this book come from numerous sources within the culture. Almost all of them first came to me while I was teaching in the classroom. So, I must first thank my students over the years who have been so stimulating to my thinking, especially Tim Reed and Vic Peterson for helping me with the manuscript. I must also acknowledge the mentors I know only through their writings: Plato, Aristotle, Kant, Nietzsche, Heidegger, Whitehead, James, Dewey, Freud, Jung, MacIntyre, and Kohut. I acknowledge my teachers at Vanderbilt, especially Charles Scott, John Compton, and Don Sherburne, for their wisdom and humaneness. David Norton was immensely encouraging and gave insightful criticism to an earlier draft. I thank Colorado College for its wise policies concerning research and teaching, its encouragement of interdisciplinary thinking, its grant of a sabbatical and other release time for writing this book, and its being as close to a liberal community of scholars as may be possible in today's world. But I find myself most indebted to two persons: Barry Goldmuntz and Marcia Dobson. Barry, with extraordinary care and empathy, led me through the darknesses of my own psyche to come once again to the light. Marcia is my colleague, wife, and soulmate. She has given me the Greeks, myth, insightful criticism on the text, conversation that is stimulating and thought-provoking, and a love so vital as to be the most cherished gift the gods could possibly bestow on any mortal. With heartfelt thanks I dedicate this book to her.

One final note: throughout the text I use an authorial "we," as though the reader were writing the book with me. This technique should not be interpreted as demanding the reader hold the same ideas that I do; rather, the "we" is an acknowledgement of the communal nature of thought. The "we," then, is an invitation to engage in the ideas presented here as live possibilities for thinking.

CHAPTER 1

INTRODUCTION:
HOW ARE WE TO DO ETHICS?

The fundamental task of any culture is to produce persons who are capable of carrying out the necessary tasks for that culture to survive and believe in itself. The crucial ingredient in this productive process is a set of values that tell the members of that culture what kind of humans they ought to be and how they ought to live and act. For most people in most cultures over the course of human existence, these values are so embedded in the fabric of social life that they go unquestioned. They are as normal a part of existence as the change of the seasons and the contours of the landscape. But at some crucial moments in the history of a culture, the regnant values become not just a matter to be lived out but a matter for inquiry. This is the moment in which ethics is born.

In our culture, it was the Greeks who first raised the question of how we as human beings ought to live. The answer they gave to it was so incredibly powerful that it has shaped the process by which our culture has produced individuals for two and a half millennia; that shaping has transformed not only the West but the entire world. The formation of this answer was the work of such thinkers as Socrates, Plato, Aristotle, the Epicureans, and the Stoics. They differed in the details they gave to the ideal (and the details are important, for sure); but they all agreed on the basic structure of what constitutes excellence in human living. Although the answer they gave went through important permutations and transformations in succeeding historical epochs, its basic thematic structure remained intact until the creation of the modern world in the eighteenth and

1

nineteenth centuries. It was then that social, economic, and ideational
forces destroyed the Greek ideal[1] and left our culture without a firm
vision of excellence that we ought, as humans, to achieve. We still
produce persons according to the old ideal, but can no longer justify
or fully believe in the ideal. It is the loss of this ideal that lies behind
the contemporary crisis of values, and overcoming this loss is the major
task we ethicists must now accomplish.

The ideal of human excellence, of how we humans should live if
we wish to live well, that the Greeks invented can be simply stated:
to live well is to live ethically. What "the moment of ethics" produced
in Greece was the commitment to remain in this state of self-conscious
awareness of values, not to just accept what the social order demanded
but to continually attempt to live according to values that had a
deeper, more fundamental source of justification than the more or less
arbitrary values of one's particular community. Socrates' dialectical
inquiries undermined old norms, and the philosophic schools of the
fourth century B.C. searched for a new, more abiding basis for value.

The quest to live ethically—to live according to values that one
has determined to be right—necessarily brings with it the values of
individualism and critical inquiry. While the Greek ethic demanded
that persons be members of a community in order to live ethically,
this living in community is far different from the kind of living in
community done by people who do not question the primary values
of their cultures. To be ethical, individuals must question the relations they have to their cultures, achieve distance from them, examine
the ground of values, and then determine what the proper relation
to the community ought to be. Above all others, Socrates gave birth
to and exemplifies ethical life. Not only did he invent a powerful
method by which he could question traditional value claims, but also
had as his mission making his fellow Athenians question the culture's
values, too, a mission he would not give up even in the face of being
put to death for it.

For us this ideal of being an individual critically searching for
values beyond those in the immediate culture may sound trite, but
in the fifth century B.C. it was a vision of a new form of human existence, a new way of organizing the psyche and relating to one's culture.
It was a path out of the devastating forms of human existence that
led to the destruction of Greece in the Peloponnesian Wars. In those
preethical forms of life people either were tied to social roles and acted
from the value structures of those roles[2] or, as Athenian drama portrayed, were driven by overwhelming emotions, desires, and psychic
forces. In neither case were people in control of their lives: they were

ruled by their social circumstances or a flux of violent, impersonal psychic forces. Socrates witnessed great heroes destroyed by immense emotional and divine forces on the dramatic stage; he constantly heard of the power of fortune (*tuche*)[3] controlling human destiny, and lived through the defeat of Athens and its Periclean ideals. He realized that as long as humans had psyches that could be pulled this way and that by the emotions and social pressures of the moment, and so long as societies were in a constant state of social turmoil due to conflict between competing factions (*stasis*), there was little hope of human happiness.

In contrast, ethical life is a life of self-mastery, a life in which individuals are able to rule themselves and to live in a community of like-minded people. The philosophers found a new ground for human action, one that was neither socially nor subjectively determined— grounds that always caused conflict between societies or individuals. This new foundation for activity was a universal and objective truth that could be apprehended by a power of reason freed from social prejudice and raised to a position of dominance within the psyche.[4] Just as the sculptor of the great west pediment of the Temple of Zeus at Olympia carved an unperturbed Apollo standing above the chaos of the battle between the centaurs and Lapiths, guaranteeing a positive outcome, so the Greek philosophers created the vision of a power of reason that could know the final verities of the world and overcome the powerful conflicting forces raging inside the psyche.

It is the merger of the individual with the universal that allows the individual to critique any particular social order, overcome the power of momentary desires, give life meaning, and achieve autonomy in a way that is harmonious with all humans achieving a like autonomy. (Although, as we shall soon see, the idea of ethical life occurring in a particular community with particular values must be balanced against the universal. This is the Greek world, not the Enlightenment.) However, the path to such a state of self-mastery is arduous. How are we to achieve self-mastery? How can we come to live ethically?

The key to attaining an ethical life for the Greeks was the proper arrangement of the psyche.[5] Without the correct organization of the capacities and powers of the psyche, ethical life is simply impossible. Hence, ethics requires a moral psychology that understands the crucial parts of the psyche and how optimally to arrange them. The optimal structuring of the psyche for the Greeks was governed by five fundamental principles.

First, the many parts of the psyche must achieve a harmonious unity such that all parts work for the good of the whole person over the course of a lifetime. Fragmentation or multiplicity in the psyche is an evil, for it causes disruption and conflict, enervates the psyche, and leads the psyche away from its final good.

Second, such a unity can be achieved only if reason is capable of attaining wisdom and directing the rest of the psyche. Emotions and desires, being bent only on their own immediate gratification, always fragment a person unless they are controlled by the power of reason; for reason is the sole capacity we have that can gain a vision of who we are as whole human beings living from the past into an indefinite future. However, our capacities to reason cannot function unless we attain knowledge. (Acting on reason based on ignorance is no better than being driven by social forces or emotions). Hence, part of ethical life must be the attainment of wisdom concerning what human beings are and what they ought to be. It follows that ethical life is also a life that involves the pursuit of philosophic and scientific wisdom.

Third, developing the power of reason is not sufficient for becoming ethical, for reason could still be overwhelmed by other forces. It is necessary that reason achieve a place of dominance in a psyche that is hierarchically organized. As Plato says, "the soul of a man within him has a better part and a worse part, and the expression self-mastery means the control of the worse by the naturally better part."[6] Hierarchy is present not only in the psyche but in every aspect of existence. For instance, in Aristotle's universe, the Unmoved Mover rules the heavens, the heavens rule earthly activity, masters rule slaves, men rule women, parents rule children, reason rules the psyche, and the psyche rules the body. It is crucial in understanding Greek ethics to see how the concepts of unity and hierarchy become merged so that one cannot be thought without the other. One of the purposes of this book is to separate the concepts and show how unity is possible without a hierarchical ordering of the elements in a system.

Fourth, the hierarchical organization of the psyche can be achieved only if we develop proper character traits, the virtues. The Greeks knew that reason alone could not accomplish the task of directing activity. For this, one needed virtues. The Greek concept of virtue (*arete*) is quite different from the one we have received from Victorian Christianity.[7] A virtue is that which enables anything to perform its function well, where the function might be a social role or whatever a thing or species alone can do or whatever it best can do. Hence, the virtue of a knife is sharpness, and the virtue of an eye is sight. For us to know what are our virtues as human beings (rather than our virtues as flute players or ship pilots), we must know what our human function is. Aristotle states it as follows:

> For just as the goodness and performance of a flute player, a sculptor, or any kind of expert, and generally of anyone who fulfills some function or performs some action, are thought to reside in his proper function, so the goodness and performance of man would seem to reside in whatever is his proper function. What can his function possibly be? Simply living? He shares that even with the plants, but we are now looking for something peculiar to man. . . . Next in line there is a life of sense perception. But this, too, man has in common with the horse, the ox, and every animal. There remains then an active life of the rational element.[8]

Here is not only the framework for the development of a theory of virtues, but also the justification for why reason is to organize the psyche. It is our natural function to become rational, and when we use our rational capacities fully, we reap happiness. What allows us to develop our reasoning capacities in both practical and theoretical affairs are the virtues. The moral virtues for Aristotle are those character traits that neither suppress the desires and emotions nor let them overwhelm us. They are character traits that give practical reason material on which to operate and the state of mind to deliberate well over what to do. It is always the mean or the moderate disposition that gives these possibilities; hence, moral virtues are defined as the mean. For instance, in reaction to the emotion of fear that arises in dangerous situations, we can either repress the emotion and face whatever is threatening us, however dangerous (rashness); be overwhelmed by the emotion whenever it occurs, and flee (cowardice); or develop the trait of courage, which lets us experience the emotion, deliberate about the possibilities, and then choose the best course of action. The character traits of rashness and cowardice do not let reason direct the psyche, for they are obsessive and allow no variability of response. It is the virtues that give us flexibility and allow our rational capacities to direct our activities in all human affairs.

While the moral virtues direct practical life, the intellectual virtues allow theoretical reason to attain its end: knowledge of the final principles (*archai*) by which nature works. This knowledge is crucial not because it gives the possibility of a technological mastery over nature, as it did for the Enlightenment philosophers and scientists, but because such knowledge joins us with these final principles and overcomes our insufficiencies as mortal human beings. When we contemplate these final verities, we become like the gods. "[T]he

activity of the divinity which surpasses all others in bliss must be
a contemplative activity, and the human activity which is most closely
akin to it is, therefore, most conducive to happiness."[9]

⑤ The fifth great principle for attaining the proper organization of
the psyche is community, for the virtues can develop only if we live
in communities that instill them, and the power of reason can develop
best in enlightened educational systems. A community is a set of
people webbed together through friendships and a shared ideal of what
is good. Unlike contemporary Western society, which assumes that
humans are in a fundamental competition with one another for scarce
resources, the Greeks found that self-fulfillment could occur only in
a social environment in which the actualization of one's individual
good provided good for the community and vice versa.[10]

The community is also responsible for fostering language, and it
is crucial for the ascendance of reason in the psyche that the proper
language be spoken. This is the language of philosophy. Whenever
Socrates encountered an ethical claim couched in ordinary language
(as illustrated in the *Meno*) or was given a poetic rendering of life (as
by Agathon in the *Symposium*), he countered with a philosophical
discourse that rendered the previous speech impotent. Plato censured
the poets, and Aristotle claimed that philosophic wisdom had a higher
place than productive (artistic) knowledge. It is little wonder that
Plato, Aristotle, Epicurus, and the Stoics all founded schools—
communities in which a philosophic ideal of ethical life could be
achieved in both language and human relations.

The proper organization of the community mirrored that of the
psyche. The community would be healthy—unified and free of factional
disputes and disruptions—only when the rational element in society
gained a hierarchical ascendancy, be this in the form of a few philosopher kings or many citizens making themselves wiser by sharing
their truths with one another in assembly.

The ideal is now complete: Humans live well and achieve happiness when they organize their psyches according to the principles of
unity, reason, hierarchy, virtue, and community. When reason rules
the psyche, rational humans govern the state, and our knowledge
reveals ultimate principles of nature, then we achieve a kind of perfect
self-mastery. This self-mastery is the zenith of ethical life and defines
what it means to live well as a human being. In this state we no longer
are buffeted by the vagaries of fortune, emotion, and social faction.
We are unified in ourselves, unified with others, and at one with
nature in knowledge. This is the great ideal that launched Western

culture on its journey to ascendancy in the world, and one that still informs how we create human beings today.

When we negatively reinforce inconsistent, nonintegrated behavior, we see the old principle of unity at work. Whenever we ask a child, "What is your favorite color [friend, flavor, activity, toy, etc.]?" we are teaching ranking, which is the primary process for organizing the psyche hierarchically. At the top of the hierarchy is still reason, as is evidenced by the two decades of education we demand of persons entering the middle and upper classes, virtually none of it having to do with the training and deepening of the emotions. Finally, we develop moderate character traits (virtues) to curb emotional outbursts and delay gratifications. We then take all that we have personally developed to the socioeconomic world, where in work we use it for both our own and other people's welfare. We are ideal human beings when we are consistent, able to rank priorities, guide our lives with reason, control our desires, and engage in productive social intercourse.

Thus, the ideal appears to be intact. But it is not. What occurs is the empty reproduction of the old ideal; there is little life or belief left in it, because every major value of the ideal has been challenged or discredited in the past two hundred years. That is, we keep producing members of the upper classes of the culture in the old way that has brought the West so much success, but there is a certain feeling of deadness to the process, a deep doubt that this really is the way human beings should be formed. This, I think, is what lies behind the contemporary crisis of values. We do not believe fully in the kind of human beings we are creating.

The first values of the Greek ideal to be severely challenged by the modern world were those of community and virtue. Although Alasdair MacIntyre[11] attributes the demise of virtue ethics and moral communities to the misguided Enlightenment project of discovering universal moral laws, history tells us that the ethics of particular moral traditions partially failed because people in such traditions could not peaceably resolve their disputes with one another when their religious and moral values differed. During the Reformation and early Enlightenment, countless religious communities entered into some of the bloodiest and most disruptive conflicts seen in Europe. Virtuous men and women supporting the values of their communities attempted to annihilate virtuous men and women of communities based on other values. Virtues and values tied to particular communities of belief were found to be ultimately destructive, and the Enlightenment philosophers sought to discover a universal moral law available to all rational humans regardless of community, just as Newton had discovered universal laws of motion that governed a serenely ordered nature.

It was not just their unresolvable disputes and the search for a universal morality that destroyed communities with strongly held traditions and virtues, for they might have sustained those positions if they could retain some isolation from the rest of the world. But with the coming of age of capitalism, this was no longer possible. With the approach of a universal economics, small communities with contained traditions and virtues uncontaminated by society at large had to disappear in favor of an ethic that, in Kant's words, would be true for any rational being anywhere in the universe.

But this hope for a rational ethics soon failed. Kant and Hume conclusively demonstrated that reason cannot know final metaphysical verities, although Kant thought it could objectively construct universal moral laws. Subsequent ethical theory demonstrated that no such absolutely valid laws can be proved. With Darwin, reason lost its aura as the faculty that distinguished humans from the beasts, the faculty that allowed them to rise above nature and be close to the divinities. Reason is for us what the claw is for the tiger; it is no more grand than that. We are inherently part of the animal realm and have no special *telos*, no final good for the species other than the good that informs all species: survival and reproduction. And as if more were needed, Nietzsche then unmasked reason for its manipulations and pretenses. He showed how reason, rather than controlling the psyche, was the pawn of a stronger impersonal force, the will to power. More important, he raised the question of whether a rationally directed psyche was capable of living as richly and deeply as a psyche not so organized. Reason was seen not only as impotent, but as life negating.

Other voices joined in the chorus condemning reason. Hume, Kant, Darwin, Kierkegaard, Nietzsche, Heidegger, Sartre, and the pragmatists did their work well. We can no longer believe that reason can penetrate to the ultimate verities of the world, especially verities that can ground moral life. Reason is at best a pragmatic tool for the organization of life and the exploitation of nature for human purposes.

Nietzsche, Sartre, Foucault, and Derrida also took issue with the values of unity and consistency, showing how such values limit the intensity of life and are liable to make us intolerant when we find values outside the ones that govern our unity. Freedom and life are intrinsically tied to multiplicity, not unity. To have a clear, unchanging set of values that give a fully closed unity is, in Nietzsche's terms, to be dead; in the words of more politically oriented thinkers, it is to be inherently biased to one's particular way of life and intolerant of other races, other classes, other cultures, and women.

Finally, feminism and minority movements have revealed to us the sins that hierarchy has perpetrated on those who were not allowed to be at the top of the system. If hierarchy demands that some rule others and take precedence over them, then we can expect in hierarchical systems large numbers of persons and things cast into dependence and secondary status. In the West these have typically been minorities, women, lower classes, and emotions and desires.

Many of these critiques of the Greek ideal coalesced in the work of Sigmund Freud. The Greek ideal had assumed that all the parts of the psyche were available to consciousness and could be harnessed by reason. Freud discovered that the psyche has unconscious processes that are not ordinarily accessible to conscious awareness and are not rationally controllable. Indeed, he found just the opposite—that the unconscious processes are so powerful they can manipulate reason to do their bidding without reason's even suspecting it. As Freud so poignantly says: with Copernicus we discovered we are not at the center of the universe, with Darwin we learned that we do not have a special place in the order of nature, and with himself we discover that we are not even masters of our own psyches. We can further say that the Greek ideal of rational dominance within the psyche not only failed to unify the psyche but helped drive many emotions and conflicts underground, increasing the bifurcation between conscious and unconscious experience. When only rational elements are allowed into conscious life, then what is unacceptable to reason must be banished to the dark hinterlands of the psyche. These unacceptable elements (such as oedipal desires, rage against one's parents, and narcissistic strivings) do not die but wage successful guerilla warfare against the citadel of rational consciousness.

Despite brilliant attempts by some of our finest contemporary ethicists to reinstate at least a part of the Greek ideal,[12] the above criticisms are a Rubicon that cannot be crossed. The belief that reason can know and ground itself in objective universal values metaphysically embodied in the universe is dead. The belief that we have a natural human *telos* that if realized will constitute excellence is dead. The belief that the locus of moral life is a small community of like-minded people is dead. The belief that reason can completely organize and direct the psyche is dead. The belief in the glory of hierarchical systems is dead. In sum, the Greek ideal, at least in its pure form, is dead.

For some, including myself, the death of this ideal has been freeing. Reason-dominated, hierarchical persons with their highly controlled emotions stifled life, limited creativity, crushed those with opposing values, exploited nature, and drove their psyches into dissembling self-relations. Yet those who now praise multiplicity, irrationality, and anarchy fail to remember the horrors of the Peloponnesian Wars and portrayals of tragic heroes. A return to these values brings only the same results: a world and psyche torn by factions.

We cannot reinstate the old ideal, but neither can we live in the absence of any unifying ideal. A new ideal needs to be developed, but on what grounds? The importation of ideals from other cultures (Native American, Asian, etc.) can seem forced and artificial. Rather, we must first turn to our own traditions, to the ashes of the consummated Greek ideal, to see if there can arise some truths unscathed by modern critiques, truths that can be a foundation for a new ideal of human excellence. Four such truths appear:

1. Happiness is only possible when we succeed in realizing an ideal of human excellence (hence, every ethic needs a theory of human excellence).

2. An ideal of human excellence must be grounded in an understanding of who we are as biologically and socially constituted human beings (hence, every ethic must have a theory of human nature).

3. Character traits are the chief determinants of action (hence, no ethic can be adequate without a theory of virtue).

4. The proper organization of the psyche is the *sine qua non* for being able to live well as a human being and act ethically (hence, every adequate ethic must have a moral psychology).

◻

1. Both Plato and Aristotle realized that there was a fundamental distinction between pleasure and happiness, and that the peculiar human state of happiness is the proper end for which humans should live.[13] Happiness, unlike pleasure, occurs only when we realize in our concrete existence an ideal of human excellence. That is, we are happy when we know we are living as we ought to. What this means is that if we have no ideal of excellence, we cannot be fully happy, regardless of what we do, for there will not be a sense of realizing an ideal. Hence, we cannot be satisfied with not replacing the Greek ideal, for without an ideal like it we are limited in our possibilities for experiencing happiness.

Unfortunately, the major schools of ethics that have developed since the demise of the Greek ideal—Kantianism, utilitarianism, Marxism, and existentialism—either do not raise the question of excellence or explicitly deny the possibility of defining it. Kant can tell us what a right act is and that we should perform right acts, but this leaves out most of the experiences of life. By Kant's criteria we are ethical only in situations where we might lie, steal, harm another human being, and so on. Kant himself states that there is no necessary relation between following moral laws and being happy; this is a position directly counter to that of Aristotle, in which the realization of ethical excellence in all areas of human life results in happiness, except under dire circumstances.

The utilitarians fare no better in helping us, for knowing that we are to maximize pleasure over pain does not give us a model for excellence. Do Socrates, Christ, and Gandhi weigh how their acts will give more or less pleasure? How silly. That the utilitarians confused pleasure with happiness was evident when John Stuart Mill admitted that some pleasures are "higher" than others. If they are, the criterion for their excellence cannot be pleasure itself, and, hence, we must go beyond utilitarianism if we are to discover what gives happiness in human living.

Marx emphasizes community over the achievement of individual excellence, and existentialists deny there is any achievement that would constitute a fitting end for human development. For Sartre, living authentically means giving up the belief that there is a final ideal to be achieved.

If contemporary ethical theories do not give us an ideal of excellence and the Greek ideal is dead, how are we to determine what constitutes human excellence? My answer to this question brings us to the second truth I wish to retain from Greek thought.

2. We can understand what it means to live well as a human being only when we understand what it means to be a biologically and socially constituted human being. The only way to know how to live well as human beings is to know who we most basically are as humans and what we most basically need. (This will be discussed in chapters 2 and 5). Excellence has always been tied to some form of realization-of-our-basic-nature ethic. Without a theory of what our basic nature is, there can be no ideal of what we as humans should become.

Yet the prevailing wisdom is that there is no such thing as a determinate human nature. The onslaught against theories of human nature has come from a number of different sources, sources that on other matters are diametrically opposed to one another but on the matter of there not being a human nature stand in agreement: Darwinism, existentialism, cultural anthropology, and behavioral psychology. With Darwin we find that there is no peculiar human nature; what activates us at the deepest level of motivation is the same as what motivates all living beings: survival and reproduction. There is nothing distinct about human nature. Cultural anthropology and behavioral psychology both hold that there is no human nature beyond Darwinian drives; that we come to be who we are as humans through cultural forces or conditioning events. Our nature is a virtual *tabula rasa*; it can be molded in almost any way.

Perhaps as a reaction against such biological and environmental determinisms, existentialists such as Nietzsche and Sartre propose that we have an ontologically prior freedom that can never be relinquished by any particular determination. No matter what we become—a middle-class businesswoman or a Kurd tribesman, we are free to choose to be other than we are. In Sartre's famous words, our "existence precedes our essence." But for us, the result is the same as the social and biological determinisms: there is no basic human nature.

These four powerful schools of thought have all but driven the question of human nature from contemporary thinking. But can we do without a theory of human nature, a theory that specifies what our basic needs are and what constitutes a proper functioning of ourselves as human beings? We have already determined that without such a theory we cannot have an ideal of human excellence. But the lack of a theory of human nature also prevents us from constructing just the opposite of a theory of excellence, namely, a theory of psychological pathology.

If we conceive of human nature as being only a social construction, then optimal functioning can be defined only in relation to social norms, and, hence, must be equated with "normal functioning," a term which at best is vague and at worst is repressive of all deviant forms of behavior. If optimal functioning is equated with normal functioning, then neurosis ("diseased" human functioning) must include such abnormal actions as those of geniuses, heroes, rebels, and eccentrics of all stripes. Sometimes, not being normal is a sign of fundamental health rather than neurosis, for the normality of a whole culture can be diseased, as in Nazi Germany. If the goal of psychotherapy is merely to produce human beings who can fit into the normal scheme of things, then it is a conservative institution, serving the reigning interests of the day. In order for psychotherapy to be more than this, it must have a theory of human nature that allows it to define both optimal and nonoptimal states without reference to present accepted modes of social behavior.

Just as we measure the health of an organ by whether it is performing its "task" or "work" in a proper way, so we need to know the "task" of the psyche in order to measure its health. What is the work of the psyche? I cannot conceive of any way to answer this question other than by positing a set of basic needs the psyche must fulfill. We can say a pathological condition exists when a person is chronically unable to meet a certain need or needs, and that excellence is attained when all the needs are being met. We can further say that a society is diseased if it systematically prevents all of its members, or a certain class of its members, from satisfying one or several of the basic needs.

What happens if we hold that there are no basic needs beyond the Darwinian ones? Suppose we find an adult unable to enter into any kind of close friendship, existing on the borders of the social world without any significant interaction with it, and having minimally developed cognitive and emotional faculties. This person is not interested in any kind of adventures or explorations, has little appreciation of cultural or natural beauty, and is more or less incapable of independent action. However, because of independent wealth, this adult is able to survive quite well with days filled with the pleasures of good food, baths, and passive entertainment along with a mild alcoholic euphoria. And, because of an aggressive sexuality fragmented off from other parts of the psyche, this person is able to place more than an average amount of genes in the next generation (with the children raised by adoptive parents).

Most everyone, from psychotherapists to ordinary observers, would, I hope, evaluate the condition of this person as pathological. But why? How can we say that anything has gone wrong with human development here unless we say that we have basic needs for such ends as intimacy, sociality, adventure, and autonomy, and that our emotional and cognitive faculties must work well in order for these needs to be satisfied? If all that motivates us are the Darwinian urges and a want for more pleasure than pain, then this adult is not a hideous deformation of what humans can be, but a model! That is, without a theory of what humans basically need, we have no grounds for preferring a society that produces people like this person (who reproduce and feel moderate pleasure) to one that develops institutions that help people become autonomous beings capable of intimacy, adventure, and social productivity, who delight in developing their powers of feeling and knowing. How can we say that children who are molested are mistreated, unless we can say that children have a need not to have their bodies violated, for such violations hinder the development of a healthy sexuality and a secure autonomous self, both fundamental human needs?

Thus, for both a theory of excellence and a theory of pathology, we need a concept of human nature that is grounded in a theory of basic needs. I will attempt to show in chapter 5 that we have ten basic needs: survival (or coming to terms with mortality), sexual identity, adventure, order, social recognition, intimacy (friendship), autonomy, knowledge, beauty, and sacredness. The emotional, cognitive, and self systems of the psyche are then all defined in reference to these needs; they must be developed adequately in order for the needs to be satisfied. Excellence in living occurs when we develop the psychic systems to the point where we are able to come to terms with death, develop a firm sexual identity, achieve a satisfying place in the social order of our choice, develop stable structures of values, put enough adventure in our lives to keep zestfully growing, have intimate friendships, autonomously direct our lives, transform our worlds into homes through knowledge, dwell in some form of sacredness, and respond to and create beauty. Excellence in human life is the complex affair of balancing these fundamental values.

I do not hold that the basic needs can be articulated only in the ways I express them. No one has ever empirically discovered a need— they are hypotheses to account for our behaviors—and, thus, any particular description is bound to have some arbitrariness in it. Are what the sociobiologists call "a need for reproductive fitness," what the psychotherapists call "a need for sexual identity," and what Plato in the *Symposium* calls "eros" the same need? I think so. Which description should be preferred? For what purpose? Each description fits a context—population geneticists cannot work with "eros"; Plato is not concerned with shifts in species populations.

Despite the impossibility of finding a "final" description for the needs, it is nonetheless necessary to have some articulation of them, for without it we cannot have a theory of human nature, or human excellence, or human pathology. What recommends my articulation of the needs is that I have not tried to be reductive and seek for the unity of the psyche in a single source of motivation, as have most philosophers and scientists. What moves us is multiple and conflicting; unity comes in developmentally organizing the psyche, not in a single goal or aim. I have been Hegelian in my approach to the needs. I find a part of the truth in many thinkers whom I attempt to synthesize into a new system (and indeed, I do not think an important articulation of a human need is left off my list—that is, if one is willing to make such connections as seeing the will to power as an aspect of autonomy). Unlike Hegel, I do not have a grand dialectical metaphysics or any claim to have discovered "the truth" about human nature. What I try to present is human nature in at least a part of its motivational complexity in hopes that this conceptual scheme might give us some possibility of living happier lives.

Although we can now see more clearly why a theory of human nature is necessary in order to have an ethic of excellence, we still must face two great problems. The first is that when we argue from what human nature is to what humans ought to do, we violate one of the accepted laws of ethical theory: an 'ought' cannot be derived from an 'is'; a value cannot be derived from a fact. Just because human beings have a nature, X, does not mean that the actualization of X is necessarily good. Suppose we are aggressive by nature; does this mean it is good to act aggressively? Such an inference is obviously problematical, but the alternative of attempting to discover how we ought to act without any knowledge of what human beings are is even more problematic. What is true about the is–ought rule is that any description of human nature, while a necessary condition for a moral claim, can never be the sufficient condition for such a claim. Before such a description can issue into a value, one must go through a process of moral reasoning that involves universalization and empathy,[14] takes into account that we live with other humans, and is quite capable of denying individual needs for the satisfaction of the needs of others, or of denying some needs in oneself so that others may be realized. Although this process of moral reasoning is necessary for the construction of ethical values, it alone is insufficient without some knowledge of what we as human beings most basically need.

Hence, in order to have an ethics of what constitutes human excellence, we must have both a theory of human nature and an understanding of the process by which legitimate ethical claims can be formulated. Sociobiologists such as E. O. Wilson think that a scientific knowledge of human nature is all that is needed for ethics,[15] while metaethicists such as R. M. Hare[16] assert that all we need, to have an ethical system, is the process of ethical thinking. I am claiming that both are necessary conditions for the formulation of ethics; neither by itself is sufficient.

The second rule my position violates is that of the autonomy of ethics. Ethics has been seen as a specific "language game" that has its own rules and structures of justification that can be understood and developed without reference to any other subject matter. This position sees the job of ethicists as the elucidation of these linguistic rules and justificatory structures. Ethics is seen as metaethics; ethicists are to relinquish their somewhat burdensome and embarrassing position of proposing certain ways of life as good and are to take on the more neutral task of elucidating ethical thinking so that people will know what they mean when they are making an ethical claim. Metaethicists do not need practical wisdom or a knowledge of human nature, but a sense of logic and how to examine language.

Metaethics has been extremely important, for we can now do ethics in a more self-consciously critical way. The work of the metaethicists, from Moore to Hare, has given us a much better conception of how moral language functions and how it differs from other languages. But understanding how ethical language functions is not enough; the tool of ethical language must be used to do the work of ethics, the work of inquiring into the question of how we ought to live as human beings.

Is it the job of ethicists to give answers to the question of how human beings ought to live, rather than just to elucidate the structures of moral language? Are we to leave this problem to others, holding that it is a question that each person must answer for herself, or are we ethicists to give guidance by proposing answers? These two alternatives are not incompatible, unless ethicists demand disciples and thoughtless adherence to their proposals. We need both an understanding of ethical language and proposals for how to live—proposals that can stimulate people to raise ethical issues for themselves more than do the rather dry texts in metaethics.

Thus, I hold that we ethicists need to relinquish our safe harbor of conceptual analysis and once again practice the art of practical wisdom. Ethics, as understood here, is a highly complex field, involving a rich history of texts and research into the numerous areas of science, social science, and the humanities that deal with human nature. We can no more expect that human beings with different occupations from ours will have the leisure or tools to encompass this material than we can expect ourselves to learn how to build airplanes or design infrastructures for skyscrapers. We need to explore all that we have recently discovered about human nature and to construct new theories of how we as humans ought to live. I say this with some embarrassment, for to claim to have practical wisdom about human living seems to involve also claiming that one's life is a model for living (assuming that one is an adult and acts according to one's knowledge and principles). This embarrassment is lessened by admitting that we are always fallible in forming ethical systems. As Robert Neville says, an ironic smile must grace the faces of ethicists,[17] for they know that ethical systems must be formulated and fully believed and yet that there are no final grounds for saying that any ethical system is right. Normative ethics is a task that sorely needs to be done and done well, even if it means putting ourselves in the uncomfortable position of claiming to have wisdom about human life in a world that never permits certainty in this area.

3. A third truth from Greek ethics has been discovered by a number of contemporary ethicists:[18] that character determines action in a more fundamental way than do rules. Rules or principles (such as the Ten Commandments) may be important in ethics, but only if one has already developed the character trait of acting according to principles. Without this trait, our reasons can generate moral rules *ad nauseam*, but they will not affect our actions. Character is, according to Aristotle, a set of dispositions we develop in response to our emotions and desires. Hence, character governs our relations not only to others but also to ourselves. Aristotle states this thesis straightforwardly when he writes that "the friendly relations which we have with our neighbors and which serve to define the various kinds of friendship seem to be derived from our relations to ourselves."[19] This doctrine that our relation to ourselves will mirror our relationships with others is seminal not only for Aristotle, but also for psychotherapy and the ethic proposed here.

We can see that the development of the proper character traits is a place where ethics and psychotherapy converge. Ethics is concerned with how to live well and with what constitutes right actions in relation to others; psychotherapy is concerned with the self's having a healthy relation to itself. These are two sides of the same coin, according to Aristotle's maxim, for we cannot treat others well without having a good self-relation, and we cannot treat ourselves well unless we are also willing to be ethical with others. The heart of Aristotle's ethical vision and the heart of the one proposed here is the development of a moral psychology, a psychology that defines what a healthy self-relationship is and then relates this pattern to living in a community of other human beings.

Ethical psychology focuses on the questions of what arrangement of the psyche is optimal and what traits of character will bring this optimal arrangement into being. These traits are called "virtues;" a virtue being any trait that enables us to live well as human beings.[20] From this definition we can see that before we can say which traits are virtues we need to know what it means to live well. And we cannot know what it means to live well as a human being until we have formulated a theory of human nature. My problem with much con-

temporary writing on the virtues is that the authors want to say what
the virtues are without developing a theory of human nature or saying what it means to live well as a human being.[21] This text proposes
a theory in which living well essentially involves developing capacities, character, and a self to satisfy our multifold basic needs. I hope
to show that if we arrange our psyches to meet our basic needs, we
will also develop ethical relations with others (see chapter 10). In
short, it is only when we become tolerant of all the psychic forces
within ourselves that we can be tolerant of all the different peoples
and perspectives in contemporary culture. Personal tolerance and
understanding and social tolerance and understanding cannot be
separated.

While there are many traits that enable us to realize our basic
needs, harmonize the psyche, and live well with one another, I am
in full agreement with Aristotle that the basic notion in all the virtues
is the mean between extremes relative to the person and situation.[22]
Or, as the maxim at Delphi said, "Nothing in excess." Character traits
that are virtues must be a mean to Aristotle because they allow us
to feel our emotions and desires without being overwhelmed by them.
They allow the sources of motivation for practical life to surface but
prevent any one of them from becoming a tyrannical, insistent drive.
Thus, with virtuous character traits we can have a full and rich set
of desires and emotions without being dominated by them. This moral
psychology is fully aligned with contemporary psychoanalytic theory
in which the self's relation to its desires and emotions ought not to
be one of either repression (deficiency) or infantile lack of control
(excess). A healthy state is when we can feel all of our feelings yet
govern our actions with knowledge and foresight of what is best for
us and others. (The virtue of moderation (*sophrosyne*) is discussed in
chapter 11.)

4. The fourth principle I think we must take from the Greeks is
that *the key to living well is the proper organization and unity of the
psyche.* What gives unity to the psyche is what we will call "the self"
or "the person," in distinction from the ego, which is the part of the
self present in conscious, rational activities. Unity of self is not a
genetic given or an entity, but a set of relations among the components
of the psyche that is an achievement of development (this development
is discussed in chapter 7). A human organism can have a more or less
unified self, from almost no self (as in severe schizophrenia) or multiple selves occupying the same body, to a strong, vital self that can
both feel emotions and desires and act on them with wisdom.

Unity of the psyche—a self—is needed to hold the multifarious parts of the psyche together, solve conflicts, and lead the human being into the future. Without a strong self powerful desires, emotions, social pressures, and compulsions can overwhelm the person and make choice impossible. This was as true for the Greeks as it is for contemporary psychotherapy. What was the evil of multiplicity and faction for Plato (see chapter 3) is neurotic fragmentation for psychotherapy today, where parts of psychic functioning become split off from the conscious workings of the self and act independently of its aim. Hence, the paramount issue in both psychic and social life is integration: integration of all the parts of the psyche and social world, no matter how low and despised these parts might be.

How are we to develop a strong self so necessary for the unity of the psyche? The lesson we have learned during the course of Western culture is that unity cannot be achieved through hierarchical organization, for hierarchy crushes diversity in the psyche and the social world. When reason is made the dominant element in the psyche, the irrational components (certain needs, desires, and emotions) get placed at the bottom of the hierarchy, and no language is created to communicate with them. They soon become repressed and forced out of the main flow of conscious life, just as the lowest classes, minorities, and women have been cast (caste) out of the mainstream of our hierarchically organized culture.

Our question now is clear: "What can we use as a model for organization that will produce unity without necessarily involving substantial repression or negation of certain parts of the psyche (or state)?" The democratic model of allowing all voices to have equal say at all times is too chaotic to give unity to the psyche, and the dialectical model of mediating opposites is inadequate to handle the complex multiple relationships within the psyche, only several of which constitute true dialectical oppositions.

The grounding idea for this text is that the ecological model for understanding natural systems that has recently been developed in the biological sciences is the optimal model for organizing the psyche.[23] Ecological organization recognizes that every element of a system is intrinsically interconnected with every other element and that all the elements have importance. How can we hierarchically arrange such elements of an ecosystem as the rainfall, the mean temperature, the carnivores, the herbivores the carnivores eat, the flora the herbivores eat, and the amount of nitrogen, phosphorus, etc., necessary for the flora to grow? The elimination or distortion of any one element affects all the elements in the ecosystem. The components of the ecosystem must also be in the right proportion to one another. Too many deer grazing an area is as disastrous as too few; too much reason in the psyche as harmful as too little. The series of feedback mechanisms which govern a web of causality in an ecosystem insure that the distorting element, the element grown out of proportion, will, in turn, be affected by the system it has altered. The parts of the psyche reason drives into the unconscious return to pervert reason.

Hence, with an ecological model for organizing the psyche, we can give each of its elements a proper place and proper proportion. There need not be any necessary systematic repression. We can have the genuine multiplicity of experience so loved by Nietzsche, along with the unity demanded by Plato and Aristotle.

We are now faced with a set of new problems. If ecology has discovered the way natural systems in fact work, and the psyche is more or less a natural system, isn't the psyche already functioning in an ecological way? Yes, the principles that govern ecological interactions in nature are always functional. A violent intrusion of a foreign element into an ecosystem can destroy it, but it will be replaced by a different ecosystem according to various ecological principles. The key for this analysis of the psyche is to develop an optimal ecological system—one that is able to support a maximum of diversity while retaining a homeostatic unity. Just as a number of ecosystems have been so severely interfered with that they have become unbalanced and have ceased to function as life sources to the species that formerly inhabited them, I will claim that the hierarchical model we have for organizing the psyche has made the psyche unable to harbor all of its "life forces." My aim is to develop a new model for organizing the psyche that will optimize its diverse powers and aspects while retaining a balanced unity.

In order to do this, we must ascertain what the components of the psychic ecosystem are and understand how they are dynamically interrelated. Part II of this book is an attempt to answer these questions and delineate what the psyche as a well-balanced, homeostatic ecosystem would be.

Even if we are able to change the way we organize the psyche into a balanced ecosystem, there is still a problem for ethics. Excellence in the West has usually been associated with hierarchical models. Being excellent is being the best, the highest member of a particular class. How can we speak of human excellence within the framework of ecology? Shouldn't we drop the notion altogether? But if the experience of happiness requires us to hold an ideal of excellence, doesn't such a position prevent us from being happy? There is obviously a tension between an ethic that is based on an ideal of human excellence and ecology as a model for arranging both the psyche and the social order. Part III of this book attempts to resolve this tension and show how, with the attainment of ecological speaking, thinking, and dwelling, we can attain a kind of excellence heretofore unrecognized in the West.

We must prepare for our discussions of the ecological constitution of the psyche and the ecological ideal of excellence by first gaining a fuller understanding of the relation between ideals of excellence and happiness, why the hierarchical model of the psyche was invented and finally failed, and the dangerous and ambivalent role ideals can play in our lives if they are not functioning correctly. These issues constitute the themes of the three chapters of Part I. However, before we can begin to deal with them, there is one last question we must face in this introduction.

How is one to write about an ecological model of the psyche? How is the reader to approach such a text? The book might be written in the style of this introduction, with its (hopefully) clear concepts, arguments, and unemotional delineation of problems and ideas. But if it were written this way, then it would only reinforce the hierarchical model of the psyche with reason as the dominant capacity. Hence, the style present in almost all ethical texts of importance since the Greeks cannot be used in ecological ethics.

This is not to say that we must throw reason entirely out as a number of recent theorists and artists seem to be saying. There is nothing wrong with reason per se. What has gone wrong is how reason has gotten out of balance. It has become too large and other elements have become too limited for the psyche to function well. Hence, this is not an antireason treatise, but one that attempts to place reason as one element among many in the psychic ecosystem.

In writing this text, I have tried to let a number of the voices in the psyche speak, not just reason. Those who demand rational argumentation may find my use of myth, metaphor, and symbol highly questionable and needing demystification, yet we know from psychoanalytic theory that these linguistic forms may carry to parts of the psyche truths that cannot be carried there by clear concepts and logical arguments.

There are other differences between an ecological text and a hierarchical text. One is the lack of a need for "parent-bashing," the process by which writers are supposed to attack the reigning authorities in the field so that their work may become dominant. In a hierarchical model, such antagonistic criticism is necessary, for the only way to get to the top of the hierarchy and gain legitimacy is through dethroning those now reigning. Ecologists, on the other hand, seek to understand how ideas from different views can cohere to form a wider system of understanding. This nonantagonistic style is one trend in feminist writing.

Ecological writing also differs from hierarchical writing in that it welcomes interdisciplinary modes of thinking. Hierarchies are field-dependent; reaching the top is something one can typically do only in a specialty. But just as many types of species, organisms, and nonorganic conditions constitute an ecosystem, so ecological writing attempts to see how a variety of perspectives can form a unified system for understanding human nature. Thus, in this treatise I examine human nature not only from the viewpoints of such disciplines as anthropology, sociobiology, psychoanalytic theory, and philosophy, but within philosophy I will try to interweave such diverse figures as Plato, Aristotle, Kant, Nietzsche, Whitehead, Wittgenstein, and Heidegger. We will not only study problems in how to live (ethics), but see how these relate to problems of language and epistemology.

Such interdisciplinary texts have two monumental problems. The first is that, at present, truth is defined as a function of following a particular methodology in a special discipline. Hence, I can claim to have truth in biology if I have followed the correct experimental procedures and put my conclusions in properly quantified empirical language, and I can claim truth in sociology if I have followed the accepted procedures for collecting data, and so forth. An interdisciplinary approach by definition transcends any particular methodology and therefore is supposedly incapable of generating truth.

The disciplines are of vital importance; they are the most concrete relations we have to reality. Yet the very basis for their success—a limited scope of inquiry—prevents them from giving us a whole vision of ourselves and the world. Without such an understanding, we cannot gather ourselves fully as human beings. A culture needs an integrated theory of human nature to help its members achieve personal integration. Theory and life cannot be separated.

It is this function of integrating various kinds of knowledge that gives us criteria for judging the adequacy of interdisciplinary thinking. Are the sources that are being integrated accepted as knowledge by at least a portion of experts working in established fields? Is the integration coherent, or are there contradictions and rough fits? Is the picture complete, or has the integration omitted problems and areas that need to be addressed for there to be a full discussion of the topic in question? Finally, is the interdisciplinary vision alive—does it speak to our experience? There are countless "complete and coherent" pictures in art galleries that we do not notice because they are dull or typical or simply don't call to us. Then we come across a painting that draws us into it, that relates in some primal way to our lived experience—a Rembrandt recalling us to our humanness, a Van Gogh revealing the swirling, dynamic chaos of life. Is the Rembrandt painting "true"? Is the Van Gogh landscape "true"? Here it is appropriate to remember Alfred North Whitehead's famous statement: "In the real world it is more important that a proposition be interesting than that it be true."

The second difficulty with interdisciplinary texts is their usual shallowness. Myriads of texts have been written on each of the problems, subjects, and thinkers of this book; for one text to attempt to encompass them all seems to doom it to superficiality. I admit that many chapters, and even pages, of this text need books to explicate them fully. But to demand that all books be specialized is to fail to understand the need the psyche has for seeing how its many facets can be integrated. If there is a depth to this book, it is the depth of a net stretched over the surface of human life. Each part of the net captures a bit of that life, a bit that I welcome other explorers to pursue in greater depth.

Not only does an ecological text spin webs over its multifarious subjects; it is also part of wider webs that include it. One of these wider nets is the movement in contemporary ethics away from the Kantianism–utilitarianism debates and the skirmishes in metaethics toward different ways of conceiving ethical life. New thinkers are introducing the centrality of character and virtues (Alasdair MacIntyre, Phillipa Foot, Edmond Pincoffs, James Wallace), the relation of ethics to developmental psychology (David Norton), and the relation of ethics to both metaphysics and the community orientation of Puritanism and Confucianism (Robert Neville). Within this group my text has most of its reverberations with MacIntyre, given our historical orientation, our love of the Greeks, and our finding failures in both deontological and utilitarian ethics. Where we essentially differ is that MacIntyre demands a choice between Nietzsche and Aristotle, while I think that both must be seen as representing fundamental truths of human existence. MacIntyre bases his ethic on a purely social construction of human nature, while I give more credence to biology, by grounding ethics in a set of basic needs, and to psychoanalytic theory, which deals with the psyche at levels other than those of consciousness. Finally, MacIntyre's ethics is fundamentally conservative, asking us to return to a way of life now gone; I am groping for an ethic that has yet to be lived.

Another part of the wider matrix is ecology itself. I add nothing to the structures of ecology already developed, but apply them for the first time to the psyche.[24] I think that such an "inner" ecology is as important as an ecological attitude toward our environments, for I do not think the latter can be sustained unless the former is achieved. We will always feel at odds with our environments if the structures of our psyches do not mirror the structures we find in nature.

I also raise the question of what kind of language is ecological language. That is, scientists and philosophers have written about ecological structures in the typical languages of science and philosophy. But these languages were constructed by a hierarchically constituted psyche in a hierarchically organized value system. They speak to only one part of the psyche and hence fail to engage the psyche in its fullness as an ecosystem. Hence previous speech about ecology has not been ecological speech. An embodiment of ecology in speech must be something other than the rational conceptual language of science; it must harmonize a chorus of different voices.

I also hope to show how ecological language and thinking are closely connected to hermeneutics as developed by such continental thinkers as Heidegger, Gadamer, and Ricoeur. Both ecological and hermeneutical thinking emphasize webs and intercontextuality; both locate the knowers in temporal traditions and see them as intrinsically intertwined with the material to be known. Both reject the notion that has characterized modern scientific epistemology: that one must achieve an unbiased, uninvolved objectivity in order to attain knowledge.

A third part of the wider web is feminism. My learning has been immeasurably enriched by the feminist thinkers of the past quarter century, and I wish the voice in this book to be in concert with theirs in the formation of a view of human nature and community that is nonhierarchical, not based in Darwinian competition, not valuing radical autonomy as the highest value, but centered, rather, on relationships and balances as fundamental.[25]

Finally, this text is an attempt to provide a more adequate notion of what constitutes human health and optimal functioning than what currently is available in the field of psychotherapy. Neither Freud's concept of the ability to work and love, nor the contemporary notion of freedom and the ability to make choices[26] is rich enough to encompass what makes up the fullness of human well-being. Also, I think that psychoanalytic theory needs a fuller, more complex theory of the self than is available even in the recent self-psychology of such theorists as Maslow and Kohut.

The preparation for our journey into the psyche is now complete. We have mapped out the territory we need to explore, attempted to say why such a journey is needed, and gotten our equipment ready. Now it is time to embark to that ancient land of Lydia and King Croesus where our voyage begins.

PART I

MEMORY

CHAPTER 2

HAPPINESS

Herodotus, the first historian of Western culture, commences his *Histories* with the story of Croesus, ruler of the most powerful empire of his day and so wealthy that the phrase "rich as Croesus" has remained in our vocabulary ever since. During the height of his reign, Croesus was visited by the Greek sage Solon, whom he escorted through his vast treasuries and then asked, "Solon, who is the happiest man you know?" Solon replied that it was Tellus, a middle-class Athenian who had a fine family, belonged to a good community, died fighting courageously for his country, and was given an honorable burial. Disturbed, Croesus asked who might be second on Solon's list. "Cleobis and Biton," Solon answered,

> two Argive youths, who when their mother had to go to the temple to celebrate a festival of Hera and the oxen were late coming home, yoked themselves to the ox-cart and pulled their mother six miles to the temple. They were much praised for this great feat of strength and virtue and their mother prayed to the goddess to grant them the greatest blessing that can fall to mortal man. After her prayer came the ceremonies of sacrifice and feasting; and the two lads, when all was over, fell asleep in the temple—and that was the end of them, for they never woke again.[1]

Rich, mighty Croesus is exasperated. "What of my own happiness? Is it so utterly contemptible that you won't even compare me with mere common folk?" Solon's response was even more confusing: "Until a person is dead, keep the word 'happy' in reserve."[2] Being a wise man, he also could have given the reply that the chorus gave to Oedipus

29

at Colonus or that the Silenus gave to King Midas: "The best thing is not to be born; however, the next best thing to this, and the first of those to which man can attain, but nevertheless only the second best, is, after being born, to die as quickly as possible."[3] Incomprehensible words to Croesus; incomprehensible words to us.

Croesus commences our history and is still present. Our culture, like Croesus, is immensely powerful and rich; yet we hardly need a Solon to unveil our unhappiness. For a century our poets, artists, philosophers, and social commentators have filled volumes delineating the alienation, depression, aimlessness, boredom, fragmentation, desperation, and superficiality of our present culture. The statistics on drug and alcohol abuse, suicides, crime, violence, and mental illness all confirm our literati's assessment. Despite our Croesus-like protestations, we are not a happy people, and the times are not happy ones.

What is happiness? How does one attain it? What could possibly be meant by the claim that the best thing is never to have been born and the next best thing is to suffer the wonderful fate of Cleobis and Biton and die young? Is this just an ancient form of nihilism? I think not. Oracular language rarely means what is literally said. That we, along with Croesus, find Solon's wisdom so impenetrable indicates that there might be something about human nature and living that Solon and the oracles understood, but that we have forgotten. This forgetfulness eventually cost Croesus his kingdom and lies at the heart of our unhappiness. What have we forgotten? Why have we forgotten it?

Forgetfulness is not an accidental property of Western culture; it is built into its very essence. The culture has created this forgetfulness in the way it has organized the psyches of the persons who live within it. The human psyche is rich and complex in its needs, faculties, emotions, and speech. It is like a nineteenth-century Bavarian castle, teeming with rooms, passageways, dark cellars, crazy nooks, soaring towers, secret hideaways, and terrifying torture chambers. Some of its rooms are filled with glorious riches, others are haunted by specters and ghosts. There are parapets of fantasy and dungeons full of wild, angry prisoners yanking at their chains, always threatening to wreak havoc on the world. In its push to achieve total coherence of personality and technological dominance over nature, the West has reduced the psyche to an efficient, small, middle-class home. Here everything is clear, controlled, and bright. Darkness does not exist, nor do dungeons or parapets. The psyche, like the modern architecture that reflects it, has become so directed toward a world that is rational, conscious, and functional that it has trouble remembering its parts that are dark, complex, and inarticulate. This psyche, in its values of technological mastery and the construction of a rational order, has become so powerful that it has transformed the world and produced a material wealth beyond the imagination of the richest of the ancient rulers. But the price paid for this success is that the psyche had to become small, bound inside the tight walls of the conscious ego, and cut off from the depth of emotion, fullness of memory, and complexity of functioning that alone can give happiness.

The purpose of this book is to restore memory: memory of what it means to be human and ways of living that give rise to genuine happiness. As contemporary psychoanalysis has shown and as Solon's stories indicate, the restoration of memory is an often perilous and painful journey to a place in which chaos is never fully eradicated, and happiness is intricately tied to grief.

In this new world there will once again be the possibility of heroism, for once again monsters and great forces capable of destroying the vulnerable psyche will haunt the world. There can be no heroes without monsters to conquer or boundaries to break. Our modern psyches have become so insular and protected inside the great walls of the rational ego that we have forgotten how to confront dark forces or how to embark on spiritual quests. Our magnificently structured egos have made failure and defeat almost impossible. But where there is no possibility of failure, neither is there the possibility of victory.

The land of heroes is, of course, Homer's world, the world that grounds Western literature and culture. The *Iliad* portrays the heroic world already in the process of self-destruction. Most of the Greek heroes are killed in battle, shipwrecked on the return to Greece, or ruined by domestic intrigue.[4] The hero who returns home to glory is Odysseus. His decade-long journey involves encounters with innumerable dangers and destructive forces, but the most powerful of these are also the most alluring and seductive: the lotus eaters, Calypso, Circe, and the Sirens. Although these foes differ in their *modi operandi*, they have the same goal: to induce Odysseus into a state of forgetfulness—forgetfulness about himself, his wife, his son, and his home. They lure and entrance by offering easy, unworrisome pleasures, drugs, sex, music, beauty, and even immortality. Odysseus alone among his men can resist, for he is the one person capable of living within memory. His reward is neither to become a god, as he might have, nor attain the riches of Croesus or the rule of an empire. His reward is to find his home. The restoration of memory is the rediscovery of home.

Our unhappiness indicates that our civilization, too, is in a process of wandering in search of a home, a sense of living in a way that is grounded and meaningful. Many have already been left on islands of no return. Some have been reduced to lives of animality in which food, sex, and material well-being are the sole ends of life. Others have tried to become gods by removing themselves from the sufferings and turmoil of the world through such mechanisms as intellectualization and drugged euphoria. Those who will survive this forced homelessness are those who have kept somewhere in their memories what it means to be human and who refuse to give up a search for home. They are not satisfied with nice, pleasant lives, lives that are fine, decent, full of wonderful goods, but lacking the crucial grounding that gives life its power and depth of meaning. These new explorers understand that the old order cannot be reinstated; that however glorious, the past is now dead, and its old meanings cannot ground a new world. They are willing to feel the emptiness of our present homelessness and have the courage not to make it a new home. They are willing to undertake the journey, once again, to try to discover what being human is all about.

Our voyage begins with the exploration of a conceptual landscape. Happiness, or the lack of it, motivates this search, and we must first understand this concept before we can go further. Our usual inability to distinguish happiness from other words for fulfillment—pleasure, joy, contentment, feeling good—lets us know that we have forgotten or become confused about what the experience of happiness is. A careful listening to our language lets us know that these terms for fulfillment are not interchangeable or synonymous. Cows and other beasts can be contented, but not happy. Pleasures come and go; happiness abides. Joy is experienced in an eternal instant; but as Aristotle says, "Happiness requires a complete lifetime: one swallow does not a spring make, nor does a single fine day; similarly, one day or a short time does not make a man blessed or happy."[5] This sense of happiness being a constant state of well-being is also indicated by its root, *hap*, which means chance, luck, fortune, or what happens to happen. While one might expect a pleasure here or there, how can one expect, in this world of change, famine, war, and pestilence, a constant state of well-being? To be happy really does require some good *hap*.

A number of paradoxes are associated with happiness, and unraveling them will help us grasp the unique experience that happiness is. Although it is nonsensical, or at best masochistic, to say "I am feeling pain but am also feeling pleasure," one can easily say

"I am in pain but ever so happy" (think of a woman giving birth). How is it possible to feel excruciating pain and happiness at the same time? A second conundrum concerning happiness is that it is quite possible to seek happiness but never find it. Why? This certainly is not true for pleasures, which are rather easy to find. How can some people who have an abundance of wealth, beauty, and other goods still be very unhappy, while some who are totally impoverished are happy? Why is it so hard to determine whether or not we are happy? How is it possible for individuals and entire peoples to be mistaken about whether they are happy? Finally, happiness appears to be both a fairly constant state of well-being and also something experienced. But experiences change and fluctuate. How can something be both an experience and also a state?

One more comparison with pleasure will give us a clue for unraveling these problems. Although we can get pleasure from almost any kind of experience, happiness has always been connected to the satisfaction of "right" desires. Not many of us would think human beings happy if they were imprisoned for their lifetimes but, while incarcerated, had the pleasure center of their brains electronically stimulated. Happiness is associated not just with activity of the psyche, but with "activity in accordance with excellence."[6] People can deserve to be happy or unhappy (because they are good or evil) in a way that one cannot deserve pleasure or joy. "Happiness is the pleasureful content of mind which results from the success or attainment of what is considered good."[7]

What is happiness? What is this state that is also an experience, both so present and so elusive, so connected to desire and ethical value structures? Happiness, I think, occurs when the concrete lived events of our lives fit the ideal of human excellence we hold. That is, most of us have an ideal, usually vague and inexplicit, about what it means to live well—what we should be accomplishing at this time in our lives, what we should be preparing for in the future, how our relationships should be developing, etc.—and when the events of our lives correspond with this ideal, a sense of well-being comes over us. Although the comparison of life to an ideal can be consciously and clearly made, it almost always occurs in the semiconscious background of experience. The possibility of this comparative judgment being in the background of any experience explains how happiness can be experientially felt over a continuous time span. All that is needed is for the events of one's life to keep fitting, more or less, the ideal of excellence; then a person can feel continuously happy. The typical vagueness of the ideal and comparison explains some of the difficulty in determining whether or not one is happy.

We can now understand why pain is compatible with happiness, for pain can be experienced as necessary in the quest for the realization of an ideal. We can also discern why happiness eludes those who seek it: searching, toil, and attainment are related to the achievement of excellence, not to the looking for happiness. When we find ourselves achieving our ideal, then happiness appears, as a gift, for it has not been sought for. We do not seek excellence primarily because it brings happiness, but because we believe the ideal to be right. However, if happiness does not occur with the achievement of an ideal, then we must suspect that something is wrong with the ideal. That is, happiness and ideals are inextricably interwoven.

We can also understand why happiness is usually regarded as the most human of ends, and why pigs can't be happy. The other forms of satisfaction do not involve the formulation of ideals of excellence. All they require is that desires be satisfied or that pleasure be present. Yet without ideals we would hardly be the species that we are. Animals can feel satisfaction but cannot construct ideals; gods can have eternal ideals but do not have mortal experience. It is only human beings that have both thought and desire, finite particular experiences and eternal universal ideals. Integrating these is our peculiarly human task, and happiness is our peculiarly human end.[8]

Now, a crucial question arises. Can human beings invent any ideal of excellence, satisfy it, and then feel happy? If people "fit" the ideal of the age and culture—the Homeric hero, Greek sage, Medieval saint, Renaissance man of learning, Enlightenment person of "bon sense," Romantic artist, rugged American individualist, Confucian family person, Samurai warrior, Buddhist monk, capitalist entrepreneur—will they be happy? Will we contemporary Westerners be happy if we fit the present ideals of professional and economic success? Those who emphasize the great plasticity and diversity in human behavior and reject the notion of a constant "human nature" will say, "Yes, any ideal will do." There is certainly some truth in this position, for the feeling of congruence of any kind, and especially of lived events to the ideal and of individual to the culture, gives deep satisfaction. Yet this cannot be the whole story, for we have innumerable examples of people who attain their cultures' ideals and do not become happy.

> Whenever Richard Cory went down town,
>   We people on the pavement looked at him:
> He was a gentleman from sole to crown,
>   Clean favored, and imperially slim.

And he was always quietly arrayed,
  And he was always human when he talked;
But still he fluttered pulses when he said,
  "Good-morning," and he glittered when he walked.

And he was rich—yes, richer than a king,
  And admirably schooled in every grace.
In fine, we thought that he was everything
  To make us wish that we were in his place.

So on we worked, and waited for the light,
  And went without the meat, and cursed the bread;
And Richard Cory, one calm summer night,
  Went home and put a bullet through his head.

E. A. Robinson

The poetic insight here is that ideals cannot be made of whole cloth or assert just any pattern of life to be good. There are genuine human needs, and if these are denied or forgotten in the ideal, then achievement of the ideal can lead to profound disappointment. Nineteenth-century Viennese society may have had certain ideals concerning sexual behavior, but, as Freud found, the structuring of life around these ideals led to not happiness but neurosis. Ideals of excellence, if they are to be worthy and guide one to happiness, must be based on fundamental human needs and capacities.

Happiness, then, comes to people when their lives meet the ideals of excellence they hold for themselves and these ideals are grounded in genuine human needs and potentialities. Hence, if we find that the people of a culture are not happy, we may suspect that something is awry with their ideal of what constitutes human excellence. This suspicion bears fruit in our examination of Western culture, for, as we have seen, the West has been in a turmoil about its ideals for over a century. The Greek ideal that humans should achieve a rigorous unity of personality by having a power of reason hierarchically guiding the other powers of the psyche died in the nineteenth century.

The results of the loss of this ideal have been devastating. The ego-dominated psyche remains, for we cannot function in a technological culture without it, but we have lost the sense of excellence it previously brought. Hence, our psyches are cut off both from the emotions that make life vital and from an ideal of human excellence that gives life meaning. The resultant boredom, fragmentation, and meaninglessness have been acutely expressed by the most insightful minds of our culture—by writers such as Kafka, Sartre, Beckett, Woolf, de Beauvoir and Camus and by artists such as Dali, Beckmann, and Ernst. The questions "Why?" and "What does it all mean?" constantly bombard us from places in our psyches that we do not understand. We tend to push the questions away and direct our attention to the immediate tasks at hand, with their limited and accomplishable goals. But the "Why?" remains and haunts our psyches with an abiding emptiness. There is no ideal of human excellence to fill us and guide us; life seems to have little purpose.

The void caused by the loss of our ideal of human excellence has been filled by another kind of ideal: the contextual ideal. A contextual ideal expresses what constitutes excellence for a specific kind of activity, such a being a professor, parent, spouse, guest, or host. The most important of these ideals (in the upper classes) seem to be those that delineate excellence in professions (what it means to be a good doctor, lawyer, salesperson, etc.). These ideals revolve around the general ideal that one is good when one is productive. However, being a productive lawyer, student, or business executive is hardly the same as achieving excellence as a human being. We can all too easily be good professionals and unfulfilled, undeveloped human beings. Contextual ideals are not ideals of what it means to be excellent in one's humanity and, hence, cannot give the kind of meaning we, as human beings, need. Thus, even though we are achieving ever greater heights of excellence in the professional world, the lack of meaning prevails.

The West will not have meaning, nor will its people be capable of genuine happiness, until it is able to believe in a new ideal of human excellence. To do this we must first determine why the old ideal of a unified rational psyche collapsed after sustaining the West for so long. Then we must carefully examine the "language" of ideals to grasp how they function, so that we can avoid their significant dangers and reap their gifts. But, most important, we must make an inquiry into human nature. This inquiry will provide us with knowledge of the basic human needs, capacities, and psychic structures upon which we will build our ideal.

Yet, to move from a knowledge of the multiple factors that make up our humanity to an ideal of human excellence means that we must have some principle for organizing the multiplicity in a system of value. To do this, we must have a model of what constitutes order. The reigning model, not only for the West but for much of the rest of the world, is that of hierarchy. According to the hierarchical model, a multiplicity is ordered when its parts are ranked, such that one item is the most important, and others have importance and place according to their rank, which is usually determined by their relation to the item selected as the first priority. It is this hierarchical model that stands behind the kind of thinking that holds that the universe has a meaningful order only if it is ruled by a single God. In such a universe everything is located in a great chain of being and has worth to the extent that it is close to (reflects, is like) God.[9] Likewise, we consider the political realm organized when there is one head of the government and other persons with ranked responsibilities in relation to this head. Thus, the state must have a president or monarch and every committee must have a chair. Hierarchy is omnipresent in the chain of command that organizes the military and in the organizational flow charts of most large institutions. The problem with the hierarchical model of ordering is that some parts get overemphasized while others get systematically discriminated against. If there is an upper class, then there must be a lower class. If reason is the highest faculty in the psyche, then the emotions and other nonrational elements must be repressed, ignored, or slighted. Thus, with a hierarchical model for order, some things will get more than is their due and others less.

If we are to satisfy all the needs of the psyche and allow it to develop to the full extent of its powers, then we must use a different principle of organization from hierarchy. The new model can be found in ecology. All the elements in an ecological system are interrelated in such a way that a homeostatic balance is achieved. Each element has a definite role to play in maintaining the balance, and if that element is lost, the ecosystem can be destroyed or severely damaged, as when coyotes are killed by ranchers, allowing rabbits to run amok, or when reason so dominates the emotions that experience loses its rich textures and becomes an arid intellectual wasteland. In ecology we do not attempt to rank elements as most important, next-most important, least important, and so on, but to grasp how each member of the environment is related to every other so as to form a working whole.

If we can discover the major elements of the human psyche and create an ideal for how they can be put into a rich, vital, working balance, direction and meaning will once again enter our world and with them the depth and fullness of experience that gives happiness. Such an ecologically organized psyche will once again find a home within itself and the world, and our journey will have found its Ithaca.

Is this merely a dream? Can we really transform the way we organize our psyches and experience the world? Aren't we always caught in the social institutions and linguistic systems of our culture, systems that currently demand that we live in hierarchy and set professional and other contextual goals above human ones?

After Solon's visit, Croesus encountered a number of misfortunes. Because he was unable to interpret a dream correctly or keep it in memory, his son Atys was killed. Because he was unable to correctly interpret the oracle "If you attack the Persians, a great kingdom will be destroyed" his own kingdom fell. But just as Croesus was about to be burned alive on a great pyre by the conquering Persians, he remembered what Solon had said, knew its truth for the first time, and thrice cried Solon's name. Cyrus, king of the Persians, was so interested in discovering who this "Solon" was that he ordered Croesus taken off the pyre. But, alas, the fire had already been lit and could not be extinguished. "When Croesus understood that Cyrus had changed his mind, and saw everyone vainly trying to master the fire, he called loudly upon Apollo with tears to come and save him from his misery. It was a clear and windless day but suddenly in answer to Croesus' prayer clouds gathered and a storm broke with such violent rain that the flames were put out."[10] The miraculously saved Croesus then lived the rest of his days as sage advisor to the Persian throne.

Transformation is possible, even if difficult to fully comprehend.

CHAPTER 3

DEATH OF A PSYCHE

Although Melville and Schopenhauer felt the darkness of its coming, and the Russian nihilists were consumed by its power, it was Nietzsche who first and most profoundly articulated the thought that sounded the death knell of the Western psyche: God is dead. In so doing, he announced that a tradition that had sustained human spirits for over two millennia could sustain them no longer and had to perish. This quiet happening was not the result of any geopolitical struggle or the whim of some king; it did not come with fireworks or as any clearly definable event. But come it did, and its coming has radically affected the lives we lead. The emptiness that followed in the wake of this death evoked grief responses that have become the dominant characteristics of our culture in this century: denial that the death occurred, in clutching to an idealized past; avoidance of feeling, by reducing the psyche to a life of materiality; a sense of being lost in a horizonless void; a desperate search for new gods and ultimate foundations; and, above all, a violent rage that has irrupted in self-destructive wars, terrorization and annihilation of scapegoats, totalitarian repression, and ferocious competitiveness at all levels of life.

Understanding this death of God, over which Nietzsche presided as high priest, is of vital importance for grasping the fundamental source of our unhappiness and moving beyond it. What died? Why did it die? Nietzsche comprehended that what had collapsed was nothing less than the way people in Western culture gave meaning and organization to the inner and outer activities of their lives. Activities might continue, but the sense of worth, of raison d'être, of being grounded, has perished. Our psyches are reflected in our cities:

39

never has any environment been the scene of more activity, and yet spotted throughout these vast, bright, productive metropolises are dark ineradicable slums, pits of violent rage, excruciating boredom, and inescapable hopelessness. Our psyches, like our cities, are in a state of radical nonintegration.

How can this happen? What are psyches such that they can be born and die, flourish and disintegrate? I will use the term *psyche* as Aristotle did, to mean "the principle of organization of a natural body having life."[1] The presence of psyche is what distinguishes a human being from a corpse. It is the organization, both conscious and unconscious, of all human needs, desires, emotions, and cognitive capacities by which we live and act in the world. Although I attempt later to delineate the archaic structure of the psyche, I find its very being, its consciousness, its preoccupation with meaning, and its ability to think, so mysterious and miraculous as to surpass any attempt at full explanation. As Heraclitus said, "You could not discover the limits of psyche, even if you traveled by every path in order to do so; such is the depth of its meaning."[2]

Human beings commence life like all other animals with a set of genetically determined needs and capacities, but they differ remarkably in the extent to which they lack an instinctual base by which to realize these needs in interaction with the environment. Rather than being a set of closed instincts, humans have developed into organisms capable of differential and open responses to an immense variety of natural and social environments. We climb trees in the forest, run through the plains, dwell in caves in the mountains, swim in the seas, build igloos in the coldest of climates and grass huts in the hottest. The variety of foods we eat makes the diet of any other species appear excessively dull. We have invented ways of living with each other from hunter-gatherer tribes to the complex technological nation states of today. If instinct, early maturation, and specialized morphology are the great enemies of plasticity, then nature has produced in us the most plastic of species.

Like the *hamartia*[3] that doomed the tragic heroes of the Greeks, this plasticity is both our species' strength and its ruin. Plasticity is the ground for consciousness, freedom, our remarkable adaptability to environments, and the variety and intensity of experiences we can have. Yet it is also that which Sartre and Nietzsche felt as the void, the groundlessness of human existence. We can do and become almost anything, but the price for this adaptability is that we can never be grounded in a set nature. At the core of our being lies nothingness. As Sartre says, "We have to deal with human reality as a being which is what it is not and which is not what it is."[4]

So, why doesn't the human species wander about in constant nausea? Why aren't we always changing our social, sexual, and natural activities? Nietzsche might have us do this, but culture would have it otherwise. We may be biologically indeterminate organisms, but we are born into determinate cultures, which, if their sets of values and institutions are fairly coherent and strong, give structure, direction, and meaning to their members. Indeed, it is difficult to conceive how our biological structures could have become as nonspecialized and noninstinctual as they have without the concomitant development of culture as the force that organizes behavior. As Konrad Lorenz writes:

> Man's whole system of innate activities and reactions is phylogenetically so constructed, so "calculated" by evolution, as to need to be complemented by cultural tradition. For instance, all the tremendous neuro-sensory apparatus of human speech is phylogenetically evolved, but so constructed that its function presupposes the existence of a culturally developed language which the infant has to learn. . . . Were it possible to rear a human being of normal genetical constitution under circumstances depriving it of all cultural tradition—which is impossible not only for ethical but also for biological reasons— the subject of the cruel experiment would be very far from representing a reconstruction of a prehuman ancestor, as yet devoid of culture. It would be a poor cripple.[5]

In sum, we have a biological set of basic needs, an emotional matrix, and capacities for prehending and acting in the world, but are not biologically determined to any particular way of organizing these needs, emotions, and capacities, nor any set way of acting in the world to satisfy those needs. It is culture that is responsible for the creation of definite types of selves with determinate patterns of behavior.

From these basic facts follow a number of salient ideas for our exploration of human excellence and happiness. First, there is no one, given structure for the human psyche; the psyche can be organized in any number of ways. The priorities we assign to the various needs, the social forms in terms of which we realize needs (such as the conditions under which societies allow sexual activity), the kinds of interactions possible between conscious and unconscious elements (for instance, for the Iroquois, dreams were critically important; for the nineteenth-century European, they were, at best, curiosities), and the balance of rational and emotional elements are some of the blocks out of which the psyche is built. These parts can be arranged in innumerable ways, and how they are arranged by a particular culture to a large extent determines the quality, depth, and focus of experience for the members of that culture. It is also possible for the blocks to fall into disarray; the psyche can go mad.

Second, cultural programming is never totally complete; individuals have more or less freedom to organize their psyches in personal, idiosyncratic ways. The extent of individual freedom present within any culture seems to depend upon the amount, diversity, and complexity of conditioning factors within that culture. Like some tribes or small towns, a society whose conditioning factors are too few or too uniform can be stifling or repressive. On the other hand, cultures whose principles, structures, and institutions have become so diverse as to be drastically incoherent can cause a general sense of aimlessness and confusion.

Third, since cultures supply the structures and directions by which humans organize their psyches, we can speak of the "Western psyche," the "Greek psyche," the "Trobriand Islander psyche," and so on, meaning by these terms the psyche-forming structures that are imparted by these cultures to their members at the most fundamental level of interaction and that, therefore, characterize the experience of the great majority of persons in those cultures.

Not being directly observable, the principles of any particular psychic structure can be ascertained only by examining the productions of its culture—its art, religion, philosophy, politics, literature, economy, and language—and then imaginatively attempting to postulate what kind of mind could make such productions. Different cultures cathect energy around different religions, laws, and so forth, not primarily because of differential environmental pressures, but because its inhabitants have different psychic structures. Cultural productions both mirror the psychic structure of the inhabitants of a culture and help create that structure. For example, Olympianism was vital in the archaic age of Greece because the gods reflected the rising sense of individual personality in distinction from the communal tribal consciousness that previously characterized the culture. As Jane Harrison says,

> But as the group system disintegrates, the individual emerges, and further, not only does the individual emerge from the group, but the human individual is more and more conscious of his sharp distinction from animals and plants, from the whole of nature that surrounds him. This twofold emergence of the individual from the group, of the human individual from the nature-world around him, is inevitably mirrored in the personality, in the individuality of the Olympian gods.[6]

In the fifth century B.C., this structuring of the self around a facet of personality was no longer adequate to encompass the growing complexity of individual and social life. Philosophy, with its more powerful model for integration and control, came to supersede Olympianism as what riveted attention. Later, one god, with a fully integrated reason and will, captivated the psyche's interest for over a millennium as it represented what persons in the West wanted their psyches to become. When they achieved this state, then that concept of God had to die as a lure for achievement.

We must be careful making such generalizations about psychic organization, however, for the problems involved with substantiating them are formidable. The productions of any culture are innumerable; some must be emphasized over others, and this emphasis can be distorting. Also, there is no way to show that any interpretation of a particular production is correct. We are in the realm of imaginative construction, not empirical demonstration. Finally, the artifacts of cultures that are economically developed overwhelmingly reflect the values of the upper classes. Do such artifacts say anything significant about the psyches of the vast majority of human beings in those cultures who do not belong to the leisured classes?

These problems make risky at best the business of generalizing about the psychic structures of people belonging to specific cultures. No generalization will hold for all the members of a culture, and the more diverse a culture is in economic and demographic structure, the less likely it is that a generalization will work. Thus, when we try to ascertain the structure of a psyche for any particular culture and age, we can only offer what Plato in the *Timaeus* called "a likely story." What follows is a brief "likely story" of the history of the Western psyche in its relation to the values of unity, multiplicity, reason, and hierarchy. The sketchiness of the story results from the fact that my major interest is in what the psyche might become rather than what it has been.

◻

What Nietzsche discovered when he proclaimed that God is dead was that the psychic structure that had collapsed was not just an important part of the psyche of Westerners, but the very ground by which the psyche organized its energies, activities, capacities, and values. At the heart of this collapsed structure was an ideal of human excellence that had persisted more or less intact for over two thousand years and, more than any other structure, defined what it meant to belong to the Western tradition.

This claim may seem strange, given that Western history has seen the growth and demise of a number of such ideals, bits and pieces of which persist as relics in contemporary culture—the Homeric warrior, Greek philosopher, Roman statesman, Christian martyr, Enlightenment scientist, Romantic artist, economic entrepreneur. But the woof underlying these ideals, weaving them into a common tradition, is a still more fundamental ideal: that each person should be a fully unified personality, this unification being achieved by making one psychic power or capacity (usually reason) and one principle within that faculty hierarchically regnant over the others. While there have been significant disputes concerning what this principle is (the Good, God, power, etc.) and how we should organize our lives around it (as philosophers, monks, scientists, etc.), that one should know and ground oneself in a first principle is unquestioned in the major tradition of the culture. In short, the fundamental value of Western culture is unity or oneness. Other values such as reason, moderation, faith, and honesty are justified to the extent that they can produce this oneness of spirit.

The ideal of unity first appeared in the earliest Pre-Socratic philosophers searching for a single substance underlying the multiplicity of natural events. It later received its full initial expression as a principle for natural, psychic, and political organization in the *Dialogues* of Plato. Before Plato there is a remarkably different concept of the self and human excellence: a self that is multicentered, with little sense of a central ego, vulnerable to strong emotional forces, and striving for ends that have little to do with rational justification or with the development of the powers of the rational ego.

We first meet this multicentered person in Homer's *Iliad*. Here are found a strange set of creatures who are similar to us in appearance, use of language, involvement in political events, and troubles in love and war, but who also talk with gods, get enthused (*en-theos*— "in-godded"), and even fight in hand-to-hand combat with gods. The other parts of the *Iliad* are understandable, but this commerce with the gods is so foreign we can barely comprehend what is happening. It is this rift with our experience that lets us see that the psyche of the Homeric hero was structured in a vastly different way than ours.

There have been a number of theories of how to interpret the gods, such as seeing them as mere poetic creatures to satisfy the craving of the Greeks for good stories, or seeing them as prescientific explanations for events that do not fit into a limited understanding of how nature works. These explanations account neither for the power and presence of the gods felt in the Homeric texts nor for the devotion of the Greeks to these gods in their practiced religion. I prefer to follow Feuerbach and see the language about the gods as expressing what the Greeks found to be the most profound psychic forces working within them—forces whose origin went beyond what little self there was in these heroes.

If we look at Olympus as a model of psychic structure, we discover a tenuous central organizing power, Zeus, and a number of other forces making strong contradictory demands. Zeus's major concern is with justice, with giving each part its due. The "parts" of Olympus that must receive their due are a rather divers crew.[7] There are forces of erotic love (Aphrodite), aggression (Ares), aesthetic sensitivity and a nonpragmatic relation to nature (Artemis), and the urge to technology and the pragmatic transformation of nature (Hephaistos). Apollo's power of light, urging toward knowledge and musical harmony, appears alongside the dark forces of Hades and earthshaking, wall-smashing, amorphous Poseidon.

Olympus is terribly confused and ambivalent about women. Demeter is the all-nourishing earth mother, fruitful, sexual, and full of grief for the cycles of life and death. Artemis is the goddess of the hunt who kills wild beasts and prurient men. A virgin, she despises Aphrodite; her world loves cool distant moonlight. Hera, the wife and equal of Zeus in many respects, is charged with a kind of rational justice in the protection of the most basic ritual and bond in culture: marriage. But her nagging, jealousy, seductiveness, and rage, and the promiscuity of her husband, manifest that this psyche is not at ease with the male–female bond of equals. These different female gods can be interpreted as different understandings of women at different stages of growing up. Demeter could be our first experience of the nourishing mother; Artemis, the mother who demands separation and refuses incestuous bonding; Hera, the controller of the household; and Aphrodite, the urge to direct our libido out of the family. Athena, the virgin goddess of war and wisdom, seems a refuge from these problems of sex and family. Born asexually from the head of Zeus, she harnesses aggression to rational ego functions, and, in so doing, helps create a new political world that overcomes the impossible problems of building political units on family and ritual structures.[8]

Indispensable to Olympus and the psyche is Hermes, who guides travelers around the world and into and out of the underworld. He is versatile, cunning, musical, the trickster, and a great favorite of Zeus. He seems to be the principle of communication between the parts of the psyche without being another part himself—he travels between conscious and unconscious, rational and emotional, dark and light,

stable and flowing parts of the psyche, and somehow, through laughter
and craftiness, keeps them in a kind of uneasy communication.
Hermes reappears later in Western life as the jester who keeps courts
and kings functioning.

Finally, there is Dionysos. He has never been accepted as an
authentic member of Olympus, but he also cannot be quite excluded.
God of joy, sorrow, laughter, tears, and drunken dance, bisexual
Dionysos never reaches the clear delineation of other gods, a delineation that a rational psyche might give him, but remains an amalgam
of Freud's eros and thanatos, reminding us of the primal driving forces
of the psyche that exist beneath any particular structuring of meaning.

The model of the multiform psyche revealed in Olympus is also
manifest in the many terms Homer uses to describe the source of
motivation or psychic activity.[9] His heroes are moved to action by the
thumos (a spirit in the chest); the *kradiē, ētor, kēr* (various hearts);
phrēn (mind in the chest, associated with the diaphragm and lungs);
and *noos* (mind). Each of these centers of motivation contains a balance
of what we would call "intellect" and "emotion," but which are not
separated for the Homeric Greeks. The absence of a central principle
ruling the psyche is reflected in the absence of locutions like "I decided
to do such and such and did it." Rather, one or another of the parts
of the self, or a god, usually "bids" the hero to do something.

Quite a psyche. While there is some central ego control, as the
presence of Zeus indicates, it is not dominating, repressive, or even
central in the way the rational ego in the psyche and the Christian
God in the universe will be later. It is responsive to each of the
numerous forces, capacities, propensities, and fears in the psyche.
Although not every Homeric hero responds to all these gods or forces,
we find in Achilles, Hector, and Odysseus humans who can intensely
love, hate, encounter mortality, feel the flux of things, gain insight,
laugh, and grieve. But the variety of forces and the intensity with
which they are felt are so great that chaos is always on the verge of
breaking out and subsuming the characters. It is no accident that the
matrix in which these Homeric heroes operate is the battlefield, or
that, at the central turning point of the war, total chaos engulfs the
battlefield as a river chases Achilles across the plains and is finally
stopped by fire (fire putting out water!). Achilles is so enraged that
he loses all his sense of balance, order, and justice, and races chaoti-
cally over the battlefield slaughtering Trojans without limit or
thought.

The madness that momentarily affects Achilles and later drives
Ajax to suicide becomes a central theme in Attic drama three hundred

years after Homer. Here the conflicts of the complex, multicentered psyche are exacerbated by a world changing from a tribal, family culture to a socioeconomic society. The tragedies are filled with persons consumed by social and psychic forces to the point of madness. Heracles goes insane and kills his wife and children. Ajax and Phaedra commit suicide. The inflexible, overly structured Pentheus cracks, dresses as a woman to spy on the Bacchantes, and is killed by his entranced mother and sisters. The great warrior Philoctetes is reduced to a fixation on his wound. Clytemnestra kills her arrogant husband and is in turn killed by her children. Creon, Theseus, and Hippolytus become so rigid that they cannot deal with the complexities of life, and make decisions that bring about the deaths of members of their families. Oedipus kills his father, sleeps with his mother, blinds himself, curses his sons to kill one another, and incestuously binds his daughter Antigone to him. Medea murders a king, a princess, and her own two children, and leaves the stage laughing. It is no wonder that in this world *sophrosyne*—moderation or balance—is seen as the most important virtue for a person to have. With *sophrosyne*, the multicentered individual is capable of living a full, balanced, intense life; without it, forces and emotions can overwhelm the psyche, reducing the person to being a slave of tyrannical impulses, and the world, to chaos.

The horrors of the disintegration of psyche and society portrayed in the world of drama irrupted into reality with the onset of the Peloponnesian wars. These wars involved not just Greek city against Greek city, but pro-Athenian democratic factions versus pro-Spartan aristocratic factions within each city. There were constant revolutions and counterrevolutions between these factions, along with sieges by one enemy or the other, depending on which faction was in control of the government. Greeks annihilated Greeks; citizens killed fellow citizens; brothers destroyed brothers. The Hellenic world disintegrated. This dissolution is tragically portrayed in Thucydides' account of how Athens fell from being, under Pericles, a state of power and elevated principles, to being one that condemned all the male citizens of the little, nonoffending island of Melos to death and its women and children to slavery. Athens finally was defeated by Sparta when it committed the folly of putting two hated enemies in joint command of the most important naval expedition of the war (and then condemned one of them to death as soon as the fleet left).

For Thucydides, the state and psyche were mirrors of each other. The rage, revenge, greed, and fantasies of glory that overwhelmed the political life of the Greek polis also overwhelmed the individuals within them. As states disintegrated and warred against each other, so were psyches in a state of internal strife and chaos.

> In peace and prosperity states and individuals have better senti-
> ments, because they do not find themselves suddenly confronted with
> imperious necessities; but war takes away the easy supply of daily
> wants, and so proves a rough master, that brings most men's char-
> acters to a level with their fortunes. . . . In the confusion into which
> life was now thrown in the cities, human nature, always rebelling
> against the laws and now its master, gladly showed itself ungoverned
> in passion, above respect for justice, and the enemy of all superiority;
> since revenge would not have been above religion, and gain above
> justice, had it not been for the fatal power of envy.[10]

Plato grew up during the Peloponnesian Wars, watched the multi-dimensional, nonunified characters go insane onstage, experienced the horrors of the wars, witnessed the atrocities of the Spartan-installed Tyranny of Thirty, and wept as the restored democracy condemned Socrates to death. He realized that the multicentered psyche with minimal rational control was too vulnerable to the passions and conflicting social influences to ground a stable, fulfilling life for either persons or states, regardless of the type of government. He was determined to articulate a new way of structuring the psyche. This theme is explicitly stated in the *Republic*, where the poets and their inadequate models of human thought, feeling, and action are to be banished from the state and replaced by philosopher-rulers whose psyches are ruled by reason, which, in turn, is grounded in objective principles.

This radical reconception of human nature away from a multi-dimensional, multicentered self to a highly unified and rationally controlled self is a major theme of the *Dialogues*. Throughout them, evil is associated with change, vulnerability, multiplicity, and ignorance; good is that which is unified, self-sufficient, permanent, and rational. Multiplicity, once the glory of the Homeric world, is now seen as the destroyer of psyches and social orders. For Plato, each person has only "one task according to his nature,"[11] and desires are described as radically atomized, each bent on its own little satisfaction without regard to the good of the whole person or the social order. A person with multiple desires not under the control of a rational principle is compared to a "leaky jar"[12] or a chariot driven out of control by a wild black stallion.[13] Likewise, a society of separate individuals, a democracy, is seen as a state in which the thirst for liberty becomes so unbounded that citizens "pay no heed to the laws written or unwritten"[14] and which collapses into anarchy.

The only defense against these tyrannical raging desires and citizens asserting their individual wills is to organize them into a unity that grasps the good of the whole and is not vulnerable to influences toward multiplicity and disintegration. A state's growth (and, by parallel construction, a person's growth) is good "so long as in its growth it consents to remain a unity."[15] Each person must do the one work for which he or she is best fitted "so the entire city may come to not a multiplicity but a unity."[16] Justice is considered a virtue for both the individual and the state because "justice brings oneness of mind."[17] Even individual virtues could be evils if they are not gathered into a "unity of virtues."

Vulnerability to multiplicity, or to any kind of change or exterior force, is weakness and can lead to a person's or state's being overwhelmed by destructive forces. Humans should seek to attain self-sufficiency rather than vulnerability. "The good must have no need of anything else to be added to it."[18] When this self-sufficiency is attained, one cannot be destroyed by internal or external forces. As Socrates says at his trial, "Nothing can harm a good man either in life or after death."[19]

But how is it possible for humans to achieve this unified, invulnerable state? It seems beyond the reach of our apparently very vulnerable, multiple, finite natures. However, Plato found in the faculty of reason precisely what he needed, for reason with the help of high spirit (*thumos*) did have the power to unify, organize, and direct the psyche.

> Does it not belong to the rational part to rule, being wise and exercising forethought in behalf of the entire soul, and to the principle of high spirit to be subject to this and its ally?[20]

What gives reason the ability and right to rule the rest of the psyche is its capability of grasping eternal, permanent, valid principles. What these principles are, how reason can come to know them, how language might or might not express them, and how they can be grounded in reality and related to a world of process are problems that deeply vexed Plato and constitute threads that bind together much of his work. The details of Plato's answers need not concern us here; what is of importance is that it is these principles that grant unity, self-sufficiency, and happiness, for when reason dwells on the eternal, unchanging principles, it takes on their nature and infuses this nature into the rest of the psyche.

It is important to see that, in adopting a hierarchical model for organizing the psyche and state, Plato rejected the democratic system present in Athens in favor of the form of political order of Sparta, Persia, and every other major state at that time. The idea that order cannot be achieved unless one part of the psyche dominates others, or one part of the state rules others, or one part of the universe creates, controls, or directs all the others, was taken up by Aristotle, the Christian theologians, and almost every other Western thinker. It has become an essential characteristic of Western thinking, although one always in tension with the democratic heritage. We do not live in a world in which order and unity are achieved by a balance of opposing elements such as Chinese yin and yang, Zoroastrian light and darkness, or Heraclitean strife. Nor do we live in that rough-and-ready Olympian world of numerous forces each of which is inextinguishable and must receive its due. We live in a universe ruled by one God, in states ruled by one king, dictator, or president, and in psyches ruled by one faculty, reason.

When the principles of hierarchy, unity, and reason are combined, we have the basis for forming a psyche centered around what has come to be known as the "rational ego." 'Ego' is used here, in consonance with the psychoanalytic tradition, to refer to the part of experience that is conscious, clear, and highly organized into geometrical perceptual patterns and logical thought structures, and that functions according a rigorous set of hierarchically ordered values. The emphasis on unity and rational order allows no foreign or disruptive material to enter experience, while the presence of a set of permanent perceptual, methodological, and normative structures defines who the person is and makes experience feel as though it were owned by someone. All experience now becomes "my experience," because it is always unified according to the same set of rational categories.

However, as we have seen, this psyche ruled by a rational ego was not a free creation. It was born in response to profound social and psychological dislocations. The fear of disintegration that underlies much of Plato's philosophy can be seen in Socrates' ferocious responses to Callicles and Thrasymachus when they advocate a free, unprincipled life of the psyche with multiple desires, but it appears most clearly in Book 8 of the *Republic*. Here Plato plots the path of social and psychic disintegration from a unified, rationally ordered state and psyche to ones dominated by aggression and greed, then declining into a lawless chaotic state of undisciplined desires, and finally terminating in a tyrannical state "of the most cruel and bitter servile servitude."[21] This last stage of disintegration resembles a state that might be described by contemporary psychoanalysts as one in which the ego functions have collapsed and become entirely dominated by compulsions from the unconscious. For Plato this descent is the natural tendency of human nature, and only a steadfast vigilance by reason to keep its objective principles in control of psychic activities can prevent it.

In dealing with social and psychic disintegration, Plato confronted one of the most profound fears of human beings. The possibility of insanity is, along with the fear of death, probably the deepest anxiety in human nature. This anxiety might even be more profound than the fears of death, because death is a necessary part of human life, with which we must come to terms, but we need never go insane yet always might. Insanity is an ever-present possibility because of our lack of a set, biological, psychic nature. The order we give to our psyches is not a necessary one; if too many conflicts arise or too many needs are not met, the structure can disintegrate.

Before Plato's time, this fear of disintegration seemed to be discharged in rituals where people could allow their personalities to disintegrate because the disintegration was carefully bounded by the structure of the ritual.[22] Disintegration was ritually lived through at various sacred times of the year and was always followed by the ritual reestablishment of a patterned life. The playwrights later attempted to adapt ritual to urban life by using annual dramatic performances as cathartic events. But Plato found these measures inadequate. They had prevented neither the destruction of Greece in the Peloponnesian Wars nor the unjust death of Socrates. His brilliant remedy for the possibility of disintegration was to abandon the method of periodic inoculation and replace it with the development of a psyche so unified and controlled by a rational ego that it could not possibly disintegrate.

From the time of its initial articulation in Plato and Aristotle, this structure of the psyche struggled for predominance in Western culture. It was never lost—especially in the writings of philosophers—but it also never fully succeeded until the seventeenth century. Mystery rites flourished in the Hellenistic world, and Romans found a pantheon of gods better able to reflect their psyches than a single deity. But with the coming of Christianity and its single, unified, self-sufficient, rational God, the tables were irrevocably turned in favor of the ego-dominated psyche. There were still heresies and tendencies to make the holy family and canon of saints into a new Olympus, but slowly these were eliminated, and with the coming of the Enlightenment and the rise of modern science, reason and unity won the day.

With this rational, unified psyche as its basis for action, the West has produced a technological culture whose power has virtually conquered and transformed the world. However, this coming into dominion of the rational ego has had its costs, as Solon might have expected. The language of domination became increasingly the primary language. What was not the rational ego lost intrinsic value and became an object for technological or political manipulation. Nature, which from neolithic times had been symbolically and conceptually associated with the sacred female (the Goddess), was reduced to mere matter, a resource to be used by males in any ways they desired. Bright, rational psyches experimented on her, found her secrets, dug into her privy parts with huge machines to extract her precious metals and minerals, and filled her air with choking gases to convert those natural materials into goods for human consumption.[23] The rational psyche, so brilliant in coming to know nature and her ways, has also produced an ecological crisis that threatens to destroy the world we live in.

Even if we are able to avert the crisis and control pollution, erosion, and depletion of resources, modern science and the rational psyche that fostered it have lost nature as a home. Insofar as we retain the rational ego as the central structure of the self, we will be aliens on our own planet. No longer can we find ourselves reflected in nature, our natures mirrored back to us, our rhythms mingled with its rhythms. We are rational creatures; nature is understood as matter. We are animate; nature is seen as inert. We are creators and explorers; nature runs in endless cycles of repetition. In becoming lord and master over nature, we have lost her as nurse and creatrix. The resulting alienation of human beings and nature is one of the most profound dislocations of our times.

Along with the drive to reduce nature to stuff and dominate it, the rational ego demanded the subjugation of all psychic activities that were not cognitive, for they have no intrinsic value for that ego. To give them any legitimate place is to open the self to the possibility of anarchy. As one of the great architects of the Enlightenment, Francis Bacon, said:

> [Men] are full of savage and unreclaimed desires, of profit, of lust, of revenge, which as long as they give ear to precepts, to laws, to religion, sweetly touched with eloquence and persuasion of books, of sermons, of harangues, so long is society and peace maintained, but if these instruments be silent, or that sedition and tumult make them not audible, all things dissolve into anarchy and confusion.[24]

The split between the rational ego and the other psychic activities is best seen in the mind/body problem, the most pressing metaphysical issue of the Enlightenment, one that continues to haunt philosophers to the present day. As first announced by Descartes, it appeared as an intellectual conundrum concerning concepts: how can the mind as pure unextended immaterial thought interact with the body—thoughtless matter extended in space. Mechanical, electrical, and chemical explanations are possible only within the material world, while logic and telepathy are models of explanation only within the mental world. There are no understandable models of interaction between the two worlds of mind and body.

But the problem is more disturbing than merely being a conceptual enigma concerning metaphysical categories. It appears that Descartes actually experienced the mind as being radically distinct from the body:

> Because, on the one side, I have a clear and distinct idea of myself inasmuch as I am only a thinking and unextended thing, and as, on the other, I possess a distinct idea of body, inasmuch as it is only an extended and unthinking thing, it is certain that this I is entirely and absolutely distinct from my body and can exist without it.[25]

Since the imagination and emotions are associated with the body, they likewise are eliminated from the self, here defined solely as rational ego.

> I further find in myself faculties employing modes of thinking peculiar to themselves, to wit, the faculties of imagination and feeling, without which I can easily conceive myself clearly and distinctly as a complete being . . . from which I infer that they are distinct from me as its modes are from a thing.[26]

The rational ego has become so dominant, so isolated from the other activities of the psyche, that it no longer believes that it has anything in common with them. While philosophers might call this "the mind/body problem," psychoanalysts see it as dissociation of thought and affect—a defense mechanism signaling an unhealthy, unintegrated psyche.

As the ego became increasingly oppressive of affects and emotions, as it came to dominate its own bodily nature just as it dominated nature, a stifling abstractness entered its expressions. Bacchanalia now appeared as sedate events on the carefully controlled, perfectly ordered canvases of Poussin, Watteau, and Fragonard. The active, emotional, involved God of the Middle Ages became a deistic mechanical genius who, once upon a time, made a perfect machine-universe and now does nothing but watch from afar. One can read the greatest philosophers of this age—Descartes, Spinoza, Leibniz, Fichte, Hegel, Berkeley, Hume—and rarely find that humans are produced through sexual reproduction. Egos write for egos and attempt to enclose themselves in a view of the world that is entirely contained and controlled by reason. As Hegel proudly proclaimed: "The real is the rational and the rational is the real."

The Enlightenment at least understood that humans had several needs—knowledge, survival, social approbation, and salvation being the main ones—and believed that reason could penetrate to ultimate realities. By the time we get to the end of the nineteenth century, though, only one drive, survival, remains, and reason has been reduced to a pragmatic tool for the exploitation of the environment to meet this need. What has intervened in the meantime is the full flourishing of the economic system spawned by the West in the late Middle Ages, capitalism, and the ascendancy of Darwinism in the nineteenth century. Capitalism put a primacy on the acquisition of material wealth as the final aim of life, and Darwinism supported this with its theory that survival, along with resources needed for survival, was the one great end of all living creatures. As Horkheimer puts it in his *Eclipse of Reason*:

> As the end result of the process, we have on the one hand the self, the abstract ego emptied of all substance except its attempt to transform everything in heaven and on earth into means for its preservation, and on the other hand an empty nature degraded to mere material, mere stuff to be dominated, without any other purpose than that of this very domination.[27]

It is upon this scene that Nietzsche comes and pronounces the death of God. This proclamation was meant by Nietzsche both as a report of a sociological fact and as a prescription: if you have not yet killed God, then you must do so. The sociological fact that Nietzsche saw so clearly was that Western society had become inherently secular: what now motivated people was mainly material and social self-aggrandizement. Religious language was still used, but it was merely window dressing to comfort the soul in times when the fear of death or of meaninglessness reared its ugly head. It no longer had any power to direct the activities or lives of Western persons. Not only religious beliefs, but beliefs in any objective principles, perished. As both Nietzsche and Freud observed, all principles are fictions—tools of the will to power or the unconscious. And the secular world understood this all too well: every principle had its limits. The rational ego, which for centuries had believed in the possibility of structuring its activities on "right" values and an "objective" view of the world, was shattered. Its skeleton was left, but not its glory.

Although Nietzsche abhorred the petty secular mind that succeeded it, he cheered the passing of the rational ego of objective principles. That ego might have served a purpose to further human power within the world at a certain time, but now it was hindering life, stifling its advance, just as the Irish elk's magnificent antlers finally became so unwieldy as to make the species extinct. Life is growth, change, death, rebirth. It is will to power. But to have power over oneself here and now means that one cannot be ruled by a past self or past decisions or codes of values imposed from without. To have power, to live, is to create; to then overcome what one has created and to create anew; only to overcome that creation and create again and again and again. Objective principles, permanent structures for understanding the world and directing activity, suffocate the power of creation. Dead planets move according to constant principles; live minds do not. Objective principles, God, offered the self great rewards—a structure of meaning with which one could have an identity and goal in life, a defense against psychic and social disintegration, and an overcoming of mortality and change—but, as Nietzsche so powerfully evinced, the costs for these goods was extremely high. It was nothing less than vitality and creativity—the very essence of life! The rational ego ruling the psyche with unchanging principles slowly choked itself to death.

Changing the psychic structure from one dominated by the rational ego (with or without objective principles) to one more open and responsive to the other elements in the psyche is a formidable task, to say the least. For Nietzsche this transformation could only occur if the person underwent a "metamorphosis of the spirit." First one must be a camel:

> What is difficult? asks the spirit that would bear much, and kneels down like a camel wanting to be well loaded. What is most difficult, O heroes, asks the spirit that would bear much, that I may take it upon myself and exult in my strength? Is it not humbling oneself to wound one's haughtiness? Letting one's folly shine to mock one's wisdom?

Or is it this: parting from our cause when it triumphs? Climbing
high mountains to tempt the tempter?

Or is it this: feeding on the acorns and grass of knowledge and for
the sake of the truth, suffering hunger in one's soul?

Or is it this: stepping into filthy waters when they are the waters
of truth, and not repulsing cold frogs and hot toads?

All these most difficult things the spirit that would bear much takes
upon itself: like the camel that, burdened, speeds into the desert,
thus the spirit speeds into its desert.[28]

Camels, in Nietzsche's metamorphosis, are characterized above
all by seriousness. They do not accept life just as it comes but ask,
"What is the best way for humans to live?" and are willing to take
on the burden of an answer. The first answers that appear when this
question is asked are the values present in society. Camels accept
these values and live them as though they were absolutely right, for
they cannot stand anything less than absolute, fully objective
principles.

But camels don't lose their seriousness. As they act on the values,
they ask if these are right; they look more carefully at the grounds
of the values, and do not accept as a legitimate ground the applause
from society. They probe their "cold frogs and hot toads," and the more
they probe, the more they discover that the ground for the values
recedes.

In the loneliest desert, however, the second metamorphosis occurs:
here the spirit becomes a lion who would conquer his freedom and
be master in his own desert. Here he seeks out his last master: he
wants to fight him and his last god; for ultimate victory he wants
to fight with the great dragon.

Who is the great dragon whom the spirit will no longer call lord
and god? "Thou shalt" is the name of the great dragon. But the spirit
of the lion says, "I will." "Thou shalt" lies in his way, sparkling like
gold, an animal covered with scales; and on every scale shines a
golden "thou shalt."[29]

The lion does not destroy values; it destroys a way of relating to
values, a way that has defined the psyche since Plato, a way that forms
the essence of the camel. The lion ceases to revere values, ceases to
find any objectivity, justification, or sacredness in them. But the lion
does not do this as so many adolescents do, merely in perverse

rebellion. No, the lion undergoes a transforming experience that enables this real change toward values to occur and ennobles it: the lion disintegrates.

> To create new values—that even the lion cannot do; but the creation of freedom for oneself for new creation—that is within the power of the lion. The creation of freedom for oneself and a Sacred "No" even to duty—for that, my brothers, the lion is needed. To assume the right to new values—that is the most terrifying assumption for a reverent spirit that would bear much. Verily, to him it is a preying, and a matter for a beast of prey. He once loved "thou shalt" as most sacred: now he must find illusion and caprice even in the most sacred, that freedom from his love may become his prey: the lion is needed for such prey.[30]

The lion descends into the void and in this grey horizonless land discovers no signposts, no markers, nothing to tell him what is right or good or worthy. Life has no meaning, no purpose. We are born and die; that is all. No better, no worse. The reverential, serious camel is annihilated.

> Why must the preying lion still become a child? The child is innocence and forgetting, a new beginning, a game, a self-propelled wheel, a first movement, a sacred "Yes." For the game of creation, my brothers, a sacred "Yes" is needed: the spirit now wills his own will, and he who had been lost to the world now conquers his own world.[31]

In the midst of the nothingness into which the lion has plunged upon killing the dragon, she finds not nothing, not a void, but life! Unencumbered by structures, the Dionysian power of life flows through one, fully, completely. "Yes, yes, yes, a thousand times, yes!" In this joy of feeling for the first time since childhood the concrete bursting stream of life rather than the abstract dead structures of values and obligations, we create our own values, create anew, forgetful of the meaninglessness of all values that the lion knows. The spirit creates values, comes to believe in those values like a camel, comes to discover that they are determining the psyche from the past and stifling life in the present, becomes the dragon and destroys the values, enters the void, rediscovers the sacred yes in the surge of life, and celebrates in the creation of new values.

The old psyche, bound and limited by unchanging rational principles and the rigorous geometry of clear consciousness, is replaced by a psychic dance of death and rebirth in a continual purposeless cycle of self-overcoming. Plato, in structuring the psyche so as to avoid self-disintegration, disjoined us from life itself, from creating destroying changing vital chaotic life itself! "One must still have chaos in oneself to be able to give birth to a dancing star."[32] Nietzsche, originally a classical philologist who explored the ritualistic roots of Greek culture, now commands the death of the Platonic psyche as the key to giving birth to a psyche open to all its multifold forces, emotions, sensitivities, and depths. His aphorisms, metaphors, and disconnected paragraphs call us to this disintegration. The way to deal with the fear of disintegration is not to avoid it, repress it, or build structures to contain it. Such tactics always fail, and the fear still controls, requiring tighter and tighter doors and locks until the conscious rational ego has to isolate itself totally within its defensive walls and elevated boundaries. Alienated, lonely, passionless, this unintegrated, enfeebled psyche had to die, had to be killed, in order for us to live. No, do not flee disintegration; that is not the way. Go through it! Disintegrate! Again and again and again. And when you come out on the other side, you, like Zarathustra, will be "one changed, radiant, laughing!"

Maybe. But not necessarily. Our mental hospitals are filled with people who disintegrated but never came out of it. Our cities are full of fragmented, shattered personalities. Our culture has seen unprecedented outbursts of war and civil violence that have left parts of it in total disintegration. The problem of lost, depressed, and disintegrated psyches had become so prevalent by the end of the nineteenth century, that it demanded the work of a Freud and the birth of a whole new school of medicine to tend to the sick psyches of our culture, to take them through and out of disintegration.

Nietzsche, for better or worse, was right in proclaiming that the old psyche had died. The attacks on first principles in all the disciplines—on Newtonian mechanics in physics, sense data and intuition in philosophy, the tonal system in music, representationalism in art and literature, and so on—and the desperate attempts to find new primitives, are evidence of this death. If Nietzsche is the philosopher of the Western psyche's demise, Freud is its scientist. He dislodged, irrevocably it seems, the rational ego from its throne of central power by demonstrating how the ego is only a pawn of the much stronger, darker forces of the irrational unconscious.

The old psyche, born from the rubble of the Peloponnesian Wars in the brilliant imagination of Plato and root cause of the West's unprecedented rise to power, wealth, and knowledge, is dead. Its principles can no longer sustain us. The happiness it gave to people who could believe in it, and who found primary needs for integration, direction, control, and order met by it, is not available to us. But as Nietzsche reveals, our culture renounced this psyche because it had become far too limiting, repressive, and downright meager, given the new, multidimensional living made possible by advanced technology.

So that humans could live, God had to die.

CHAPTER 4

IDEALS

The ideal of being a person fully unified around an absolute principle, such as God, died at the end of the nineteenth century. This did not generate a birth of radically free spirits, as Nietzsche had hoped, but instead created a void of meaning. This ideal was not replaced by another ideal of what it means to live excellently as a human being, but rather, a myriad of ideals for contextual excellence rushed in to fill the vacuum. Ideals of contextual excellence define what constitutes worth in given particular activities. We may no longer know what it means to be a good human being, but we do know what it means to be a good lawyer, businessperson, parent, connoisseur of restaurants and foods, buyer of goods, driver of vehicles, and so forth. These ideals explain why we are rarely at a loss for what to do, even if we do not have a general ideal of human excellence to guide us.

For the middle and upper classes, the most important of the contextual ideals have become those of work or profession. We consider ourselves successful and living well if we achieve excellence in our chosen fields of work and have a very difficult time thinking well of ourselves when we do not do well in them. Recently, the hold of professional ideals of excellence has become so commanding that they have virtually become ideals for human excellence. To be a first-rate professional is to be a good human being.

That is, the language of ideals, along with most everything else in contemporary life, has been co-opted by the economy and is now basically a tool used to propel economic life. For better or worse, Marx has won the day in his general philosophy, even if his specific programs have been rejected by the West, for the culture has accepted

61

the notion that economics is the central activity in human existence and that all other activities are secondary.

While the number of professional ideals is as numerous as the professions, they tend to share at least two common values: productivity and efficiency. To be good at a job means to be productive at it, and productivity is, in turn, dependent on the ability to act efficiently. For a large portion of the populace, productivity has, in fact, become the ultimate value. We are worthy when we are productive. Activities that have no product, such as a walk along a mountain stream or an afternoon's chat with a friend, might be enjoyed but cannot be fit into a scheme of excellence. The health of the nation is not measured in Aristotle's terms of whether or not the populace is happy, but in terms of the gross national product.

The key to being productive is to be efficient, where efficiency means to do a given task in the least amount of time possible using the least amount of expendable resources. Efficiency, in turn, requires one to be absolutely concentrated on the task at hand and to allow no diversions to pull one from its demands. Hence, efficiency often turns work into a mechanical activity, where there is no room to linger and enjoy a creative moment, appreciate the aesthetic aspects of a situation, or engage in human dialogue. Efficiency has become such a dominant value that it has broken out of the workplace to govern almost all activity from education to the preparation of food. Contemporary architecture in particular gives us the message that form must follow function, and hence that life is functional and we are functionaries. There shall be no place for frills and baroque curls, no hidden passageways, no turrets for lonely imagination, no disorder, no playfulness, no overflowing of spirit. Life is work. To work is to be productive, and being productive involves making oneself into an efficient, usually mechanical, agent for the economy.

Efficient productivity can be so draining and stressful that it pushes us to the opposite extreme in those parts of life that fall outside of work. Leisure time is filled with activities whose only end is to give us low-grade, nondisturbing pleasure. Alcohol, drugs, and mindless diversions have become significant features of our cultural landscape. Amusement—activity devoid of the muses—drugs us into soporific forgetfulness, and television has replaced the hearth as the center of the home. Productive activity and mindless diversions have one thing in common: neither allows the human beings engaged in them to experience and enjoy the multiple depths and richnesses we have as human beings. We have become specialized and compartmentalized and have forgotten how to bring ourselves as full human beings to our activities.

The absence of a sustaining ideal of human excellence, and the omnipresence of productive economic ideals, have had a devastating effect on one of the most important practices of the culture: child-rearing. Parents understand that if their children are going to become successes in the contemporary economic world, they will need to learn how to master skills and subvert their own needs in favor of the demands of the institutions for which they are working. Skill learning and self-discipline become paramount virtues, regardless of their effects on the well-being of the child as a human being. Indeed, what constitutes well-being in distinction from success in the professional world is a question that is all but forgotten. As soon as children can utter intelligible sounds, they are hearing the alphabet sung to them and the first ten integers spoken in forceful tones. As soon as they show a modicum of muscular control, they are asked to master excretory functions. The quickness by which these and other early skills are learned is held to be a key indicator for success later in life. Unfortunately, the most powerful reinforcer for the learning of these skills, and the one easiest to come by for the parental trainers, is the giving and withholding of love and approval.

The outcome of this system of childrearing is often the development of highly successful skill-learners and achievement-oriented persons. But the cost is severe, for it involves the development of persons who severely lack feelings of self-worth. What children "learn" from their personal interactions preparatory for cultural existence is that ideals are the repository of worth and that they will have worth and be loved only insofar as they can attain the ideals. Rather than having their own needs responded to, children must meet the needs of the ideals and of the parents and institutions that impose them.

The tragedy of this situation is that the attainment of ideals can never give self-worth. A person is a finite particular being whose needs and wants are idiosyncratic; ideals, on the other hand, are universals, statements of right or good for everyone who is in the activity over which the ideal rules. The particular can never be fully subsumed under the universal. Hence, individuals who commence with the notion that as particulars they are worthless will never be convinced otherwise by the attainment of an ideal, for they still know that it is the *ideal* that has value, and not they themselves.

Although negative self-images are deleterious on the level of personal fulfillment, causing such ills as depression, masochism, and a tendency toward self-destructive behavior; on the socioeconomic level they can be quite valuable. For one thing, they produce high achievers, people desperate to attain increasingly difficult goals to prove that they really are not worthless. A straight-A report card, captain of a team, dean's list, junior vice-president in charge of regional sales, and so on up the ladder—each attainment carries the hope that self-worth will finally be achieved, but it never is. Defeat is not admitted, the accomplishment just wasn't grand enough, and the hope remains that the next achievement will be the one that finally wins self-worth. Thus are many executives produced and destroyed as they push beyond their limits for a goal that they are not conscious of and cannot attain.

Negative self-images also fuel the economy by producing an insatiable consumer psychology. Distrustful of satisfaction from human beings, we hope that the acquisition of material goods can fill the emptiness. It never does, but there is always the possibility that not enough opulence has been achieved, and the insatiability continues, generated by the emptiness within and the general ideal of material success from without.

This insidious psychology of ideals has come under severe attack in the twentieth century. Ideals are seen as demanding a stultifying conformity and unity, thereby negating multiplicity, individuality, and creativity. Karen Horney understood that in many forms of neurosis the "real self" is rejected in favor of an "idealized self."[1] The idealized self is an image of perfection, an image that tells a person how she ought to feel in any particular circumstance rather than allowing her to freely feel what she in fact does. The idealized self demands that one's acts and thoughts conform exactly to a standard. Since a finite particular person cannot become a standard of perfection, and since a person with a negative self-image will, by necessity, always be subverting herself, the perfect image is never attained, and the psyche fills with guilt and oppression.

There has also been a political outcry against ideals. Since ideals always posit one way of life as best, they are almost always biased toward a particular socioeconomic class, either in material conditions needed to fulfill the ideal or in a kind of upbringing that already inculcates the ideal. Whether they favor a social aristocracy or an "aristocracy of talent," ideals appear to be antidemocratic. Too often idealists become fanatics,[2] intolerant of dissenting views and values of others. If people or things do not conform to the ideal, then they do not have worth, and, like the Jews to the Nazis or the American Indians to the European Christian settlers, can be annihilated without qualms. The cry now is for regionalism, multicenteredness, and tolerance for the vast variety of ways that humans can live.

The attacks against ideals, and in particular against the ideal of unity, has been carried even further by contemporary linguistic philosophers. Wittgenstein attempted to show that questions like "What is the good?" or "What constitutes human excellence?" are meaningless. Language carries meaning only when it is part of specific contexts. We can answer "What is a good knife?" or "What is a good parent?" but never questions that go beyond the boundaries of specific contexts. He further proclaimed that there was no final ideal language into which all legitimate truth claims could be translated. There are numerous language games, each with its own set of rules and functions, and these cannot be reduced to some "higher" or more general language.[3]

French semiologists, such as Jacques Derrida, concur. There is no single meaning to a text, no final realities that can be grasped and represented in language. Life is a play of supplements swirling around an absent center, to be enjoyed, encountered, and not negated by the imposition of general ideals and final meanings.[4] Play, freedom, manyness, release from guilt, release from the tyranny of Platonic forms are the life-enhancing shouts from these despisers of ideals. Let the different parts of the psyche have more free play, let the mind free-associate so that the various parts of experience that have been repressed or denied or lowered in status can return and enter full psychic interplay.

This critique of ideals is correct and a corrective. In fact, ideals have tended to crush vitality, creativity, and diversity. But while the antagonists of ideals understand and illumine the dangers of over-structuring life with ideals, they do not see clearly the dangers of multiplicity and a multiply-directed psyche (or state). Plato did not invent the rational psyche, unified around a single ideal, in response to nothing. The atrocities of the Peloponnesian Wars were real; the excesses and fickleness of the Athenian democracy were self-destructive. Multiplicity may seem wonderful until one meets a schizophrenic whose psyche has disintegrated into a chaos of fragments, or unless one belongs to a state that is unable to function because of factions. Such entities are not rich and vital. They are poor cripples.

What is needed to prevent the psyche from falling into fragmentation is, according to recent psychoanalytic theorists such as Erik Erikson and Heinz Kohut, a personal identity or "nuclear self." A person has a personal identity[5] when (a) she has a sense of self-affirmation engendered by effective mirroring and love in early childhood,[6] (b) an integration of "constitutional givens, idiosyncratic libidinal needs, favored capacities, significant identifications, effective defenses, successful sublimations, and consistent roles,"[7] and (c) a coherent set of ideals.[8] These factors all differ from each other and one cannot substitute for another.

The development of an archaic feeling of self-worth and the integration of the parts of the psyche are largely unconscious processes whose outcomes are greatly dependent upon the presence of loving parents and effective role models. These two processes give the bases for having a self and asserting oneself in the world without guilt or self-negation. What ideals give is a unification of conscious cognitive processes with these unconscious unifications. The first two unifications are based upon a mimetic representation of others in oneself and hence look toward the past and what has been. Ideals propel us into the future. They are our vision of what we might become if we can gather our energies and talents and transform ourselves and our worlds to bring the vision into being. Ideals are the dynamic part of personal identity and push us into journeys of discovery and creation far beyond what is possible with the first two unifications alone. If the ideals are fragmented, shallow, or constantly changing, the chances are that this journey into an ever fuller and richer self will also be fragmented, shallow, or so fickle that not much depth of self is produced.

Ideals also help to overcome one of the most persistent problems in the development of self: selfishness. All healthy children will be, for some years, genuinely selfish. They will assert their own needs and demands with little recognition of the needs of others. If these needs and demands are met and the child feels affirmed as someone worthy, then there is a springboard for overcoming this early narcissism to develop a deeper self able to interact sensitively and responsively in a world of others. However, giving up this early selfishness to become a being able to engage in reciprocal human social interactions is never an easy matter. Since ideals are always expressed in universal terms (what is right, good, excellent), they help us overcome this constant tendency to selfishness by demanding that we consider more than just what we want to do, but what it is right to do.[9] Insofar as ideals carry meaning and can be shared by others in a community, they act as mediators between the personal and the social.

Ideals also combat the urgency and power of immediate desires. When we have no ideals, it is extremely hard to resist impulses that want satisfaction in the moment but that have no foresight as to what is good for us or our communities in the future. With ideals, we can deny impulses because we understand and have a commitment to a vision beyond immediate situations.

Ideals can overcome the meaninglessness of a life devoted to nothing more than personal satisfaction. Selfishness can reap pleasure in vast quantities, but it carries little meaning. What is human life all about? Our pleasure getting is the same as pigeons pecking bars for food pellets or cats lying in the sun. Pleasures are felt immediacies; in themselves they carry no meaning. Meaning comes only in terms of universals. Ideals can give a person a sense of worth far beyond her or his insignificant particularity by locating that particularity in a universal goal. There is a smallness and pettiness in human lives that have no ideals; giving oneself a universal value and striving to achieve it, especially when such achievement involves personal sacrifice, is the only way human life is granted dignity.

Finally, the realization of one's ideal can, in large part, overcome the narcissistic injuries of separation that occur in childhood and restore one to a sense of wholeness. The achievement of wholeness by questing after one's ideal is, according to C. Fred Alford, a healthy way to express one's narcissistic eros, while the loss of one's ideal and retreat to infantile ways of merging is a regressive form of eros.[10]

◻

We are now faced with a dilemma. The critics of ideals assert that these permanent structures negate particularity, vitality, diversity of experience, and the possibility of growth. However, other theorists claim that without a set of stable values it is doubtful that a person could achieve a personal identity, meaningful growth into the future, or a significant depth of experience. How can we have both diversity of experience and unity of self? How can we both have the permanence and stability that ideals give and not get caught in rigid, monotonal living?

These conundrums can be solved only if we change our traditional thinking about ideals. First, we must realize what ideals can and cannot do in giving a sense of unity and worth to the psyche. The achievement of an ideal can never replace the grounding sense of worth given in early childhood, nor can it give the kind of grounding connectedness that develops from early mirroring and identification processes. The organization of psychic activity around consciously held ideals is a very important unification, but always a secondary one in terms of maturation. When ideals are used to attempt to do the work of these more archaic forms of unity, the order that comes to the psyche is defensive and repressive. That is, ideals will act as an escape from an earlier psychic world that did not achieve integration. The ideal is grasped as the one way to escape the turmoil of this primitive fragmentation. One suspects of idealists who pursue their values with fanatical fervor that they hold their ideals in this defensive way and are fleeing something rather than genuinely pursuing a goal. Ideals serving a defensive purpose are often rigid, insensitive, and sadistic because they are being used for the unconscious purpose of combating anger, sadness, and chaos in the psyches of people who were not given the affirmation they needed.

It is my belief that the ideal of human excellence that has governed the West since Plato, was created mainly for defensive purposes. In their attempts to impose a unity on what they considered to be a wild and unmanageable psyche, Western thinkers since Plato have constructed ideals from the viewpoint of the rational ego and have given heed to only its needs: power, control, productivity, and knowledge. Although these ideals have led to an immensely successful technological culture with its increased material well-being and health for millions upon millions of people, they have not led to increased happiness, for they have been forgetful of other needs and capacities. Part of us is very satisfied in this culture; but many other sides of ourselves are left unknown and unfulfilled.

What is called for is the development of an ideal of human excellence that is responsive to the full panoply of human needs and capacities, an ideal that is nonrepressive and nonauthoritarian, and that does not controvert multiplicity, creativity, and openness. It must be directive, but it cannot be so closed that it denies the many worthy ways of living that exist. It will be an ideal that does not constrict life into patterns of conformity but, like a path through the forest opening onto a wide mountain meadow dancing with flowers of every hue and shape and uplifted to boundless sky, leads us to the rich and variegated textures of experience.

How can this be? How can ideals be unifying and directive and yet remain open to multiplicity and creativity? The key to solving this problem is the replacement of the hierarchical notion of unity, which has dominated Western ideals since Plato, with the new and vital way of understanding the organization of systems that has been developed in the biological sciences: ecology.

In ecological systems, unity is not achieved by some force or organism dominating or controlling all the others. Rather, the parts of the whole achieve a natural homeostatic balance through a process of mutual adaptation. There are no absolutely dominant factors in an ecosystem. What "rules" the savannah? Is it the lion or the sun or the amount of nitrogen in the soil, which determines whether the grasses will grow, the grasses that are eaten by gazelles, which in turn the lions devour? If the soil composition is changed or the temperature or rainfall or presence of some crucial microorganism alters, then the savannah might no longer be, nor might the king of the beasts.

The parts of an ecological system are intrinsically interrelated, such that to change one part is to change all the others and the nature of the system. That is, if we are going to greatly enlarge the realm of reason and rational control in the ecosystem of the psyche, then we can predict that this will have profound negative repercussions on the emotions, other cognitive capacities, and needs that reason has difficulty recognizing, such as those for beauty, sacredness, and intimacy. Unlike other ecosystems, in which the growth of a dominant form of plant life, such as a forest of Douglas firs, can simply destroy the vast variety of botanical forms that preceded it, the parts of the psyche dominated by rational consciousness do not die but become repressed. As repressed, unconscious elements fragment off from the major structure of personality, they can wreak havoc on the psyche. In other words, when the functioning systems of the psyche get thrown out of ecological balance, what results is not a new and different ecosystem, as happens in nature, but a distorted and self-destructive system. The ego-dominated psyche is like those ecological niches in which a new animal is introduced that has no natural predators and that multiples so bountifully that it destroys the food supply necessary to sustain it. Such an animal is out of ecological balance; such a psyche is doomed to forms of self-destruction.

In ecology there is always a proper proportion of elements. Too much light or phosphorus or water can be as devastating as too little. The amount of light needed to make petunias bloom would keep chrysanthemums from ever flowering. This notion of balance and proportion, of each thing and function having its boundaries that it cannot exceed without causing violence, is the central ethical notion in the Greek dramatists, Pre-Socratic philosophers, and Aristotle. It is the fundamental principle of order in ecology.

With ecology we have a way of integrating diversity without negation or repression, a way of incorporating change within order, and an ideal of order that can encompass such large variations as the differences between a rain forest and a desert. Our new ideal of human excellence will be based upon the premise that the psyche is happiest and healthiest when it works as an integrated ecosystem. That is, the psyche will be able to achieve its fullest depths of experiential intensity when each of its parts is performing its proper function and all of the parts are proportionally balanced so as to mutually enhance one another.

To elucidate how the psyche can function as an ecosystem, we must first discover its basic components and then determine how these components can form a system of reciprocal and harmonious interaction. When we understand what ways of thinking, speaking, and dwelling can best bring about this ecological state of the psyche, then we will know what excellence in human living really is.

❏

'Ecology' is formed of two Greek words, *oikos* and *logos*. *Oikos* means "home," but *logos* is an almost impossible word to translate. It is, perhaps, best defined as the presence of meaning, such that when logos is present in the world or in words, meaning occurs—rather than a senseless heap of stuff or a string of meaningless sounds. Ecology, which studies what makes a particular environment a habitat for a species of plant or animal, might help us understand how to make homes of ourselves such that meaning can enter our lives and ground our language.

PART II

PSYCHE

CHAPTER 5

BASIC NEEDS

At the heart of our new ecological concept of the psyche is a theory of multiple basic needs. These needs are the ultimate source of all human activity and the reason why all the other systems of the psyche function the way they do. We cannot understand anything about the psyche unless we know what these basic needs are, how they function, and how they interrelate. The aim of all activity and of all psychic structures is their satisfaction.

Basic needs have four essential properties. (a) They are intentional. That is, they generate activity toward certain goals such as survival, reproduction, adventure, or knowledge. (b) They are not reducible either to some more all-encompassing need or to one another. (c) They are that which all normal human beings, given the appropriate conditions, seek to fulfill. (d) When they are chronically unfulfilled, we are in a state of deprivation and suffer harm in the sense of not being able to function optimally as human organisms.[1] This deprivation is often felt with varying degrees of intensity as a lack, incompleteness, or as something just "not being right" with our lives.

In understanding basic needs, we must distinguish between desires (wants) and needs. Any particular desire or want can be arbitrary, extravagant, misplaced, deficient, untimely, and so on. That is, no particular desire carries any warrant that it should be satisfied. A need is different, for if a need is not satisfied over time, then the human organism is injured and becomes less capable of optimal functioning. A child might desire a certain toy, such as an expensive doll, and we as parents can deny this desire without guilt or remorse, for no intrinsic harm is done. However, the same child needs love, protec-

73

tion, consistency, and empathic mirroring. These cannot be denied the child without injury to the ability of the psyche to function.

However, the matter is more complicated than needs versus desires, for basic needs usually express themselves through particular desires. For instance, we do not feel the need to survive, but desires at particular times for this drink, this kind of food, a warm coat. Any of these desires may be denied without significant harm, except in dire circumstances, but they cannot as a set be denied. I might not need this piece of chocolate cake, but I do need to eat. Hence, a first step in the justification of a desire is to show that it satisfies a basic need and does so better than other desires that also express that need. However, since we have multiple needs, we also have to understand the relation of a given desire to all the needs. That is, my desire to live in a completely secure, sterile room that is impervious to nuclear radiation and stocked with canned goods to last fifty years might enable me to survive longer than would any other desire expressing this need, but satisfying that desire would frustrate my needs for adventure, beauty, knowledge, social esteem, and so on.

Hence, to say that a desire should be satisfied means that it satisfies a specific basic need and either has positive effects on other needs or at least causes them less harm than other desires of the set that would satisfy the basic need. We should add that we live in communities and the needs of others also must be taken into account (see chapter 10).

Without this distinction between desire and need, all desires must appear to be on an equal footing, distinguishable only by their intensity or ability to produce pleasure. Yet neither intensity nor pleasure is a measure of whether a particular desire is the best way to satisfy the needs. Without a language of needs, we can become lost in a sea of desires and wants, each demanding to be satisfied, each promising pleasure as the reward for satisfaction. The failure to distinguish between desire and need is, to me, one of the primary failures of utilitarianism. When the basic needs ground our activity, we attain happiness; when we live to satisfy desires, we reap pleasure, often to the detriment of our happiness.

While the West has produced a number of profound theories concerning what the basic needs are, almost all of these theories have been captured by Plato's value of unity, or "oneness." Thus we find almost every theorist of the West asserting that such-and-such is the one ultimate drive or the one most important need. This prepossession with oneness goes all the way from Plato's saying in the *Symposium* that our most basic need is for beauty, to sociobiologist E. O. Wilson's recent claim that all living creatures have one final aim: reproductive fitness. Other theorists have proposed such ends as power, social recognition, autonomy, survival, knowledge, immortality, and unity with God, as the ultimate ones. These mono-drive theories are often brilliant portrayals of this or that aspect of human nature, but one has the feeling that the illumined landscape is enveloped by a sea of dark forgetfulness. Always when one need is claimed as basic, some modes of experience must be discredited, or at best seen as sublimated alternatives for frustrated primal drives. Rationalists like Aristotle and Descartes, who hold the search for knowledge to be primary, find sexual activity unworthy, albeit necessary, for the continuance of the species. On the other hand, for those like Freud who find the basal urge to be sexual libido, "the whole edifice of civilization becomes a mere substitute for the impossibility of incest."[2] Religious experience is a fraud for those who emphasize survival and economic activity as fundamental (Marx), while economic activity is seen as crass and degenerate by those who claim primacy for the need of sacredness. The need for order and permanence is abjured by lovers of adventure such as Nietzsche, while good Parmenideans and Platonists will have us seek nothing but eternal, never-changing structures.

Once we free ourselves from the category of oneness, we can see that the psyche must, in fact, have a number of basic needs. It is the multiplicity of the basic needs that explains why the psyche is so complex, why human activity is so diverse and many-faceted, why it is so difficult to find a pattern of living that is fully satisfying, and why so many of our need theorists are compelling even though they contradict one another. Each has found a part of the truth and explored it in depth.

Once we escape the compulsion to look for the "one" basic need, we encounter a number of problems in determining what the basic needs are. How many are there: three? eight? seventy-two? Why one number rather than another? 'One' has meaning because it is the principle of unity, but no higher number (except maybe two, which is the principle of duality, or three, which is the dialectical unification of duality) carries any justification or primary reason why the psyche has this number of needs and only this number. There is no magic number to guide our search.

Nor are there any undeniable signs of basic needs. Basic needs do not appear to individuals with little name tags saying "You need more social recognition," "You need more adventure," or "Your parents are domineering, you need more autonomy;" we must determine them from the observation of behavior. If a need is genuine, then all humans must have it and express it in their behaviors. But the behaviors that express needs can be extremely diverse, and some needs can be effectively repressed by a culture; and the indications of this repression, hard to determine. That is, the bases of all behavior are obtuse and dark. Despite some claims made by scientists, we never empirically encounter a basic need. We see only humans behaving in this way and that and invent theories as to the causes of the behavior. All "causes" are theoretical constructions.

How can one justify that something is a basic need? I am tempted to offer sociobiological explanations for the needs, showing how individuals who developed each need would be more likely to pass genes to the next generation than those who did not. It is fairly easy to imagine why the needs to be social, balance order and adventure, develop intimacy (pair-bonding), develop autonomy (self-reliance), and gain knowledge would aid survival and reproductive fitness. E. O. Wilson gives a strong argument as to why a need for sacredness or religion would help societies form and survive,[3] and one can see that those with a sense of beauty would be more likely to reach harmonic solutions to conflicting tendencies than those who didn't, and hence be selected for. I think that these reasonings are probably true, but am loath to offer them as justifications. I share Steven Jay Gould's hesitations about these new "just so stories" and agree that genes (and needs) come in pools and can't be easily explained in isolation from one another.[4] Also, I do not want to give the impression that survival and reproductive fitness are more primary needs than the other eight. Once a need has been selected for and is part of the gene pool, it is as intrinsic a part of our "human nature" as the inclusive fitness needs. If in the future one or several of the needs is selected against, then evolution will be on its way to producing a new species. What I take from sociobiology is the important idea that there are genetic predispositions to human behavior.

The following construction of a theory of basic needs is founded upon three sources: the findings of the special sciences, the ideas of great theorists and writers of our past, and a phenomenological examination of lived experience. The special sciences provide us with a wealth of empirical data about human behavior and are a rich source of theoretical speculation. However, each field will, by the necessity of its own specialized objectives, study only a limited aspect of human activity and will construct its theories of motivation within these strictures. The profound insights of great philosophers and writers can broaden the scope of our considerations beyond the narrow confines of scientific methodologies. If any need has been supported by a special science, school of thought, or thinker, I try to use or refer to their justifications. Within these arenas I have found a number of very convincing cases for why certain needs should be considered basic. What is not convincing is when these authors attempt to prove that the need they are working with is the only basic need.

But the final test for any theory is its ability to explicate and make articulate our own lived experience. Logic, empirical evidence, and conceptual clarity are all important aspects in the justification of a theory, but it is in the cauldron of lived experience that theory either lives or dies. I invite readers to ask the following question for each of the proposed needs: "Would I be willing to forego entirely the satisfaction of this need, if I could be assured that all the other needs would be fully satisfied?" A negative reply indicates the primacy of the need. Personally, I could not will to live without the experiences connected with all of these needs—they all seem essential to being human.

What are our basic needs? We need to survive and come to terms with our sexuality, to balance order and adventure, to have both intimate friends and a place in the wider social order, to attain autonomy and the kind of knowledge that makes us feel at home in the world, to live in beauty and have sacredness touch our lives. Each of these needs requires a separate volume to explore it fully. All I can do in this book is to give minimal sketches of the essential structure of each need. These schematic sketches are hardly justifiable as pieces of philosophy, but their expansion would frustrate the primary intention of this book to offer an overview of the elements of the psyche that we need to take into account in forming an ecological conception of the psyche.

The Basic Needs

1. Survival

> My heart is sore pained within me: and the terrors of death are fallen upon me.
>
>   (Psalms 89.47–48)

> Ay, but to die, and go we know not where;
> To lie in cold obstruction and to rot;
> This sensible warm motion to become
> A kneaded clod; and the delighted spirit

To bathe in fiery floods, or to reside
In thrilling region of thick-ribbed ice;
To be imprison'd in the viewless winds,
And blown with restless violence round about
The pendent world; or to be worse than worst
Of those than lawless and incertain thought
Imagine howling; 'tis too horible!
The weariest and most loathed worldly life
That age, ache, penury, and imprisonment
Can lay on nature is a paradise
To what we fear of death.

(Shakespeare, *Measure for Measure*)

The need to survive is probably the most accepted of our basic needs. This need actualizes itself in specific desires for food, shelter, warmth, security, health, and so forth. Survival is not more primary than the other needs in the sense that they can be reduced to it; nonetheless, we must meet our survival requirements before the other needs come into play. It is difficult to satisfy any need while dead. This does not mean that survival is always the most important need and cannot be overridden by others. Heroes have willingly died for the sake of social recognition, and martyrs have chosen death rather than betray the realm of the sacred.

Although this drive to survive seems straightforward, it becomes highly problematic in human beings. Unlike any other living thing, we are conscious of our mortal natures and know that at some time we will die. The combination of the fundamental desire to survive with the firmest knowledge of impending death transforms the need to survive into the need to come to terms with mortality. For most of the world, this deepest of human problems is solved by denying that we are, in fact, mortal. Many religions and philosophers have tried to show us "the way" to the understanding that our finite mortal natures are illusions and that behind this illusion we are one with God or partake of eternal, ceaseless forces.

Whether we follow one of these "ways" or the path of secular humanism, which asserts the reality of this world here and now, we still need to face our mortality and ourselves as "beings-unto-death." Without such an encounter with death, a constant semi-conscious fear or anxiety can plague us for a lifetime and circumscribe our abilities to be fully vital. Not confronting this fear of death induces repressions of all the emotions that deal with loss (grief, sadness, anger) and isolates us from the world of changing particulars in which we live. Defenses such as indifference to life (Camus, *The Stranger*), abstract intellectualism, and emotional aloofness are all common ways we have of denying that we live in a world of flux, death, and birth.

This facing of death is not merely entertaining the idea that we are going to die (intellectualism), but the intuitive experiencing of the nothingness within one, and the ability to say "Yes" in the same moment. One must affirm death before one can fully affirm life. Thus, satisfying the need to survive is not quite as biologically mechanical as getting enough food, shelter, and protection. At the deepest level it involves incorporating death into one's very being.[5]

2. Reproductive Fitness

> Urge and urge and urge,
> Always the procreant urge of the world.
> Out of the dimness opposite equals advance, always
>   substance and increase, always sex,
> Always a knit of identity, always distinction,
>   always a bread of life.
>
> To elaborate is no avail, learn'd and unlearn'd
>   feel that it is so.

(Whitman, *Song of Myself*)

The need for reproductive fitness is, in the concepts of recent population geneticists and evolutionary theorists, the need to have one's genes passed on to future generations. For these fields, reproductive fitness has supplanted survival as the fundamental biological urge, for when the two conflict, it is the reproductive urge that needs to win if the species is to persist. We survive to reproduce. Reproductive activity in general lowers the ability of an individual to survive, insofar as it saps energy and time one could be using to gather resources and makes one more vulnerable to predators. In a number of cases, such as for the female salmon or the male praying mantis, reproduction means certain death. But the urge to mate pushes one onward. "A thousand deaths do I propose to achieve her whom I love."[6]

While we reject the notion that reproductive fitness is the "one" basic need, we certainly must recognize, despite what most of our philosophers have said, that we are sexual beings and have a primary sexual need. At a simple straightforward level this need reveals itself in the urge for sexual intercourse and the joy in having children. Indeed, if a poll were taken asking what has made most people happy over time, the having of children would probably be the most common answer. But, like our need for survival, the need for reproductive fitness is more complex than first meets the biologist's eye. Genital sexuality is only a part of our sexuality, and according to a number of psychoanalytic theorists, far from the most important part. As Freud has shown, sexuality assumes vitally important nongenital forms in childhood. In these early years, sexuality is felt as the craving for bodily stimulation and affection (polymorphous perversity). If there is not enough caressing, hugging, and being physically cherished (or too much stimulation of the wrong kind), then the child's sexual growth can become fixated at an early stage, and the person can fail to develop into someone who can have an intimate relationship with another person as an adult.[7]

As adults our sexual need is directed not only toward genital satisfaction but also toward the development of a sexual identity. In fact, many psychoanalytic theorists believe that the attainment of a sexual identity is far more important in satisfying the sexual need than genital experience. There are numerous people who are sexually hyperactive (nymphomaniacs, satyrs) or who spawn innumerable children, that are not sexually fulfilled, while others who are continent are fulfilled. Those who are sexually fulfilled seem to have developed a strong sexual identity, while those who aren't do not have this identity.

What it means to have a gender identity—what it means to be a female or a male—is the subject of a violent debate at present, with positions ranging from the sociobiological claim that gender radically determines personality traits and behavior to one that holds that the only difference gender makes is in the configuration of bodily parts—gender has nothing to do with character, behavior, or patterns of thinking, all of which are functions of social conditioning.

From these debates, two conclusions emerge. First, the attainment of a sexual identity is vital in the development of psychological health, and, second, that sexual identities cannot be specified in terms of traits. Although we can certainly disagree with Freud that all neuroses are rooted in sexual disturbances, we must also remain impressed with the high correlation between neurosis and sexual problems that psychoanalysis has revealed. It seems that to engage fully in the adult activities of intimacy, generativity, and autonomy[8] we need to have a firm sexual identity.

The problem is that such a sexual identity cannot be defined. That is, there seem to be no character traits that are invariant across cultures that could define male behavior or female behavior. Those that appear as the most likely candidates for ubiquitous traits can be explained by the almost universal social function of the woman's caring for home and children due to the convenience of mammary feeding. When this function can be shared, as in technological societies, we find more uniform trait development in the sexes.

Perhaps the most we can say about what it means to have a sexual identity is that a man or a woman becomes comfortable with and accepting of the fact that he or she is a sexual animal and comes to love the particular body he or she has, a body primarily defined by sexual organs. While it is easy to say "accept yourself as a sexual animal and love your particular body with its penis, pubic hair, and testicles, or breasts, vagina, and full hips," in our culture, which has such a long history of emphasizing the mind over body, reason over the desires, and productive expertise over reproductive involvement, it is an exceedingly troublesome task.

This difficulty in accepting ourselves as sexual beings and cherishing our bodies is in part due to our bodies' revealing our inherent mortality. To accept our bodies as who we essentially are is also to accept our corruptibility. We do not live forever; children, the fruits of sexual fitness, replace us and serve as constant reminders of our growth unto death. To become fully sexual is to join the world of finite changing particulars. Birth and death govern this world; it is the world of tragedy but also the only world in which a genuine zest and vitality for living is possible. When we are in love the whole world becomes alive. The trees dance, the birds sing as never before, the air is full of vital spirits, colors shimmer, and excitement fills every pore of our skin. Here is life; here is sex.

3. Order

We all need a certain base level of order in our lives. Some people can tolerate more chaos than others, but if the bottom line of order is threatened, fear and anxiety—the two most unbearable and debilitating of the emotions—arise, warning us to return our affairs to a more structured form. Order is security, change and chaos insecurity. Indeed, *mad* is derived from the past participle of the Indogermanic verb *mai*—"to change"! In most cosmogonic myths (which are also myths about the creation of psyche), the universe is created by order being imposed on chaos. Chaos is death, hell, madness. Order comes and the world is created.

This need for order is felt at every level of our existence, from our unconscious biological functioning to our conscious world of conceptual constructions. Physically this need for order is expressed in the organism's incessantly seeking a homeostatic condition. The white blood cells produced to fight disease must be destroyed after the disease is conquered to return the blood to its normal count. The adrenalin that gives us added strength and acuteness of perception in times of fear will poison the body if it remains.

Psychologically, this need for order is expressed in our unconscious drive to rid ourselves of cognitive dissonance. As Festinger has shown,[9] we must make sense of our world and will do anything to keep dissonance out of our conceptual structures. For instance, if a child conceives of herself as being a wonderful, important person, and of her parents as nourishing, competent, loving people, but yet finds certain needs chronically unfulfilled, then something in her view of the world must give way. The nonfulfillment cannot be blamed on chance, for a world with that much left to chance is too frightening for a vulnerable child, nor can the parents (at least at an early age) be found at fault, for they must be seen as competent and nourishing in order for the child to have her primary need for safety met. The only path left is for the child to conceive of herself as unworthy to have all her needs met, and a negative self-identity begins to be formed. Without the need for order, the whole affair might remain a case of moderate deprivation. But with our need to understand the "whys" of the world and to put these into a coherent framework, the deprivation becomes the ground for a lifelong complex.

Socially, the need for order is manifest in our transformation of almost all human interactions into recognizable contexts with set roles, scripts, and structures of interaction. Human beings are too complex and unpredictable to meet person to person. If Martin Buber's I–Thou relation is one in which two persons face one another as persons outside of any role structures, then such experiences must be exceedingly rare, possible only in relationships of the greatest trust. We need the security and expectations that recognizable contexts and roles give us. When we, like characters in a Kafka story, cannot discern what the context is—what its rules are, what roles people are playing, what its goals are, what is expected of us—we become anxious to the point of madness.

The social order of roles, institutions, and contexts is contained within a wider system of symbolic order, which, at its most profound levels, organizes space, time, and experience for the members of a culture. This structure of ultimate values, icons, and categories is the net that captures what William James called "the booming, buzzing confusion" of life and gives it meaning and order. When the symbolic order of a culture is broken or in a stage of significant transition, its members can descend into chaos, anxiety, and dread. Eliade relates a story of the nomadic Achilpa tribe whose central symbol, a pole representing the *axis mundi*, broke: "They wandered about aimlessly for a time, and finally lay down on the ground together and waited for death to overtake them."[10] The environment had not changed; food, water, and shelter were available. Everything was the same as before, except a stick had broken. But that stick was the center of the symbolic world. Without it, life had no meaning or organization.

There have been numerous symbolic orders governing the lives of humans. These orders seem to have lives of their own. Many have died, some have grown and adapted to changing conditions, some have remained rigid, some are moribund. What keeps one symbolic system alive while another dies has been a matter of intense research and debate, but aside from chance events, there appear to be three crucial factors involved. The first involves the internal coherence of the system itself. If a system of values is inconsistent in some fundamental way (e.g., it contains both "all persons are created equal" and "nonwhite, nonmale persons are not to be given equal opportunity or status"), the incoherence will either slowly drain life out of the system or cause an upheaval that will destroy the culture or result in a more consistent order. The second factor is that each symbolic system can be more or less adaptive to the conditions of the environment. Since conditions vary widely and change—sometimes slowly, sometimes with catastrophic quickness—there is no "right" or eternally valid set of symbols. Each symbolic order must adapt to its own peculiar circumstances. The third factor is that symbol systems can be more or less responsive to the full manifold of human needs. All structures must satisfy some human needs (especially the need for survival), but there is a great divergence in the degree to which they can meet all of them in depth. If some needs remain chronically unsatisfied in a culture, then we can expect to see some agitation to alter the system to meet those needs or a slowly dying interest in the system itself.

Belonging to a culture whose symbolic order is alive and coherent is one of fate's greatest gifts. Here the community is spirited and full of zest for its own mission. Such is not the case for our culture, which is presently struggling with inconsistencies of values, nonadaptiveness to changed environmental conditions, and lack of fulfillment for needs outside the sphere of the rational ego. If we are to transcend the moribund symbols of the culture and create new forms of vital meaning, we need to be aware of the upheavals in our symbolic order and the forms of despair and meaninglessness they cause. An old culture is dying; a new one is being born.

4. Adventure

> A race preserves its vigour so long as it harbours a real contrast
> between what has been and what may be; and so long as it is nerved
> by the vigour to adventure beyond the safeties of the past. Without
> adventure civilization is in full decay.
>
> (Whitehead, *Adventures of Ideas*)

Diametrically opposed to our need for order is the equally important need for change and adventure—a need to break the patterns
of the past and seek new experiences. Without this need for adventure, order could trap us in deadly routines. Like the need for order,
the zest for adventure has roots much deeper than the human psyche.
Hartshorne attributes variations in bird songs to this need,[11] and even
those bastions of conditioned order, the rats, seem to have a yen for
discovery:

> It was predicted that a rat which had found food down one arm of
> a maze would inevitably return to that arm in search of a reward.
> The response was conditioned. Unfortunately for theory, rats, being
> full of curiosity, frequently explore the rest of the maze, when replaced
> at the entry, instead of immediately going for the reward. No one
> was surprised at this except the psychologists.[12]

Adventure takes us out of the strictures of order and throws us
into change. For philosophers as far apart in time as Heraclitus and
Whitehead and in culture as the Buddha and Bergson, change and
process are the heart of existence. "Everything flows and nothing
abides; everything gives way and nothing stays fixed."[13] It is in those
moments between old and new structures, in those moments of flow
and change, that we find ourselves in the presence of the real, the
throbbing vital energy that flows through all beings.

Come! Dance! Greet Dionysos in song and wine and movement!
Let go of your structures, your pedestrian habits, your orderly morals.
Darkness falls, fires rage. The mountains shake with wind. The
streams crash down, down, down the mountain in joyous never-ceasing
revel. Come! Join the dance! Round and round and round. Flesh on
flesh; drums pounding the immortal rhythms of the heart; feet
mimicking the destruction and creation of the world. Kill! Destroy!
Return to the chaos whence you came. How can new worlds be made
without chaos? How can new selves be born without the deaths of the
old?

In the interstices of structures, in the gaps in texts, in the breaks of order, in the moments of sacred time when the routines of profane time are put aside for the holy reenactment, lies life—unfinished, flowing, regenerative.

Existentialist philosopher Jean-Paul Sartre asserts that no structure can ever encompass a human being, a "for-itself." We are defined by our consciousness, and consciousness is not a thing, not a structure. It is sheer activity, vitality, process, always intending objects and structures in its search for order and stability and always transcending those structures. For Sartre this insatiable and unsatisfiable striving to become ordered and stable (to become an "in-itself") condemns human experience to nausea. But for Nietzsche and other process philosophers, this striving beyond the present is the cause for rejoicing and pronouncing the Sacred Yes.

Sartre and Nietzsche are both right; both emotions are in place when we enter the world of change. Nausea, the feeling of weightlessness, of having no center, is evoked by change, for in change the structures that ground us disappear, and new ones have yet to appear. Nausea recalls us to our essentially open nature and reminds us that while we need to have some structure to our psyches, no particular order is essential. Change, if it is real, throws us into the more or less unknown, and thus will often have as its emotional companions anxiety, dread, fear, and nausea.

But adventure also evokes excitement. Structures may give life security, but they make experience formulaic. Intensity wanes until some adventure or change comes that awakens our eyes from seeing their typical patterns of expectations and makes us want to think and feel anew. Without adventure, we are in full decay.

Along with anxiety and excitement, adventure also evokes the emotion of grief. There is no birth without death, no change without loss, no loss without grief. This is a fact that our culture has problems accepting. We like to feel the excitement of adventure, even its tension and fright, but not its grief and loss. The failure to allow grief into the process of adventure dooms many of our adventures to triviality: a change of place, a change of activity, but no real change in values, character structure, or modes of experiencing.

Whether the need for order or that for adventure is "more basic" has been the subject of heated debates from the time Heraclitus asserted that change was primary and Parmenides replied that nothing ever changed, all was a single order. Ecological thinking accepts that we have needs for both, that neither is more basic than the other, and that they are meant to balance one another. Under some conditions and in the context of certain life histories, the need for order will be ascendant; under other conditions, the need for adventure. A life of unopposed order would make us inflexible and unable to adapt to the conditions of the world, while a life of pure adventure without order is insanity. Nature has done well in balancing these needs and giving us the emotions that tell us when they are out of balance: anxiety curbs adventure; boredom and restlessness let us know when we are too stable.

5. Intimate Love

> One turf shall serve as a pillow for us both;
> One heart, one bed, two bosoms, and one troth.

(Shakespeare, *A Midsummer-Night's Dream*)

Without friends no one would choose to live, though he had all other goods.

(Aristotle, *Nicomachean Ethics*)

The need for intimacy is the need to participate in a human relationship that is mutual, singular, empathic, and caring; a relationship in which we are not variables or roles, not replaceable by other human beings. As humans we are not satisfied with social relations that are merely functional, pleasurable, or partial in the sense that they involve just parts of ourselves. We need to be in a "special" personal relationship that involves us to the cores of our beings. We want to be so closely bonded to another human being that experience loses its sense of isolation and garbs itself in the joys of shared experience. This sharing is, as Dewey says, one of the greatest joys known to human beings.

Intimacy is a singular relationship. That is, neither the relation nor a partner in the relation can be replaced by any other relation or person. Often we fall in love with an image or an ideal, use other people to fit that image and then pretend we love them as individuals when we are really only in love with an archetype. If one person leaves the relation he can be replaced easily with another. Freud found that this was particularly true for people who had not worked through their oedipal desires. They kept searching for mother or father surrogates, and anyone who reminded them of parental traits and was willing to play the complex oedipal game then became the object of love. Likewise, when we love our children intimately, one child cannot be replaced by another. Our relationships are individuated to the child and its idiosyncratic wants and character structure. Every child needs such a relationship and feels hurt and rejected by a relation that seems to be a generalized response to a typical child.

The second characteristic of an intimate relation is that each person is known and affirmed as a whole human being. The father who affirms only the obedient, charming, nonassertive part of his daughter does not love his daughter but is fundamentally manipulating her to fit his own desires. The wife who affirms only the competitive, aggressive aspects of her husband is, likewise, only affirming a vehicle for the satisfaction of her own desires. If we love a person only when they have "good" feelings—excitement, love, joy, interest—and not when they are sad, angry, afraid, or narcissistically self-possessed, then we are loving them only conditionally. We are giving the message "You will be loved only if you are happy or loving or beautiful," rather than "I love and affirm you as a whole person." Such a conditional relation pressures the other person to repress or deny the unaffirmed feelings and enhances the possibility of fragmentation rather than integration.

The sharing of experience that forms the heart of an intimate relationship is grounded in the ability of the partners to empathize with one another. Empathy is experiencing another person's feelings with the same feeling-tone as that person. It is a mimetic form of knowing in which we repeat in ourselves what is being felt by the other, either consciously or unconsciously. We feel the other's joy joyfully, anger angrily. Sharing at the deepest level is this mimetic reenactment of feeling. Empathy is union. It is what is intimate in intimacy.

Empathy is bordered by two poles: overidentification and objectification. When it goes over into one or the other of these poles, intimacy is lost. In overidentification the empathizer becomes so fused with the beloved that she loses her own identity. With such an over-identification the lover can give no help to the beloved if a situation is difficult and perspective is needed. Intimacy is destroyed, for now there are no longer two persons sharing an experience, but just the overwhelming experience itself. In objectification we gain knowledge about another person without participating in how that person experiences herself. The person is known as an object, in the way a geologist might know the properties of a certain mineral. There is a connectedness in the knowing process, but a coldness in the refusal to empathize at the level of emotion. The Nazis knew the Jews had a desire to live but could not empathize with this desire. If they had, they could not have done what they did. Thus, genuine empathy requires that the individuals both retain their separate identities yet mimetically participate in the feelings of one another.

Finally, intimacy demands that a commitment be made to attempt to sustain the relation through all adversity and time. Here a philosopher can add nothing to Shakespeare:

> Love is not love
> Which alters when it alteration finds,
> Or bends with the remover to remove:
> O, no! it is an ever-fixed mark
> That looks on tempests and is never shaken;
> It is a star to every wandering bark,
> Whose worth's unknown, although his height be taken.
> Love's not Time's fool, though rosy lips and cheeks
> Within his bending sickle's compass come;
> Love alters not with his brief hours and weeks,
> But bears it out even to the edge of doom.
>   If this be error and upon me proved,
> I never writ, nor no man ever loved.

(Sonnet CXVI)

Intimate friendship is such a cherished good because it satisfies the two seemingly opposed needs for individuation and connectedness. Unlike all other social contexts, which attempt to impose a set of values and to demand that one play a role, intimacy does not impose roles or a set of values. Here we are affirmed as full persons, in all our multiplicities, foibles, and strengths. This affirmation helps us break the bondage of social conditioning and assert ourselves as individuals without having to suffer the loss of connectedness that plagues all other paths to autonomy. To have been loved intimately as a child is perhaps the greatest of all gifts that nature can bestow by way of luck, for such a love is the basis for growth into an integrated, full human being. The absence of love in an otherwise successful adult life, like Faust's, can doom it to a slowly growing glacier of cold despair and isolation.

Our culture has constructed the institution of "romantic love," in which the needs for intimacy and sexuality are fused. When this fusion is successful, the result is an enormous heightening in the intensity of experience. Bodies and souls intertwine in a vortex of such profound involvement that all other experiences pale in comparison. Such a conjunction of needs, while powerful, is not necessary; intimacy need not be sexual (at least in the genital meaning of that term).

According to Erich Fromm, our culture has not done well with this need for intimacy. "No objective observer of our Western life can doubt that love—brotherly love, motherly love, and erotic love—is a relatively rare phenomenon, and that its place is taken by a number of forms of pseudo-love which are in reality so many forms of the disintegration of love."[14] The core of the problem is in the way our culture has structured the psyche to emphasize the rational ego. The function of the ego is to direct life in as controlled and objective a manner as possible, which it can do only if it can achieve distance from involved connectedness of the emotions. But intimacy is grounded in an emotional connectedness to another person. As such, intimacy is a constant critique of the Western psyche and always in tension with it. As Carmen says to Esmiraldo, if you want to go to your job, you can just forget about me. One of the tasks of a new ecological ethic is to reconstruct the psyche to allow intimacy to flourish.

6. Social Recognition

> People don't realize how much they rely on recognition as a proof they exist.
>
> (John Fowles, *Mantissa*)

When we turn to the moral and psychological literature of the Enlightenment, we find as a common theme that the most basic human need is for social approbation. Pascal, Malebranche, Hume, Hobbes, Locke, Johnson, Lord Halifax, La Bruyère, Rousseau, Adam Smith, Wolff, Butler, Voltaire, and others of lesser fame all find this need for esteem in the eyes of others, and a derivative esteem in one's own eyes, to be the basis of human action, both good and evil. We can also find verification for this need as far back as Homer, where the chief good in life for a warrior was fame, and as close to the present as Thorstein Veblen. We do not, according to Veblen, seek goods mainly for survival or consumption, but because "the possession of wealth confers honour."[15] While as ecological thinkers we do not accept that this need for social recognition is the only or primary one, we understand that we are social beings and must have some recognized place in our social order. As Aristotle says, any person who lives outside society must be either "a beast or a god."

The latest expression of this position is ethogenic social psychology, especially the work of its two leading practitioners, Irving Goffman and Rom Harré. For Harré, "The pursuit of reputation in the eyes of others is the overriding preoccupation of human life."[16] We achieve social recognition by proving to others that we can follow the values and rules of social institutions and practices, play the roles they demand, and give accounts of what we are doing in socially legitimated narratives. Our moral careers (Goffman's term) are the histories of how well we meet the challenges of the social institutions and practices of which we partake. If we are successful, then our social esteem rises; if unsuccessful, it falls. If we deal with challenges in ways not condoned by institutions, we either become innovators of a new social order or get stigmatized and cast out.

In social life, unlike intimacy, we are not persons, but personas. We wear masks and play roles. We are always performing and monitoring our performance to make sure we are successful. If the revelation of who we are, regardless of foibles and folly, is essential in intimacy, the opposite is the case for social life. We must carefully manage the impressions we make. Indeed, Goffman sees the management of self-image as the preeminent activity in human life.[17] Such management ought not be understood as deceit or a moral defect, for we are social beings and must find a place in the realm of social reputations.

The need for social recognition is at the heart of two of the most crucial problems of our culture. The first is the extreme tension and unhappiness caused when the system for social recognition is attached to a hierarchical status structure. In a hierarchical status structure, a few will have high status, but most will be taught to think poorly of themselves for their low position in society. Further, if the statuses are arranged according to wealth, as they tend to be in contemporary culture, and there is no boundary as to how much wealth an individual can have, then no one can be happy. Veblen saw this problem clearly:

> The desire for wealth can scarcely be satiated in any individual instance, and evidently a satiation of the average or general desire for wealth is out of the question. However widely, or equally, or "fairly," it may be distributed, no general increase of the community's wealth can make any approach to satiating this need, the ground of which is the desire of everyone to excel everyone else in the accumulation of goods.[18]

What might a system of statuses be in an ecological framework? In ecology we recognize the worth of all the parts that make the whole function and realize that garbage collectors, company presidents, maids, senators, clerks, and lawyers are all necessary parts of the ecosystem and deserve more or less equal recognition. We do not have to rank. That is a compulsion of the old hierarchical psyche that finds order only in systems organized around the "one" or "the best." A system of social recognition need not delegate large numbers of people to a realm of lowered self esteem because they belong to a lower class. There will no longer be a "lower" class.

The second problem with social recognition is that social identities can, for people with weakly developed personal identities, usurp the entire personality structure. The many social roles we play can lead to personal fragmentation and an inability to generate a strong central self able to critique social contexts. Rather than finding ourselves with some control over activities and institutions, we discover ourselves determined by them. As mere social beings, we are more or less like Adolph Eichmann, the Nazi who directed the deportation of Jews in Germany and other occupied countries to concentration camps. Eichmann did his job well and followed the values and procedures of the contexts of which he was a part. He was a superb social functionary. He had no self to break through the practices that reduced persons to things and activities to tasks to be done efficiently. When Hannah Arendt went to Eichmann's trial seeking an understanding of evil, what she found was not some great demonic force but the banality of a person reduced to a social identity.[19] Unless the need for social recognition is balanced by the need to gain autonomy, there is the peril of becoming a mere pawn in the hands of social forces.

7. Autonomy

> Give me liberty or give me death.
>
> (Thomas Paine)

Like a bulb wishing to burst through the soil that protected it against the ravages of winter, humans desire to leave the dependency of childhood and burst into the sunlight of autonomy. We need to gain an increasing freedom to direct our own activities and lives and we find submission to others to be intolerable. Just as states cannot endure subjugation to a foreign power, neither can healthy individuals accept lives of bondage.

Probably no other end has been more celebrated in the Western tradition than this notion of freedom. From Pericles proclaiming Athens's superiority "because we are free" through such luminaries as Plato, Aristotle, Epicurus, Locke, Rousseau, Spinoza, Jefferson, Hegel, Fichte, Nietzsche, and Sartre, the value of personal and political autonomy has been a generating force for much of our social and political change. Autonomy is also an essential value in defining health for psychoanalytic theory:

> The freedom to define oneself and the capacity to exercise this personal freedom become the essentially human. And if this capacity for self-definition be man's essence, all those aspects of man which interfere with this capacity to engage in such a self-definitional pursuit are viewed as pathological, all aspects which further this undertaking are his healthy facets. If one posits such an essence, health becomes defined by the degree to which a person is free to perceive himself as an independently acting and reacting unit, experiences consciously the choices at his disposal, and makes choices with a conscious sense of responsibility for them.[20]

Although there has been close to unanimous agreement that freedom is a fundamental need of humans, there has been wide controversy over what constitutes freedom and how it is to be achieved. Thinkers from the Greeks to the Enlightenment emphasized that autonomy was the result of a rigorous self-development that included an ability to control the emotions and exercise the powers of deliberative thought. Since the Enlightenment, we have tended to locate freedom in environmental possibilities rather than in the powers of the self. If the environment has significant possibilities open to the agent, then the agent is free. Psychoanalytic theory has added a new twist in claiming that unconscious compulsions are the major hindrances to freedom. Compulsions can make us unable to act on what our conscious minds advise and can distort our reasoning, wants, and perceptions so significantly as to make choice impossible. These unconscious urges and repetitive patterns have been isolated from the workings of a central self, and like the delinquents and criminals who have been isolated from the mainstream of society, victimize the self or society that is unable to incorporate them.

All three positions have an aspect of the truth: we are free when (a) there are significant opportunities for choice in our environments, (b) we are not determined by unconscious compulsions, and (c) we have developed the necessary cognitive powers to make choices. The first condition is met by societies in which there are enough conflicting socializing forces to avoid authoritarian rigidity, and numerous roles requiring adult responsibility in the economic, social, and political spheres. It has been the aim of democratic polities since the Enlightenment to foster such an environment.

The key to the reduction of compulsions is, according to recent psychologists, the development of a self that is flexible and rich enough to encompass the vast diversity of emotions, needs, and thoughts that we have. As Erikson says:

> Psychologically speaking, a gradually accruing ego identity is the only safeguard against the anarchy of drives as well as the autocracy of conscience, that is, the cruel overconscientiousness which is the inner residue in the adult of his past inequality in regard to his parent.[21]

This theory agrees with that of Aristotle, who held that unless we develop moderate character traits that allow us to feel but not be overwhelmed by emotions and desires, it makes no difference how well we reason about actions or how free our environments are. We will still be slaves to our fragmentary passions. We cannot be free without an integrated self. How such a vital and flexible self can be developed is the subject of chapter 7.

However, even if our environments are full of opportunities for adult responsibility and we are free of interior compulsions, we still would not be free if we had no way of formulating our own values. Autonomy dawns when we refuse to accept values just because they are maintained by the reigning cultural authorities, and enter a critical process for determining which values we accept as our own. While the use of such a critical method may result in the same choice that one would have precritically made, the very process of deliberating and choosing carefully is the experience that most deeply satisfies our need for independence.

The questioning of regnant social values and the construction of personal values evokes a profound discontinuity between the self and society and the self and its past self. It is in this discontinuity that freedom is found, according to such philosophers as Nietzsche, Sartre, and Kant. Without such ruptures we would merely be the products of socialization forces. Yet we must remember, along with Aristotle, Spinoza, and Erikson, that autonomy also requires continuity. Without a continuous and steady growth in our deliberative faculties, knowledge of the world, and understanding of ourselves, there would be no possibility of exercising choice that amounts to more than whimsy.

There must also be a continuity between one's personal identity and the social order, for the self cannot be fully developed without social approbation, nor can the need for social recognition be satisfied without such accommodation. Erikson writes:

> If. . .we speak of the community's response to the young individual's need to be "recognized" by those around him, we mean something beyond a mere recognition of achievement; for it is of great relevance to the young individual's identity formation that he be responded

to, and be given function and status as a person whose gradual growth
and transformation make sense to those who begin to make sense
to him. . . . Such recognition provides an entirely indispensable support to the ego.[22]

These continuities of self and society and of self with self are no
merry waltzes of unending compatibility. The social order constantly
threatens to turn persons into social functionaries, and ever-present
regressive tendencies can turn the self into a prisoner of its own past.
Discontinuity is needed in the development of autonomy. This is not
to say that life must be constant struggle, questioning, and turmoil
in order to be free. A life of indefiniteness and perpetual change is
as unhealthy as a life caught in rigid unchanging structures. Neither
is free; both are forms of escape from the responsibility of becoming
a definite self with a recognizable identity that has the courage to
grow and change. Having an identity and being able to critically
challenge oneself to new forms of life and thought are not only not
incompatible, they require each another. Real change needs the
security of an identity, and a personal identity could not realize its
complexities and tensions without the dynamics of discontinuity. The
path up the mountain is continuous, but endures many switchbacks
in its course.

8. Knowledge

> All men by nature desire to know.
>
> (Aristotle, *Metaphysics*)

This first line of the *Metaphysics* has been echoed again and again
throughout the history of our culture. The quest for knowledge and
learning for the sake of learning has been proclaimed by writers of
all ages as *the* telos of human life. Knowledge supposedly distinguishes
us from the beasts and thereby gives us our defining characteristic
and function: we are homo sapiens, the beast that knows. Not only
do we seek knowledge for its own sake, but most of our other needs
seem to require some knowledge in order to be satisfied. We need
knowledge of nature to survive, knowledge of ourselves and others
to have intimacy and autonomy, knowledge of social norms and
patterns to gain social recognition, and so on. Some have even held
that if we attain a certain sacred knowledge, it will make us immortal.

As important as knowledge is as a tool for the satisfaction of other
needs, it is not this function that concerns us here. Such knowledge

is like food, a necessity for survival but not itself what I am calling a primary need. For knowledge to be a primary need, it must be sought as an end in itself. While it was self-evident to Aristotle that human beings had a natural wonder and desire to understand the world in which they lived, it is not so for us. Modern wisdom declares that what we call knowledge is really just interpretation, and that interpretations are sprung from deeper needs for power or prestige. Pragmatists, sceptics, Nietzscheans, and semiologists join hands in proclaiming the nonprimitiveness of the need for knowledge. As Nietzsche has Zarathustra say, "You too, lover of knowledge, are only a path and footprint of my will; verily, my will to power walks also on the heels of your will to truth."[23]

This doubt concerning the genuineness of our need for knowledge comes in part from our lack of understanding of what knowledge is and how it functions. Our culture has been captured by one peculiar definition of knowledge that has distorted our comprehension of it. For us, knowledge must have empirical verification, be attained by an objective (emotionally uninvolved) agent, and fit into a logically coherent framework. This concept of knowledge has been extremely powerful and lies at the root of the scientific and industrial revolutions of our culture. But it also might not have given us knowledge in the deepest ways we need it. What is knowledge? Why do we need it?

The myths concerning the coming of knowledge to the world of humans reveal a profound ambiguity. On the one hand, we find a set of myths in which wisdom-bringers—Athena, the Muses, Prometheus, Solon, Newton, et al.—dispel darkness and bring light and salvation to the world. However, there is another set of myths that disclose fear and disaster in the attainment of knowledge. Adam and Eve ate from the tree of knowledge and were banished from paradise. Oedipus, the seer who penetrated the riddle of the Sphinx, pushed his quest for knowledge so far that he uncovered his own unbearable pollution. Semele, mother of Dionysos, asked to see Zeus as he really was and was thunderbolted to death.

The ambiguity in the myths about knowledge reveal that this need is intimately connected with one of the deepest, most problematical structures of our nature: the nondetermination of our behavior by instincts. Rather than relying on instincts to direct our activities, we must acquire knowledge. This nondetermination is, in one way, our glorious openness and ground for all that we have created, but in another way, it is felt as being "unnatural" and alienated from the earth. All other animals have habitats where their instincts allow them to live. We, by nature, have no home, but must gather knowledge about places and use this knowledge to transform the earth into a habitat. Thus, the quest for knowledge is full of ambiguous emotions because it both reveals how homeless we are and gives us the tools for creating our own peculiarly human habitations. Adam and Eve cannot live instinctively in a natural paradise with no cares. We have been wrenched from being at home in nature and now must seek knowledge to transform an alien nature into a home.

That the search for knowledge is fundamentally the same as the search for home is revealed in the most profound vehicle of memory, language. For the Greeks, *noos* ("mind" or "intelligence") and *noesis* ("knowledge", a state of knowing that is immediate and final) have the same root as *nostos*—the longing for home.[24] Odysseus, the hero with the most *noos* in the Homeric epics, is also the person with the strongest *nostos*. His intelligence and relationship to Athena, goddess of wise counsel, are what enable him to return home when all others fail.

Knowledge has truth as its object. In English, *truth* stems from *troth* or "trust" and was originally connected with fidelity and faithfulness. These terms find their root meanings in relationships of the home—being faithful to the clan and one's spouse such that one can be trusted. To live in truth is to live in a world of trust, a world that will not arbitrarily destroy one and in which one fits. There is a mutual trust between the inhabitants and the habitat. This is the state of knowledge and of being at home.

Knowledge gives us home. Knowledge can transform an unknown foreign world that is dangerous in its unknownness into a safe, sustaining habitat. When we know what foods there are to eat, what dangers lie in what areas and how to avoid them, how to find shelter, how to move within the area safely and efficiently, where there is a beauty that renews us, and so forth, we then have a place we can trust, a home. Knowledge is a fundamental need because it transforms the foreign into home, where the foreign can be ourselves, a place, the earth, the universe—anything. We have a need to live in the familiar (the family), and knowledge is what makes anything familiar.

Yet the paradox remains, for we can never fully find a home. A home, in the deepest sense, mirrors us. It reflects us back to ourselves and says that we are inherently part of it, in harmony with its deepest laws and patterns. But we begin the search for knowledge in ignorance, in homelessness. What we are is homeless beings seeking a home. No home can ever mirror back to us our primal state of being homeless. Our need for knowledge is always fraught with ambiguity.

The problem with contemporary knowledge is that it has attempted to deny both the ambiguity in the search for knowledge and the relation of knowledge to home. The mathematical and mechanical world that has come to be the truth of our age may indeed feel like a home to the abstract, disembodied, rational ego, but it is hardly a home for our emotions and such needs as those for beauty and sacredness. The scientists loved the new world of the Enlightenment, but the Romantics revolted in horror at this antiseptic, colorless, emotionless, meaningless world of mechanical atoms. The technology this new knowledge has given us has made life easier and more secure in a number of ways, but it has presented, in the form of atomic weapons, the most insecure world ever experienced. We live in a world in which we know more than ever before, but very little of the "knowledge" means much, because it belongs within a framework that does not make the world a home for us.

Meaningful knowledge will come when we once again open up to our homelessness and begin to think on what we really need for the earth to be a home. This thinking will recall the fullness of our human nature, our multiple needs and emotions, and that we begin our search in ignorance. It is a thinking that itself can be a home, for it attempts not to settle the ambiguities of our nature, but to dwell in them. Heidegger is the contemporary philosopher who has explored this kind of thinking in the greatest depth. His words need to be heard.

> However hard and bitter, however hampering and threatening the lack of houses remains, the *real plight of dwelling* does not lie merely in a lack of houses. The real plight of dwelling is indeed older than the world wars with their destruction, older also than the increase of the earth's population and the condition of the industrial workers. The real dwelling plight lies in this, that mortals ever search anew for the nature of dwelling, that they *must ever learn to dwell.* What if man's homelessness consists in this, that man still does not even think of the *real* plight of dwelling as *the* plight. Yet as soon as man *gives thought* to his homelessness, it is a misery no longer. Rightly considered and kept well in mind, it is the sole summons that *calls* mortals into their dwelling.[25]

> But how else can mortals answer this summons than by trying on *their* part, on their own, to bring dwelling to the fullness of its nature? This they accomplish when they build out of dwelling, and think for the sake of dwelling.[26]

9. Sacredness

By the need for sacredness I mean the need to experience or be in the presence of the ultimate, of something that is not exchangeable for any other good and that is experienced as a ground for other existences, while nothing further grounds it. In contrast, the secular is the marketplace where everything has its price and exchange value. The market is centered on the individual's desires and his or her exchange of goods and services to satisfy them. The sacred is focused on the ultimate, not the self, and there is no bargaining or exchange.[27]

In this age of secular bounty and religious impoverishment, forgetfulness of our need for sacredness comes easily. This forgetfulness is aided by recent theories that attempt to reduce sacredness to psychological or social phenomena and deny that there is a genuine need for self-transcendence and apprehension of the sacred. Religious practices are "explained" as being adaptive in helping societies and individuals survive, being effective opiates, or satisfying unconscious compulsions. Persons who claim to have experienced something ultimate in an epiphanous moment are seen as having only projected the feeling of social cohesion, satisfied a wish-fulfillment for an ultimate parent, or relieved guilt for a primal oedipal murder. Religion is at best an illusion; at worst, an evil that destroys the possibility for human peace and vitality.

The universality of religious phenomena, and the depth of satisfaction that is found in the experience of the sacred, call for a nonreductive, noncynical approach to matters of self-transcendence. When we focus on the satisfaction of our mundane, individualized goals, we are restless, constantly pushing to get something or somewhere. Needs other than sacredness can never be fully satisfied; we must continually work at gathering resources, keeping the order, breaking stifling patterns, responding to our intimate friends, overcoming infantile regressiveness in order to mature, gaining knowledge of the ever-changing world, monitoring ourselves in social contexts, and so on. Always there is labor, goods to be exchanged, institutions to be satisfied. Indeed, labor is the essence of secular life, and our contemporary emphasis on work as the primary human function manifests how secular we have become. The call to the sacred is the call to let-be and be.

> Come unto me, all ye that labor and are heavy laden, and I will give you rest.
>
> (Matt. 11:28)

In the world of secular activity, the will is the basic faculty. The self is constantly acting to satisfy its desires and needs. The need for sacredness is the overcoming of self-centered willing, and reposing in that which resides through time and change. Even that master philosopher of will, Nietzsche, found that for will to be free, it had to give up its own willing. For Nietzsche this is done by experiencing time as eternal recurrence, by experiencing the world as repeating itself again and again through endless time.

> Everything goes, everything comes back; eternally rolls the wheel of being. Everything dies, everything blossoms again; eternally runs the year of being. Everything breaks, everything is joined anew; eternally the same house of being is built. Everything parts, everything greets every other thing again; eternally the ring of being remains faithful to itself. In every Now, being begins; round every Here rolls the sphere of There. The middle is everywhere. Bent is the path of eternity.[28]

In experiencing time as eternal recurrence, the will realizes the foolishness of all ends and goals. Nothing will ever be changed. If the overman comes, he will be followed again by the rabble. Willing makes no real difference, and in this numinous insight, Zarathustra's will is released from itself, and Zarathustra is able, finally, to dwell on the earth.

Eternal recurrence is, of course, only one account of what is met in the numinous experience. There are many others—for instance, Heidegger's Being, Tillich's ground of Being, the Christian monotheistic personal God, the Hindu multiplicity of gods and goddesses, the Native American's Wakonda, Emerson's Oversoul, Hegel's Geist, and Heraclitus's Logos. The paths to the sacred are equally numerous: meditation, self-flagellation, ritual dance, mastery of sacred texts, descent into hopelessness, communing with nature, and so on. What seems common in these theories and reports of sacred experiences is that the ultimate comes as a gift. We don't deserve what is holy, nor can we earn it. It appears gratuitously. We might work at ways of improving the chances of the sacred experiences occurring, but there is no guaranteed final result. Work is how we achieve secular goals; sacredness is *sui generis*, as when the meaning of a poem dawns on us or a natural landscape becomes infused with beauty and meaning.

A second common feature of the numinous experience is the loss of self-centeredness in the face of the ultimate. We feel, as Otto says, "the emotion of a creature, submerged and overwhelmed by its own nothingness in contrast to that which is supreme above all creatures."[29] The loss of significance in the experience of the holy is not, however, felt as a negation, for the profound connectedness of the individual to the ultimate is also revealed. This sense of primary union, which goes beyond the power of categories to understand and words to describe, is what gives the experience its transcendent nature.

A person who has been touched by sacredness has two traits that are absent from those whose lives are grounded in the secular: thankfulness and peace. These characteristics are tonal qualities that infuse the entirety of a person's way of acting, feeling, and thinking.

Thankfulness is dwelling in the memory of the world and self as gift. The thankful person responds to the gift of the numinous with a thankfulness for all that is. Contrasted to thankfulness as a way of being in the world is the trait that grounds ethics, namely, justice. The root concept of justice is "desert"—that which a person is due. Different theories find different kinds of people deserving of different kinds of rewards and punishments, but always there is something deserved. Thankfulness transcends justice by understanding that no one deserves anything: all is a gift. Thankfulness does not eliminate justice, which is necessary for the world of practical activity, but it does allow one to overcome the anger, tensions, and limitations of living in the world of "good and evil." Thankfulness is a state that transvalues all values without hostility or rebellion.

Peacefulness is a state of fully accepting the world and ourselves as we are. The world and ourselves no longer need to be transformed or changed. We no longer need to strive to realize our potentialities. Death can no longer negate life, nor can bad luck destroy it. Life needs nothing more; it is complete. Whitehead understands this quality:

> (Peace) is a positive feeling which crowns the 'life and motion' of the soul. It is hard to define and difficult to speak of. It is not a hope for the future, nor is it an interest in present details. It is a broadening of feeling due to the emergence of some deep metaphysical insight, unverbalized and yet momentous in its coordination of values. Its first effect is the removal of the stress of acquisitive feeling arising from the soul's preoccupation with itself. Thus Peace carries with it a surpassing of personality.[30]

Because sacredness gives one a sense of belonging, of completeness, of peacefulness, of connectedness to the ultimate, it has been seen as the most important need. When sacredness comes into a person's life, mortality seems overcome, the world becomes a home, the insistent push of the other needs vanishes, and with it the necessity of labor. Sacredness "puts out" Croesus' fire (desire) and allows him to dwell wisely on the earth. When we are close to the holy, we can feel whole, at one with the world and ourselves. 'Holy' shares the same root as 'whole' in the Gothic 'hails'—safety, health, physical integrity. It seems that when we cease being bent on the satisfaction of this or that particular need and gather ourselves in self-acceptance, wholeness and integrity come. It is because sacredness gives this sense of wholeness and completion that it has so often been deemed the one and only worthy human end.

But it is not the only worthy end. People who limit their potentialities to dwelling in the sacred can be as incomplete as humans who center their lives on sex, social recognition, or the appropriation of resources. We are not just beings-toward-God; we are also sexual, social, individualized persons living in particular places at particular times. Insofar as the experience of the sacred makes any place a home, it cannot make this singular place a home. That comes by gaining knowledge of the particular place and harmonizing one's habits to fit it. Likewise, the sacred might overcome dread of death in one way, but it does not produce the bread necessary for sustained life. Our need for sacredness is one of our needs, not our only one. Sacredness may be present in all our experiences as a tone or background, but is not itself all experiences. The importance of this tonal quality, however, should not be underestimated. It gives a liberating perspective when the little things in life threaten to overwhelm us. Peace and thankfulness grace a person's life with joy as no other qualities can.

10. Beauty

Love is the love of beauty.

(Plato, *Symposium*)

The teleology of the Universe is directed to the production of Beauty. . . .The real world is good when it is beautiful.

(Whitehead, *Adventures of Ideas*)

From its unequaled exposition in Plato's *Symposium*, through its worship by the Romantics, to its grounding of Whitehead's vast metaphysical system, the desire for beauty has been recognized as a basic human need. Ugliness lowers our spirits. When our surroundings—social, physical, or cultural—are dreary or misshapened, we feel less adventurous, less sexual, and less like probing for knowledge, pushing into autonomy, or surviving. Beauty, on the other hand, calls us into life and fills us with excitement and zest. The profound response we have to the presence or absence of beauty reveals that we have a fundamental need to live in beauty.

The need for beauty is the need for harmony in the environment, in oneself, and between the environment and oneself.[31] Aesthetic harmony occurs when a number of separate elements flow together to form a whole without losing the strength of their individual details. In a high mountain meadow the peaks soar in their rugged majesties while the flowers delicately dance to the music of winds. A marmot lollops across our path; a pippit flutters away. Each detail carries its own vitality, but each blends with the others to form a whole that adds to each detail. A mountain seen from the window of a car is not the same mountain as one seen from an alpine knoll that one has arduously climbed. Beauty is about interrelationships and the harmonies among things.

While this kind of complete aesthetic experience is unusual and clearly demarcated from ordinary experience, it is, nonetheless, on a continuum with all of our experiences. Every experience involves some kind of unification of diverse elements and is, in this sense, aesthetic. Thus, the need for beauty is not just the need for unified experiences (which we always have), but a need for increased intensity within these harmonies. There are, of course, several kinds of experience that elicit intensity—sudden sharp pain, horror, disgust, anxiety, and so on—which we would not ordinarily term "aesthetic," for they lack any involvement with the 'beautiful'. Aesthetic intensity seems to demand that the elements experienced be contained within a patterned contrast (to use Whitehead's words) in which there is both variety and harmony.

In this light, the aesthetic can be located between the realm of harmonies, with such minor contrasts as to produce only low-grade pleasures, and the realm of ruptures, dislocations, and annoying inconsistences, as when a loud tourist in Bermuda shorts invades the sacred space of Chartres or a telephone wire disrupts an otherwise beautiful view. In general we can say that the deeper and more complex the contrasts are between the elements in the experience, without their breaking into destructive ruptures, the greater the aesthetic intensity provoked. Sometimes the complexities are hidden in the recesses of consciousness. We see a ladyslipper hidden in the forest shade. For an instant our heads stop their incessant clamoring, and we become fully present to this simple flower. The complexities here lie in the realm of archetypal metaphor: brightness arising out of gloom, ephemerality combined with an undaunted burst of life, a bright spot of color focusing a vast undifferentiated world, sexuality in shape. These metaphors are themselves complex and can resonate in all the parts of the psyche rather than being isolated in one sector, such as rational consciousness.

Patterned contrasts seem to arise most frequently when we are able to balance receptivity and creativity. The aesthetic occurs when we let the vibrant unclothed particulars of the world flow into experience and organize them in fresh, evocative ways. Such a balance is uncommon, for we have tendencies, on the one hand, to be overreceptive and let the world do all the work, and on the other hand, to be overactive in our forcing the details into preconceived, expected patterns. When we are too passive in experience, it remains shallow, unable to evoke deeper, fuller resonances in the psyche. Surfaces aren't penetrated; original insights are not achieved; and most important, the creative activity of the self is absent from the experience. Overcontrol occurs when our structures of perception and belief dominate the rich particulars of the world and force them into expected patterns. We experience only what our rigid structures of anticipation allow us. Whatever doesn't fit is repressed, cast out, or devalued. We can't dwell in the symbolic richness of the ladyslipper, but must classify it, *calypso bulbosa*. The world is now in order, and we walk on, untouched. While such patterns of expectations make the world safe and ever-harmonious, they turn life into a dull sameness. The aesthetic is created when the self and the world, subject and object, meet in a dynamic, cross-fertilizing matrix of interaction.

Our need for beauty has, for the most part, been scorned or trivialized by modern culture. Industrial forces have blighted the land, and aesthetic concerns have continuously been overridden by economic consideration. At a deeper level, the whole hierarchical way of organizing the psyche, values, and institutions is unaesthetic, for it demands that some individuals have much greater importance than others. Rather than a complex set of interrelations forming an aesthetic whole, we achieve unity by raising some elements to dominance and reducing others to submission or nonexistence. In contrast, beauty and ecological structuring are kindred notions, both concerned with interactive harmonies, for ecology stresses the interdependence of all the elements of an ecosystem and the importance of each to the whole.

Likewise, there is an intrinsic relation between beauty, ecology, and psychological health, for health is defined in terms of the various parts of the psyche being able to interact and communicate with one another. The neurotic psyche is fragmented, and experiences are prevented from resonating throughout the multiplex levels and realms of feeling, ideation, memory, and meaning. This fragmentation not only divides the psyche against itself, it prevents the psyche from having a depth of aesthetic enjoyment. The fragmented psyche is a piece of disharmonious ugliness. Thus, we might revise Whitehead and say that not only the world but the psyche is good when it is beautiful.

CHAPTER 6

EMOTIONS, CAPACITIES, CHARACTER

Basic needs form the foundation for all psychic functioning. To satisfy them we enter into our vast variety of individual and social activities—from tiddlywinks to philosophy, from sexual foreplay to religious prayer. Needs, however, do not have the power of self-satisfaction, nor do the organisms of which they are a part. Satisfaction comes only through a successful interaction of the human organism with its natural and social environments. The psyche does not enter these interactions unprepared. It comes equipped with a highly complex system for monitoring and adjusting itself to the world, a system that involves capacities for knowing the conditions of self and world, emotional predispositions to respond to those conditions, and a propensity to organize successful patterns of responses into stable adaptive structures of behavior, namely, habits or character traits.

Although capacities for knowledge, the emotions, and character can be separated for the sake of analysis, in life they are inseparably intertwined. Our emotions are dependent upon the appraisals of situations made by our cognitive faculties, but in turn the emotions organize the field of perception into salient and background features and focus memories necessary for knowledge. Our characters are created from early successful cognitive–emotional responses, but the formed character then shapes all of our cognitions and emotions. The fearful person scans the environment for any sign of danger and is predisposed to withdraw, while the secure person scans the same environment looking for interesting possibilities of exploration.

105

As analysis must begin somewhere, let us start with the emotions, for in many ways they are the glue that binds the psyche and world together. The primary function of the emotions is to monitor the relationship between the organism's needs and the environment and to predispose the organism to certain reactive behaviors. If the environment is appraised as safe and accommodating to the needs, our emotional response is one of interest, joy, or happiness, and our predisposition is to explore or relax. If the environment is thought to be one of deprivation, we then feel angry and have a tendency to aggress. If we feel threatened, we become fearful and withdraw. When we emotionally respond to the world in these ways, we are connected to and involved in it, often to the point of being unable to extricate ourselves. Emotions spin threads to every part of ourselves and the world, situating us in a vast web of interdependencies.

The contemporary malaise of feeling alienated, distant, bored, and isolated from the world and ourselves is an effect of the repression of the emotions that has been occurring in the West ever since the Greek thinkers launched their full-scale attack on them. Aristotle was the most lenient, allowing moderate and balanced emotional responses to be part of a good life, but the others were harsher. Plato grouped the emotions with desires; he saw them as a disruptive, never-ending cycle of deprivation/gratification and would permit only the pure pleasures of the intellect to be part of excellence in human living. The Cynics and Stoics were more brutal: passions for them were contrary to nature and needed to be extirpated. Epicurus found the life of constant tranquility or cheerful serenity to be the goal of human existence, and counseled overcoming the disruptive emotional responses as a means to this end. The Patristic, Medieval, and Renaissance periods did little to change this negative evaluation of the emotions, and by the Enlightenment the emotions were ripe to be cast out of the rational mind by Descartes and tossed into a valueless, mechanical body. Despite strong dissenting voices, such as those of Hume and Rousseau, the major trend followed Descartes. Emotions, along with desires and feelings, were typically grouped in a lower part of the psyche that went largely unanalyzed and unappreciated. The development of reason and the moral will were the focus of most philosophic texts; the disruptive animal emotions were to be controlled and harnessed so the ends of reason and will could be achieved.[1]

By the end of the nineteenth century, the negation of the emotions had become so pronounced that a number of new lines of inquiry into the emotions began. One was the study of emotional expressions and responses as evolved behavior and, therefore, as having important adaptive functions; initiated by Darwin's *The Expression of the Emotions in Man and Animals*, this line continues strongly today in ethology and sociobiology. William James commenced another trend with his research into the physiological structures associated with the emotions. A third line of inquiry was begun by the psychoanalytic tradition, with its profound study of the dynamics of the emotions and how these dynamics affect the rest of human activity.

These three lines of inquiry have produced in the last century a remarkable broadening of our knowledge concerning the functioning of emotions. Although some dissenters hold that emotions are primarily social creations, there seems to be widespread agreement that (a) emotions have biological origins and exist because they are adaptive; (b) emotions are highly complex processes involving perception, appraisal, feeling, dispositions to respond, and feedback mechanisms capable of altering any part of the process; (c) a small number of basic emotions form the basis from which other emotions can be built, much as many colors are created by mixing the three basic ones;[2] (d) each basic emotion has its own particular physiological structure, function, and etiological profile; and (e) the primary expressions of the emotions and the ability to interpret these expressions are universal constants for human beings. Although the above conclusions have a strong bias toward a biological understanding of the emotions, most theorists would also agree that culture is a vitally important influence on how we appraise situations, express our emotions, understand and conceptualize what we are feeling, and respond to the action tendencies present in the emotions. We might share emotions with other animals, but it is also true that as "one goes up the phylogenetic scale variability increases, and that such variability results from the growing dependence in higher mammals on learning and symbolic thought and the lessening dependence on wired-in stimulus-response linkages."[3]

Emotions begin with the perception and appraisal of some interior and/or exterior stimuli. Depending on the appraisal, a specific emotional response is triggered. If the situation is appraised as dangerous, fear is evoked; if the appraisal is one of being chastised for breaking a group's mores, shame; and so on. Some appraisals in later life can be consciously considered, but most appraisals are unconscious, extremely quick, and quite complex, involving an assessment of one's needs, one's abilities to act or cope with the environment, and the environment's relation or potential relation to one's needs.

There seem to be some appraisals that are biologically given. A baby deprived (of food, love, or security) does not "learn" that it is; it inherently knows it and expresses its distress by crying or screaming. There is also evidence that we have innate mechanisms for decoding and understanding the emotional expressions of others. But most of our appraisals are based on learning. As the great British empiricists of the Enlightenment found, learning occurs mainly through the process of association (now termed "conditioned response"). We experience certain factors in the environment that are then followed by certain consequences, and this connection forms the basis of appraisal and emotional response in future situations when those factors occur again. The child who has once been bitten by a dog will usually appraise later dog-situations as dangerous and respond with fear until enough counterexperience convinces him otherwise. Thus, each emotion has a vast system of roots spread throughout the dark loam of the psyche. These roots constitute the history of the emotion in the person. They are the memory of the experiences, encounters, and relationships that have earlier called forth the emotion, and that form the basis for present evaluations and responses. Although the goal of psychoanalysis is to uncover unfavorable and irrational correlations from the past so that emotions in the present can be free, such a state is an idealized goal, never capable of pure attainment. The tree is never without roots.

Once a situation has been appraised, a particular emotional complex is activated that involves experiential, neurophysiological, motor-expressive, memory, and reactive components. That is, we have a set of differentiated emotions, each of which is activated by a certain appraisal and issues into its own distinctive behavioral and experiential patterns. While there are debates concerning which emotions are basic and which are secondary,[4] the following seem to be major candidates for the basic emotions.

Interest/Anticipation: An emotion based on the appraisal of a situation as safe and/or stimulating. Its action tendency is exploration. This emotion is the most common of the "positive" emotions and motivates learning, development, and creative experimentation.

Joy/Enjoyment/Acceptance/Trust: An emotional complex in which there is a sharp reduction of stimuli and tension, and a concomitant feeling of harmony within oneself and with the world. Interest propels one to explore and experiment on the world; this emotion, on the other hand, allows one to let it be, to dwell in restfulness. When this state of rest occurs, it seems to fill us with a sense of self-worth and well-being, a contentment that is crucial for further exploration and growth. It is evident that this emotion is central in the numinous experience of the sacred. Erikson also finds basic trust and acceptance to be the crucial emotion in early bonding and all subsequent felicitous relations to others.

Surprise: A quick, sudden, transient emotion that clears the nervous and cognitive systems for a fresh response to the stimulus situation.[5] Its action tendency is keen observation. This emotion is important for reorientation to changes in ourselves and our environments. People who experience a number of unpleasant surprises often learn to fear surprise and develop defenses to control their perception of the environment so that surprises cannot occur. Unfortunately, such security is bought at the price of not being open to the vitality inherent in flux.

Anger: This emotion occurs when we feel ourselves deprived or prevented from doing what we want. Anger has the action tendency of aggression against the depriving or offending object. Such aggressiveness can be a stimulus for the emotion of fear, especially if the aggression is directed against a primary source of nourishment and protection—fear either of retaliation from the superior source or fear that the aggression will be successful (as children can often feel with their magical sense of power) and destroy the source of nurturance. In these cases where anger evokes fear, the aggression is often displaced onto a safer object, such as little brothers, sisters, pets, or oneself in self-destructive acts. Such displacement often does not rid us of the anger felt, and it can continue to haunt us in its attacks on inappropriate others for long stretches of time. On the other hand, the direct feeling and expression of anger against the offending person can fill one with a feeling of power and self-assurance. This powerfulness in turn can lead to a heightened sense of self-worth and vitality.

Sadness: The emotion we feel in response to loss. It serves the adaptive function of heightening the importance of bonding by letting us know how much another person or thing has meant to us and signaling to others that we are not well and are in need of compensating bonding. Expressions of sadness tend to innately evoke caring responses in others.

Grief is the joining of sadness and anger, for in situations of loss we feel not only emptiness but also deprivation. Grief is an ambiguous emotional state, for sadness makes us feel the preciousness of the lost person and beckons us to fold into ourselves, like an animal curled up for protection, but anger urges us to rage against the lost person for depriving us of herself. Hence, we both want the grief object and want to destroy it; we want to become passive and to strike out. This ambiguity makes grief an extremely difficult emotion to feel, yet being able to feel grief is necessary if we are to grow and live in a world of change. All change involves loss; grief is the portal by which we leave the past and enter the future. Life is a vale of tears, but the tears cleanse and open us to the exhilaration of time.

Fear: The response to situations appraised as dangerous and with which we have inadequate abilities to cope. Fear is the most toxic of the emotions, causing such stress in the organism that people and animals have been literally frightened to death. It provokes the opposite response from anger in its tendency toward flight. Fear can be provoked not only by external dangers but also by internal stimuli, such as when a person feels murderous rage against a parent or sexual libido for an inappropriate person. It can be caused by the absence of a source of security or by a symbolic or structural likeness to a previous fearsome event. In addition, we seem to have some natural fears, more prominent when young but still active in adulthood, of loud noises, darkness, wild animals, and excessive strangeness or chaos.

It is obvious how fear is adaptive in protecting us from dangers. But the toxicity of the emotion makes it necessary to avoid the emotion as much as possible. Some theorists have hypothesized that the noises, sudden motions, immense numbers of strangers, and high crime rates of our modern cities are responsible for a chronic low-level fear that eventually makes the organisms living in them unstable and vulnerable to heart attacks, diseases, and psychological troubles. A similar kind of stress is experienced by neurotics who carry with them a chronic fear of their own emotions and "unacceptable" thoughts.

Disgust: The emotion we feel when we evaluate a situation as being one of psychological or physical deterioration. We are disgusted at the smell of spoiled food, the sight of a spoiled child, or seeing a beautiful landscape that has been spoiled by industrial exploitation. The action tendency of this emotion is to reject the disgusting substance or person, usually by avoidance but sometimes by extirpation. Disgust, along with the defense mechansim of projection, is often used as a way of attempting to rid ourselves of unacceptable feelings. For example, when one feels too much sexual attraction for an incestuous object, a reaction formation can occur in which one feels all sexual acts to be disgusting, or all men to be disgusting in their ravenous desires for women, or all women to be depraved in their pro- miscuous lusts.

Contempt: The emotion felt when one appraises another person, race, nation, etc., as being inferior. Contempt leads to rejecting behavior or, when combined with anger, hostility. It can be adaptive for rallying one's energies for aggressive assertion in a competitive situation, for defense, or as a compensation for a weak self-image.

Contempt, disgust, and anger form what Izard calls the "hostility triad," in that they all involve a readiness to aggress against an offending object and can be mutually supportive in the massing of aggressive power.

There has been much discussion in recent literature about whether humans are innately aggressive or not. The analysis here holds that aggression is neither a basic need nor a basic emotional response. Rather, it is an action tendency connected with the emotions of anger, disgust, and contempt. If there were no situations that evoked anger, disgust, or contempt, there would be no aggression. Since such a state is impossible to imagine, as all life involves loss and deprivation, aggression will remain a common part of human existence. Yet it can be reduced significantly by minimizing situations that produce the hostile emotions and by channeling debilitating and provocative physical aggression into other kinds of aggressive expression.

Shame: The feeling of nakedness, helplessness, alienation, and lack of dignity before the eyes of a community whose mores we have broken. In shame we become painfully self-aware, lose hold of our abilities to reason, and fervently desire to crawl into the nearest hole and disappear forever. The adaptive function of shame is evident: it promotes social coherence by making individuals sensitive to the opinions of others and to the structure of values in the community. Although shame may seem to negate autonomy, it does not. When in the throes of shame's painfully heightened self-consciousness, we can become aware of ourselves as selves in distinction from an ordinary melting with others in typical social contexts. "Shame-lessness" is usually not an autonomous assertion of the self in the face of a repressive society, but an angry aggressive response that indicates that there has been significant deprivation from others.

Guilt: An internalized emotion we feel when we have (a) learned and accepted certain moral or social values and (b) developed enough self-critical ability to grasp (usually unconsciously) that there is a discrepancy between our behavior and the values. Shame always occurs before the eyes of others. Guilt, on the other hand, is an emotion concerning the self's relation to itself. The self is judge, juror, and accused, with the accused being found guilty and punished. Guilt is the emotion through which Freud's superego, the internalized punishing parent, does its work. Guilt is often felt when we separate from our parents or other persons in order to individuate, because we have learned and accepted in the past that it is "natural" or "right" for us to belong to these people or be obedient to them. To separate is to break the old moral order.

When excessive, guilt helps produce the negative self-images that are at the heart of so much neurosis and self-negating behavior. We must be consistent: if we have an assessment of ourselves as bad, then we must do bad things. With such self-defeating propensities in guilt, one might wonder why it developed as a basic emotion. The hypothesis is that guilt acts as an inner police force that enables social cohesion to persist despite individuation.

Happiness: The other emotion that is structured around ideals, but which is diametrically opposed to guilt. This affect occurs when we find that our behavior, and more importantly our characters, meet the ideals we hold for them. While most psychological theorists tend to lump happiness with excitement or joy, it is clear from the earlier analysis of happiness (chapter 2) that happiness is not just being interested or contented, but is what we feel when there is a congruence of the ideal and the actual. However, as was previously discussed, happiness ensues fully only when the ideal is based in the satisfaction of the needs.

This list is not meant to be final or exclusive. There may be other emotions that belong on it, such as jealousy or envy, but it is not clear yet whether these are merely functions of a certain kind of social organization or biology. What is important is to know that the psyche comes into the world with a set of differentiated emotional responses, each of which will be evoked depending on how the organism is relating to the environment in the quest to satisfy its needs. One might wonder why love is not on the list. I consider love to be a highly complex state involving our need for intimacy, the emotions of excitement, trust, and happiness, and the predominance of the capacity for empathy. All of these factors are crucial in order for us to feel love and to be in love.

These discrete emotions are the primary indicators of the relations of our needs to the environment. They are vital in providing us with information about ourselves and the world and in generating initial action tendencies. The other important monitoring system is that of pleasure and pain. This is a more encompassing but less directive organization than the discrete emotions. In general, organisms feel pleasure when the activities in which they are engaged are need fulfilling, pain when they are not. Pleasure and pain interact with the emotions in ways that can amplify, prolong, or attenuate them. Excitement and joy are usually accompanied by pleasure, which tends to keep us in these situations, while pain makes us want to terminate our sorrows and fears as soon as they have run their courses.

Along with understanding that the emotions are differential responses to the organism–environment interaction, there are two other theorems concerning the emotions that are significant for understanding how the psyche functions. First, each emotion involves a complete process from perception/appraisal to reaction/action. If this process is stymied or blocked at any point, a number of pathological symptoms can occur, such as undifferentiated arousal, chronic muscular tension, maladaptive behavior, and repression.[6]

Second, each emotion can be felt with more or less intensity. Sometimes the change in intensity can feel like a change to a different emotion, such as low-intensity anger being experienced as irritation and high-intensity anger being experienced as rage. The more intensely an emotion is felt, the more clearly we can discern what we are feeling. People who constantly experience emotions at a low intensity tend to be confused about what they are feeling and not know whether they are excited or afraid, sad or bored. We can also repress emotions at various intensities. That is, a person who represses anger usually does not repress any ability to experience anger, but only anger at a certain level of intensity.

Although the following hypothesis has not been verified or refuted by any studies I know of, I put it forth as an intriguing possible dynamic structure of the emotional system. If we have repressed an emotion at a certain level of intensity, then we will be anxious about feeling any emotion at that or a more intense level. In other words, repression of any emotion at a level of intensity will lead to a repression of all the emotions at that level. What is repressed is the level of intensity itself.

This hypothesis seems to be counterindicated by numerous examples of people who, for instance, can't feel love, but rage intensely at everything in the world, or who can't feel anger, but seem to be buoyant, full of surprise, love, interest, and so on. In order to handle cases like the enraged person, it is necessary to distinguish between "acting out" an emotion and feeling an emotion. When one acts out an emotion, one follows the action tendency of the emotion without really feeling the emotion. The emotion is only partially evoked by the situation; the reaction is an overdetermined response in the present to prevent feeling the real rage that exists in the unconscious. Thus, acting out is not feeling an emotion, but a defense against such feeling. Anger and aggression are being used to immunize the person against the rage. But defenses are not emotions; they at best are pseudo-emotions. The rage is not really felt.

In the type of case in which the positive emotions seem to function normally but there is an absence of rage and hostility, I am convinced that people can fool themselves into thinking they are feeling emotions, as a defense against their depression and repressed feelings. Such feelings have a manic character to them. On the surface they appear strong and vital feelings, but on further examination they turn out to be thin unconnected responses. The emotions are "acted," not felt.

If this hypothesis is correct, then it is crucial not to repress any emotion, for such a repression can destroy the functioning of the whole emotional system. For the emotional system to work well, we must be able to differentiate the emotions we are feeling and how strongly we are feeling them. If there is substantial repression of one basic emotion, then the person is condemned to a more or less monotonal emotional existence and loses the most vital monitoring system we have for evaluating our state of psychological health.

When significant repression of the emotions occurs, the web that holds the organism together and relates it to the world is broken. We feel isolated and disconnected, both from ourselves and the world. We cannot determine what we need or want, or whether we are in a satisfying or unsatisfying relation to the environment. Further, the repressed emotions don't disappear but remain underground in the psyche, requiring increased amounts of energy to keep them chained but nonetheless breaking out here and there in overdetermined and inappropriate reactions to events. The organism is now diseased, unable to know or satisfy its needs, unable to weave together the fragmented parts of the self, unable to see the reality of its relation to the world.

To live well—to be able to recognize and satisfy the needs—we must have a fully functioning system of emotions.

Yet even if the emotions are strong and vital, there can still be significant psychic malfunctioning if the appraisals that generate the emotions are erroneous. For our interactions with the environment to be successful, we must have knowledge of ourselves and our world. We gain knowledge about how to interact successfully with the environment by developing our various capacities for knowledge. Two of the most primitive and, for the most part, unconscious capacities for knowledge have already been mentioned: biological mechanisms for decoding certain key stimuli (such as emotional expressions) and associative learning that issues into conditioned responses. The three other major capacities we have for gaining knowledge are mimesis, intuition, and conscious reasoning.

Mimesis is a capacity for knowledge in which we learn by copying the behaviors of others or by empathically repeating in ourselves what others are feeling. This capacity is invaluable in giving us knowledge of how to do things, and it can be either an unconscious process, as when we learn to respond to the world by copying our parents' responses, or a conscious procedure, as when we watch others doing something and then try it ourselves.

Although there is a tradition in Western culture of understanding intuition as the ability to grasp essences unavailable to the synthetic workings of perception and reasoning, I interpret it as the ability we have to unconsciously assimilate a large quantity of data, instantaneously assess it, and have an insight thrust into consciousness. When we just "see" or "know" that a certain solution is right or that a certain person is the mate we've been seeking, intuition is at work. When we try to say why the particular solution or person is right, we can only elucidate a set of universals (I love her because she is intelligent, good-looking, caring, interesting, etc.) that could apply equally well to a number of individuals. Intuition is the process that lets us know the particularity of individuals and things, while ratiocination gives us universals, similarities, connections, structures. Reason also tends to be abstract, clear, and devoid of emotional input. Intuition, on the other hand, lives in the dark webs of the unconscious where it ingresses into our needs, character, emotions, history, long-forgotten associations, and so on. This full connectedness to all the psychic functions and the ontogenetic development of the individual makes intuition a deep, rich, and dangerous source of knowledge. It is dangerous because if unconscious elements are diseased they can easily distort intuition. How often has intuition told a boy that he has just met the right person—the girl of his dreams—only to have it turn out that she is an oedipal surrogate and the relation, rather than being full of bliss, is tortured with ambivalence.[7]

Intuition is similar to biological decoding mechanisms, associative learning, and mimesis in its grounding in unconscious processes. All of these capacities develop in the experiences and pressures of childhood and can become maladaptive at later points in life. We tend to unconsciously generalize early associations and come to expect that all situations will be structurally similar to those of childhood. All women will be like mother, all men like father. We tend to repeat the behaviors of our parents through learned mimesis, even if these actions were inadequate for the parents and are for us, too. We tend to intuit as "right," structures that repeat successes of childhood but that may not work in adult settings.

The one major capacity we have for correcting these psychological and epistemological problems is the power of conscious reasoning. Unlike our other cognitive capacities, which we have by nature, critical thinking must be learned through training or education. It develops later in life than the first four capacities and is much less involved in the forming of situation appraisals for emotional responses. It is precisely this distance from the emotions and the unconscious that allows critical reason to gain some sense of whether they are diseased or not. While Freud said that reason can be merely the slave of the passions, he also maintained that one of the keys to a successful therapeutic recovery was the presence of critical rational powers.

Critical reasoning is a complex set of processes and takes different forms in different situations. These processes include empirical observation, imagination of possibilities, formulations of general hypotheses to solve problems and unify disparate particulars, weighing the pros and cons of proposals, synthesizing information from different fields, and analyzing particulars within general structures of understanding. Each of these processes is itself complex and takes extensive training and practice to master. Each can be applied more or less extensively to various situations and more or less thoroughly. In general, the more kinds of situations, psychological structures, and cultural patterns we can bring under the purview of critical reason and the more thoroughly we can apply the processes, the more powerful a role this cognitive capacity can play in our lives.

What reasoning can do that the other forms of cognition can't is to free us from our bondage to the familiar. The other forms of cognition, especially associative learning and mimesis, create conceptual, perceptual, and evaluative structures of expectations. These structures mold experience into familiar repetitive patterns that are typical for the members of a culture and that make the world orderly and safe. The world is as we expect it to be, and we keep doing things just as we learned to do them. Critical reasoning has the power to unearth these patterns of expectations and create new ways of experiencing. It does this either by demanding we apply an impersonal and noncultural, "objective" set of categories to the world (those of empirical science, for instance) or by initiating a probing critique of our values, our views of reality, or our understandings of what it is to be human, a member of a certain family and culture, of a certain gender, and so forth. Critical reason can even examine itself and inquire into the grounds for the possibility of reason. The deeper it probes into the structural basis of experience, the more we can be liberated to explore new possibilities of experience beyond those of childhood and culture. With the development of critical reason we can move from living merely consciously to living self-consciously.

Yet the matter is not quite as simple as having one's life liberated by learning how to think critically. There are far too many cases of persons knowing what they ought to do or even wanting to do it, but being unable to do it. The dessert is eaten, the alcoholic beverage consumed, the affair consummated, the angry words spoken. It is these experiences that let us see the truth that Aristotle knew so well and that was forgotten with the overestimation of the powers of reason in the Enlightenment: reason can only direct action if there is a set of character traits, or habits, that allow this to occur. Without the proper character traits, people can have the most highly developed ratiocinative abilities possible and it will do them little good in living well. If reason bids a self-indulgent person to curb his excessive desires, the self-indulgence will simply override the dictum. Reason might be the most powerful tool available to humans, but, as the Greeks knew, character is fate.

A character trait is any general way we have of responding to situations. Character traits are habits that organize emotions, needs, and capacities in general patterns of response. Habits have received a bad press in our culture ever since the Romantics crowned spontaneity as the highest human virtue. But the presence of 'habit' in such words as *habitation, inhabitant, and inhabit* reveals that there is no living, no dwelling in a place, without habits. A place can be inhabited only by creatures whose habits are in a harmonious relation to the patterns of the environment. Without habits or character traits our psyches would be a chaotic mess, our behavior unpredictable, and lives with others impossible. As William James said, habits are the flywheel upon which the world turns.

Unlike our needs, emotions, and primitive cognitive capacities, which are biologically given, there are no set character traits. Aristotle was right when he wrote: "Neither by nature, then, nor contrary to nature do the virtues arise in us; rather we are adapted by nature to receive them, and are made perfect by habit."[8] The forges in which our most important character traits are molded are situations that evoke our basic emotions. In response to situations of danger and the emotional response of fear, we can develop the traits of being courageous, rash, or passive, depending upon how we get reinforced by the outcome of our actions and upon the models we have around us. A little girl breaks one of her father's cherished Chinese vases and fears a terrible outburst of aggression. Like her mother, she lowers her eyes, slumps her body, mumbles words of apology, and thereby

averts the danger. This successful action will be a step in the formation of the character trait of passivity and appeasement in situations
of danger.

Character traits can remain situation-specific and be mobilized
only in certain types of events (e.g., passivity only in situations of
danger), or they can become more or less general ways of acting (e.g.,
passivity in all facets of life). These general and specific character
traits are the core of who we are as persons. Emotions, needs, and
capacities are common to all persons, but how we organize them, what
we emphasize, how and what we allow ourselves to feel, and how we
solve problematic situations is determined by the particular set of
character traits we develop. Dour or funny, serious or supercilious,
rigid or relaxed, intuitive or logical, sexy or prudish, assertive or
cowardly—character is who we are. As Emerson says, "We pass for
what we are. Character teaches above our wills."[9]

What kind of character traits will allow our emotions and cognitive
capacities to optimally function in satisfying the basic needs? A complete answer to this question must await the development of an
ecological concept of the psyche, but in general we may say that
Aristotle was right in holding that a virtuous character trait "consists in observing the mean relative to us, a mean which is defined
by a rational principle, such as a man of practical wisdom would use
to determine it."[10] The mean is what allows a person to feel the emotions without being overwhelmed by them and their impulses to
immediate action so that her rational capacities can clarify the situation, weigh the possibilities, and choose the most appropriate action,
given her complex multiple needs stretching into an indefinite future.
The mean, thus, escapes both repression (what Aristotle calls "deficiency") and infantile lack of control (excess). On these points, I find
Aristotle's moral psychology in complete agreement with contemporary psychotherapy in its definition of emotional health.

It appears that my moral psychology, aside from the careful
specification of basic needs, is fundamentally Aristotelian: moderate
character traits, developed rational capacities, balanced and
thoughtful satisfaction of the basic human needs. But at this point
we must depart from Aristotle's moral psychology for three crucial
reasons. First, Aristotle's moral psychology rests on a teleological
biology that sees our natural function as the development of our
rational capacities. Not only is this kind of natural functionalism no
longer believable, but it also overemphasizes the place of reason in
the psyche.

Second, Aristotle had no conception of the unconscious dynamics of the psyche—of how trauma, conflicts of emotions, and chronic neglect in childhood can distort the functioning of the psyche and immobilize its rational capacities. The unconscious does not work according to logical, reasonable principles, and highly conceptual, abstract language cannot communicate with it. Yet the unconscious dynamics of the psyche must be integrated with its conscious functions, for the psyche to be whole. Hence, we must introduce a different kind of thinking and language as primary in the psyche, if we are to have a moral psychology that can incorporate both conscious and unconscious elements.

Third and most importantly, Aristotle did not have an adequate concept of self or of the stages of self-development. He defined the moral psychology of individuals primarily in terms of their character traits, rational capacities, and social relations, all of which are developed through proper social reinforcement and exemplary education. But what provides the unity for these traits and capacities? Are the traits and capacities fully constitutive of the self, or is there a self that transcends and grounds them? It seems that for Aristotle and some contemporary virtue ethicists, the final grounds for moral psychology are character traits and capacities. However, contemporary psychoanalytic theorists, especially those doing self psychology and ego psychology, in examining the difference between healthy functioning persons and those with forms of neurosis, have found that persons with highly developed capacities and virtuous traits can, nonetheless, live shallow, unhappy lives full of ambivalent acts (which in one light are virtuous, but in another carry hidden aggressions), if they have not developed a firm unified self. For these theorists, it is not the virtues but the construction of a firm nuclear self that is the ultimate ground for optimal human living. If a strong self is constructed, it will develop virtues; but the converse does not follow. The presence of virtues does not indicate a strong self, for the virtues can be brittle, used for manipulation, and harbor unconscious aggressions. Their exercise seems to offer little happiness to those without strong selves, for they must use virtuous behavior as a proof of a self-worth they know they do not have. While part of this self may be formed through reinforcement and education, a crucial archaic ground for the self requires a different kind of relation between child and parent than either reinforcement or education. Our age has seen numerous examples of people (including some noted evangelists) who, while being trained to be virtuous and wanting to be virtuous, are compelled by unconscious forces to commit immoral acts.

❏

This chapter and the previous one on basic needs have been schematic. They are intended to be a map of the basic constituents of the psyche with which a moral psychology must deal. In sum, we have discovered that human beings have a set of basic needs whose satisfaction is the aim of all activity. The keys to the satisfaction of the needs are a set of vital emotions and developed cognitive capacities. Further, the emotions and cognitive capacities function well only when we have virtuous character traits. But the virtues, in turn, must rest in a self-affirming, flexible, unified self, one capable of integrating conscious and unconscious elements, entertaining strong conflicts of feelings, and dealing with complex needs in a complex environment. In sum, the ultimate ground for the development of the virtues, the healthy functioning of the emotions, the meaningful (rather than abstract) employment of the cognitive faculties, and ultimately, the balanced satisfaction of the needs is the construction of the self. It is now time to cease being schematic and turn to the heart of our ecological moral psychology: the construction of the self.

CHAPTER 7

THE MAKING OF PSYCHE

Chaos. This is the condition of our psyches as they are thrown into the world at birth. Conflicting multiple needs, strong emotions changing with the flux of events, opposing messages from different cognitive capacities. No center to the self...No self. No way to rein in the swirling flux, to order the world. Creation myths from every corner of the earth recall this initial state, for the creation of the world and psyche are one. In the beginning "the earth was without form, and void; and darkness was upon the face of the deep." The chaos is variously represented as a wind-egg (Chinese), churning waters (Hindu), raging winds (Phoenician), formless dragons (Babylonian, Chinese), writhing serpents (Hindu), or a pregnant woman falling through space with no place to give birth (Huron). The Orphics sang: "Night, it is you I hymn, mother of gods and men. The ground of all being is night." And drawing upon ancient myth, Aristophanes wrote:

> There was Chaos at first
> >   and Night and Space
> >   and Tartaros.
> There was no Earth.
> >   No Heaven was.
> >   But sable-winged Night
> Laid her wind-egg there
> >   in the boundless lap
> >   of infinite dark.[1]

The intensity of this initial chaos should not be underestimated. Our safely ordered adult psyches tend to live in forgetfulness of this primal chaos and the Herculean struggle of early childhood to subdue the hundred-headed hydra that lives within. Only in moments when we lose control of an emotion, or face a profound deprivation, or suddenly find our psychic structures unable to cope with the world is this primeval abyss recalled. The making of psyche is the transformation of the original chaos of needs, emotions, and capacities into some kind of organized whole.

But how? The creation myths have a number of answers. Some myths, such as that of Pan-Ku in China, relate how chaos itself throws up a figure who gives form to the world. Other stories hold that order enters the world with the development of language. "In the beginning was the Word." In still others (as in the Aristophanes myth) there is a primal force of love or desire that bonds with chaos to form creatures. More commonly there is a great Earth Mother giving birth and a great Sky God parting the waters or killing the dragons.

All these myths recall us to first truths. Because we are capable of associative learning, the chaos slowly transforms itself into connected pieces. Love clarifies the world by pulling certain special persons and objects out of an undifferentiated background and focusing experience around them. The Great Mother and Father nourish, affirm, mirror, protect, and act as ideals luring us to self-formation. And language turns an inarticulate welter of objects into a world with meaning and order. Parents, learning, desire, and language: all are necessary for the creation of psyche.

These forces can bring order to the psyche in any number of ways, but the way that has been predominant in the West and most other cultures has been through the creation of "persons." A person is a human organism that has developed a unified set of ambitions, ideals, skills, and character traits that give the organism an experiential and behavioral continuity through time. This set of characteristics, which may be called the "personality" or "self" of the organism, is the receptacle or matrix within which most of a person's experiences occur; it is what gives experiences the sense that they are "owned" or "had" by someone. It is the "I" in Descartes's "I think therefore I am."

When a human organism becomes a person, it attains a central structural core of interests, traits, emphases and deemphases of various of the needs, emotions, and capacities. This core organizes the experiences and activities of the organism both in the moment and through time. During every waking moment our senses are open to a teeming multiplicity of data; it is the personality structure that arranges the data into foreground and background, into objects and horizons for objects. It is also the personal core that provides the continuity from what we have been in the past to what we will be in the future.

'Personhood' is not a thing or a substance, but an organization of psychic components. As such we can be more or less persons, for we can be more or less unified. In general, the more psychic fragmentation there is, the less we are capable of being persons. The limiting case is the schizophrenic who seems to lose this central core altogether. Also, our personhoods can be more or less social or individuated. The more social we are, the more we share common characteristics with others in our society and the more we identify our future and past with the social future and past. Individuation occurs when our personal cores have a different history and different values from others in our society. Finally, our personal core can be more or less present in the ordering of experience. When it is fully present, experience has the feeling of belonging to us and feeling very familiar. We are in control of experience. When experience breaks loose from personal control it can either be wonderfully fresh or very frightening, as when we cannot control an emotion or a compulsive desire. Here other forces are in control of the psyche rather than the person. The more these forces remain outside of the influence of the central core of personality, the more anxiety we feel about being overwhelmed and thrown back into our primal chaos.

The development of organisms into persons gives the organisms a way of organizing the vast complexity of psychic factors into a unity that is not constantly at odds with itself nor a pawn in the hands of environmental fluctuations. The continuity through time that personal order gives releases one from the bondage of the immediate. We can imagine that we will be a part of the future and that we will have interests in that future. With this awareness of future interests is born the impetus for delayed satisfactions and the possibility of planning into the future. Perhaps more than any other factor, this ability to think and plan into the future has taken our species out of a continuity with nature and thrust us into a world of immense power for controlling natural forces and creating artificial worlds—for better or worse. Such an ability could never have occurred without the development of a stable personal order within the organism.

The development of self creates a new kind of experience: self-consciousness. Self-consciousness is not just the awareness of a self having an experience of the world rather than the world merely appearing in a field of consciousness, for the world as object is utterly altered. Objects in conscious experiences have the characteristics of being concrete and immediately present in the field of awareness, while those in self-conscious experiences are felt as distant, separated, and abstract. The world is experienced as "other" than us, as apart from us. The distance and abstraction of objects are functions of experience being structured by a self that lives from the past into the future. Objects are no longer merely what they are in the here-now, but deeply interwoven with memories from the past and projections of future possibilities. The tree before me is where I first kissed a sweetheart, a possibility for shelter if a storm should come, lumber if the future demands building, a place of climbing for future children. These memories and possibilities are present in consciousness, even if unarticulated, and the object becomes stretched through time and filled as much with what it is not as with what it is. This realm of possibility now calls upon the psyche to actualize the possibilities, and pragmatic will is created.

Thus, the ordering of psyche into a person is an event of the most far-ranging consequences. It opens up the future, and with this, will, self-consciousness, and power over nature. The sadness of this creation is that innocence is lost. The garden of Eden must be abandoned, and we receive the peculiar human gift of knowing that the future will bring our own deaths. Death is born with the coming of persons into the world.

Some minimal concept of personal identity seems to be necessary for the formation of human societies. The basic structure of society, the kinship system, cannot exist unless one can differentiate oneself, brothers, sisters, mother, father, children, and so on (no matter how these be defined). However, the sense of personal identity here may be minimal, and the organisms could keep as a fundamental structure their social identities. That is, most of the key characteristics of any person in the tribe will be shared with all other persons in the tribe. The most important continuity will be seen as the tribal continuity, and the most important future, the future of the tribe. If the structure of the tribe collapses, then so do the individual psyches of the members of the tribe. The development of complex socioeconomic systems both helps create and is dependent upon the development of a fuller, more individuated sense of personal identity in its members. Differentiated roles calling for different skills, living patterns, and so forth, demands that the social order have individuated members, but members who, while not under the domination of a strict social code, will nonetheless be consistent and accountable for their actions. Indeed, without the social discovery of individual personal order as a way of organizing the psyche, there probably would have been no development from Stone Age ritual cultures into modern historical ones.

The centrality of personal order in a Western human's becoming a functioning independent agent is why Freud and the rest of the psychoanalytic movement had to move from a drive psychology to an ego or self psychology. Libido is only one drive, and its being more or less repressed is not a matter of ultimate concern if a number of the other needs are being met. However, nothing could be more important than the creation of a strong central personal order that can unify the diverse psychic components and direct the activities of the organism with wisdom and vigor. Libidinal injuries are serious not just because they confuse our sexuality but because they wound our sense of self-worth.

The unification of the psyche into a person is, in our culture, a highly complex affair involving at least three subunifications. The first of these occurs in the initial years of life and involves the child's gaining a positive self-image and an embryonic ordering of ambitions and ideals. This synthesis is achieved when the child receives an affirmative mirroring of itself by its parents (or parent substitutes) and is able to identify with a calm, integrated, "omnipotent" person.[2] The mirroring of a child back to itself gives the child both a profound affirmation in the primordial language of affirmation, mimesis, and an initial reflection back to itself that it is real and important. The model acts as an ideal-to-be-realized, a lure for a like-synthesis of the psychic parts in the child. The model also gives the feeling of protection and safety to the child, necessary ingredients for early exploration of abilities and capacities. Finally, the parents, while recognizing that the child is not yet a person, will nonetheless treat it as one. That is, they will treat it as though it had a continuous identity and continuity to its behavior and character. They will expect the child to be consistent and to gain increasing control over its bodily functions, desires, and emotional reactions. That is, they expect the child to develop a unified center of personality and through such expectations help create that center.

If these childrearing processes go well, the child achieves an archaic unity of the psyche that involves four components. First, the child develops positive self-feelings (a positive self-image). This is Kohut's grandiose pole of the nuclear self.[3] It harbors our ambitions, strivings, and core feelings about our self-worth. Second, the child develops a basic trust that the world will respond to its communications and demands. For Erikson, developing basic trust is the first task for all human beings and is necessary for a healthy interaction with the world, especially in social and intimate relations.[4] Third, the child develops enough coherence in the relation of needs, emotions, and cognitive capacities with the responses of the world to start forming patterns of meaning. Fourth, the child develops a rudimentary set of ideals. This is Kohut's idealized pole of the self.[5] It contains the nascent values and hopes of what the self can become.

One can see that this archaic synthesis is not simple but contains a dynamic tension between the grandiose pole of self-esteem and the pole of idealized values. The grandiose pole is particular and contains feelings that the child is perfect just as it is; the idealized pole contains the formulation of an ideal—a universal—which stands in opposition to the perfection of the grandiose pole and calls for further development. This archaic psychology explains why the self is so dynamic, and gives credence to Hegel's notion of the self as emerging through a series of dialectical oppositions in which particularity and universality keep adjusting to one another in an attempt to achieve wholeness.

Kohut calls this archaic unity the "nuclear self," for it is the foundation on which all later unifications will be built. The creation of a nuclear self is not to be considered an all-or-nothing affair; it is always more or less. But whether one has more or less is a matter of utmost importance; for if the archaic unity is weak, then the latter unifications must be partially compensatory and will lack the flexibility that allows life to have vital diversity.

The nuclear self of Kohut is what, I think, the daimon is for philosopher David Norton.[6] Norton holds that we become happy and fulfilled only when we are able to express and develop our idiosyncratic inner natures, our daimons. While Norton seems to hold that these natures are biologically given, it would not alter his philosophy much to associate them with Kohut's notion of the nuclear self being a combination of biological givens with early social construction. Both agree that this first synthesis of the self is what may be called our "essential self," and it is in satisfying and fully developing the ambitions and ideals of this self that we get our deepest sense of fulfillment and of "realizing our natures."

Although archaic unification lays the basis for the development of persons in all cultures, it is insufficient for producing the kind of personal order necessary for functioning in complex socioeconomic cultures. Two secondary syntheses are required: a narrative ordering[7] and a structural unity. A narrative is simply a story that follows a character through a series of events. As such it gives the organism a thread by which to weave together disparate moments of time and enables the person to have a personal history apart from the social history of the tribe. Narrative order first appears in the West (if not everywhere) with hero myths. In the *Iliad*, human organisms become persons when they have narrative stories that can be told about them. When, on the battlefield, Diomedes asks Glaukos who he is, Glaukos does not give his social status or military rank, but his paternal family history for five generations. When Diomedes discovers that their family histories cross (his father had entertained Glaukos's grandfather), they cannot fight. Rather, they exchange armor, an act indicating that they have exchangeable selves by having intertwined stories. The self *is* the story told about one; to not have a story is to not be a person. Thousands of nameless human organisms without stories are slaughtered at Troy, but they are of no more concern than other animals. They are not yet persons.

What makes a series of events into a narrative story? How does the narrative structure create a kind of human being different from the kind created by the preceding ritual structure? Ritual is the celebration of repetition, while narrative demands linear change and development through time. Ritual asks, "How can we be joined to the earth and community?" while narrative asks, "What distinguishes this individual from all others? What makes this particular story worth hearing?" Ritual merges individuals into the group; narrative separates individuals from groups. Although heroes, as Joseph Campbell has shown,[3] all have something in common, nonetheless each hero is different—Achilles is not Ajax, is not Diomedes, is not Hector. This is just to say that the process of narrative individuation might have a common structure, but it does produce individuals.

Stories are told at first through an oral tradition by poets and only later by individuals about themselves. By creating narrative templates, the poet both figuratively and literally creates the world of persons. It is therefore true to say that Homer and the Bible are the parents of our culture, for they gave us our first narrative structures, our first paradigms for personal synthesis beyond archaic and ritual unity. The power of the great reformers in the first millennium B.C.—Zoroaster, Buddha, Socrates, Confucius, and Christ—resides not so much in what they said as in the fact that they lived and spoke new kinds of narrative structures, structures that more deeply met people's needs than the heroic narratives and that were available to everyone. No longer did one have to have a distinguished lineage, wealth, physical prowess, and political power to be a person. Anyone could embark on the spiritual journeys they advocated, have a story to tell about it, and thus gain personhood.

To have a narrative order, then, we must be able to narrate, at least to ourselves, a story about ourselves. But what constitutes a "legitimate" story?[9] Here the individual and community are enmeshed, for while each individual might have a different story in details, the structure of the story must relate to the set of possible stories available in the culture. Telling the story of a religious journey to salvation is possible only in a society where this kind of narrative is acceptable. Told to a group of committed secularists, the story goes unheard or is ridiculed.

The power of narrative-templates in a culture can be poignantly felt during a transitional state when one kind of story becomes illegitimate and another takes its place. Such a transition has recently occurred in the templates available for middle- and upper-middle-class women in Western culture. A quarter of a century ago, there was one predominant story-type for women in these classes: fall in love, marry, support a husband on his road to professional success, raise children to be productive citizens, and run an efficient household. If a woman had to or wanted to work in one of the limited occupations open to her, she had to supply some further explanations. Today, this wife/mother narrative is not acceptable, or is at best a narrative of the third or fourth rank. Being only a spouse or a parent is considered dull and boring; having access to and succeeding in the previously male-controlled domain of professional narratives is what is legitimate.

This arrangement, in which the culture provides a stock of story-templates and individuals fill in the details, has allowed the development of differentiated persons while simultaneously exerting social conformity. Even those who rebel against the sanctioned story structures of their cultures usually do so within the safety of a rebel subculture that has its own set of narratives. The wider message of this tale is that personal identity, insofar as it concerns the construction of a personal narrative, is not an individual achievement apart from the social order, but occurs within socially prescribed boundaries. As Erikson says, one cannot gain a personal identity unless that identity is recognized by others in a community.[10] But one's identity will not be recognized unless one "makes sense" to the community, and this is best done by indicating how one's particular story fits the set of legitimate stories of the community.[11]

Although a narrative added to a nuclear self can give a sufficient unity for persons in simple, stable social orders, it is not, by itself, an adequate basis for psychic unity in a complex, rapidly changing culture. In these latter kinds of society, narratives can come into being and pass away with a suddenness that can destroy persons who have no other identity to rely on: the old soldier who can only repeat *ad nauseam* the war in which he was a hero; the rugged homesteader who has been replaced by mass farming technology; the housewife whose children have left, and with them, her raison d'être. And although narratives can give a general continuity through time, they are incapable of solving specific problems that arise within the narrative framework. I might choose the narrative of being a college teacher, but this does not tell me whether I should teach at a major university or a small college, or whether I should specialize in this area or that. Finally, life has become so multidimensional and complex that narratives cannot organize or even relate to numerous events that happen in our daily lives. One's chosen narrative might be to achieve professional excellence in a certain field, but this will hardly help one in situations of intimacy, childrearing, mountain climbing, and so on.

In short, narratives are too narrow to give unity to the vast multiplicity of events and problems we ordinarily encounter in complex societies, and they do not have the power of self-critique that is necessary in an open, fluctuating social milieu. That is, narratives are inherently conservative and constrict us into old images or old continuities even when a change of narrative could be life-enhancing. Plato and Aristotle understood these problems at the beginning of modern culture and counseled the replacement of the poetic/narrative structure with a higher level structure. In Plato's *Republic*, the poets and their heroic narratives are exiled while the philosophers with their rationally ordered psyches are made rulers. In Aristotle's *Ethics*, poetic forms of thinking and living are made secondary to a psyche structured in terms of practical and theoretical wisdom.

The higher level structural organization of the psyche centers in epistemic and normative systems for resolving any inner or outer conflict. Epistemic systems give us methodologies for accepting or rejecting the extraordinary multiplicity of beliefs that assault us every day in a modern society, while normative systems critically organize our values and allow us to make ethical, aesthetic, and other practical choices. These systems, when strong, can determine almost every aspect of conscious experience, from what we consistently focus on in the realm of perception, to what and whom we listen to in the conversational matrix of the community, to whom we fall in love with and what we eat. The ultra business person looks at Pikes Peak and sees real estate; the religious mystic sees a monument to God's power and strength.

This structural unity will be termed the "ego," and conscious experiences organized by it will be termed "ego consciousness." When the narrative order is chosen by using epistemic and normative structures, it also becomes part of the ego.

How this structural unification is achieved is no mystery: it is conditioned by the values of the culture. In particular, the type of structural order developed in individual psyches typically depends, as Marx said, upon the economic modes of production and the location of a person within the class structure. If the economic system needs from its middle classes attentive, quantitatively astute (with a concomitant deemphasis on qualitative sensitivity), emotionally stable, punctual, responsible people capable of significantly delayed gratifications and resistance to pleasureful temptations of the moment, then it will develop institutions (schools) and reward systems (social status and salaries) to produce individuals who have a quasi empirical/mathematical epistemology and a normative system that favors the abovementioned values.

While archaic unity tends to be unconscious and relates to every part of the psyche, the higher level structural synthesis is primarily for the organization of conscious processes, although it itself is usually not fully available to consciousness. As a secondary unity relating to conscious choices and the conscious direction of activity, the ego can be constructed without a strong nuclear self or a clear narrative direction. As such, it can act both as a unity for conscious life and as a defense against unconscious anarchy. Although secondary unities can be quite successful at both conscious direction and defensive protection, split-off parts of the self that are not recognized by the ego structure can conflict with it, use the structures as tools for their own irrational purposes, or undo the rational deeds of the ego through "inexplicable" rash behavior or "chance" events.

Thus, a person is not just a simple unification of psychic parts and ambitions but a complex synthesis of at least three other unifications—the archaic, narrative, and ego. Fullness in a person comes when these three unities cohere with and support one another in such a way that the nuclear self gives a foundation and impetus to embark on a fulfilling narrative that can achieve the archaic ideals, and the structural unity gives the person the psychic wherewithal to achieve the goals of the narrative, while simultaneously being able to critique and overcome it if a more satisfying life history becomes available. This is the ideal. More often than not, it seems, the three subunities are incomplete and do not cohere well with each other. How many of us suffer profound inner battles between an unfinished nuclear self crying to remain a child and be mirrored, a part that harbors romantic visions of narrative grandeur, and a part that attempts to realistically solve the problems of the day and keep order in the house?

These three unifications, which transform us from early chaos, dependency, and demands for instant gratification to autonomous, self-regulating, self-articulating persons, all occur within a wider framework of metaphors concerned with "making" or "growth" that touch the process at every point and deeply influence its outcome. The most prominent of these metaphors in the West is that of the journey. From the *Odyssey* through the *Aeneid, Divine Comedy, Parsifal, Pilgrim's Progress,* and *Faust* to Joyce's *Ulysses,* much of the great literature of our culture has attempted to define, dramatize, and idealize the process of becoming a person.[12] Although each of these literary journeys symbolizes a different path to personhood, there are many congruent elements. The traveler usually leaves home and returns to the same place, but now for the first time it is his home. Almost always the would-be hero must descend into the primal chaos (Hades, for Odysseus and Aeneas; the Inferno, for Dante; Walpurgis Nacht, for Faust; and a Mabbot Street whorehouse, for Leopold Bloom), overcome powerful earth mothers (Circe, Dido, Sirens, witches, whores) who wish to oedipally lure the heroes back to an undifferentiated childhood, defy overbearing parental authority (Cyclops, Aeneas's father), and repress desires for immediate gratification (something Odysseus's men cannot do and that kills them). Almost always group intelligence and planning lead to disaster, while the person capable of independent judgment and action heroically survives. However, the hero is usually not alone, but aided into and through the chaos by a wise guide—Athena, for Odysseus; Venus, for Aeneas; Virgil, for Dante; Mephisto, for Faust. This metaphor of the guided journey underpins the psychotherapeutic process in which therapists lead patients into the dark chaos of their pasts, help them break the bondage to their parents, and guide them back to the light of an autonomous adult world.

The metaphor of the journey emphasizes that the process of individuation is neither strictly biological nor mechanically social. It is full of dangers, diversions, and pitfalls. Many, if not most, get waylaid somewhere along the way and do not reach the fullness of selfhood. If and when we finally achieve an autonomous adulthood, we should feel as Odysseus does upon reaching Ithaca, a genuine sense of completion and wholeness, an exhilaration at finally becoming who we really are.[13] In psychological terms, this wholeness is achieved when the ambitions and ideals of the nuclear self are realized in our narrative histories.

Another set of metaphors that deeply affect the way we develop into persons is that connected with "making." That is, how we go about making persons depends upon the models of making we have in mind. These models originate in the crafts, and it makes no small difference what crafts we take to be paradigmatic. For instance, weaving presents a model of gathering various threads and intertwining them into a whole; but forging hammers out recalcitrant material through force to form a finished product. The building crafts demand a preestablished blueprint and a serial process of working from the foundation to the top, step by step, one layer after another. On the other hand, the artistic crafts tend to be more open-ended, the work often being allowed to shape itself in the process of creation. Our childrearing and educational practices will obviously be very different depending on which model of making we take to be primary in the creation of persons.

Finally, there is a mythic background that holds that we only really grow up when we fall in love with a person outside the family and thereby leave the oedipally predisposed eros of childhood and enter an adult genital world. The paradigmatic myth for this process is, fittingly, that of Eros (Amor) and Psyche. Psyche is the youngest of a king's three daughters and so beautiful that people come from the world over to see her, meanwhile neglecting the altars of Aphrodite. Naturally, Aphrodite is enraged and sends her son, Eros, to make Psyche fall in love with a hideous man. However, Eros falls in love with Psyche, builds her a magical palace in the woods that provides instantaneously for all her needs, sleeps with her every night, and gives her the one instruction that she must never try to see him. Psyche is blissfully happy, but her envious sisters convince her that her lover is a monster and that she needs to discover who he is. So Psyche holds a lamp over the sleeping Eros, sees that he is the most beautiful of men, falls desperately in love with him, and in so doing lets a drop of hot oil fall. Eros awakens. He tells Psyche that her mistrust has ruined their love and departs. Psyche is shattered and begins wandering the world in search of Eros (here the metaphor of the journey appears). She finally comes to the home of Aphrodite, who sets her four impossible tasks: to separate into types numerous seeds heaped in a chaotic pile, to gather golden wool from a flock of sheep that absorbs the heat of the day and is deadly violent, to fetch waters from a stream that flows from an unreachable mountain height and is guarded by dragons, and to descend into the underworld to bring back a magical potion of beauty from Persephone. Psyche's conscious and rational powers are unequipped to accomplish any of these tasks, but ants come and separate the grain for her, a river reed tells her to wait until evening to gather the wool, Zeus's eagle fetches the water, and a tower in Aphrodite's palace informs her how to successfully enter and leave the underworld. Psyche still fails in one last deed. On her return from the underworld, she is curious to see what Persephone has put in the box that will give beauty. She opens the box and is enveloped by endless sleep. But Eros, who has finally recovered from his wound of hot oil, comes and rouses her. They are married, and their first offspring is a daughter, Pleasure.

The most general insight to be gained from this complex tale (which is the basis of a marvelous C. S. Lewis novel, *Till We Have Faces*) is that love awakens the desire to leave childhood structures and individuate. This theme can also be found in Plato's *Symposium*, where love leads to higher and fuller realms of integration, and in Dante's *Divine Comedy*, where Beatrice evokes Dante's eros and leads him to a full development of his powers and a union with God. What is at stake in the conflict between Aphrodite and Psyche (who is structurally identical with Aphrodite) is whether love is to be an impersonal force that remains outside the boundaries of personal order or whether it is to be bonded to the development of persons. Love (Eros) favors the latter as being more satisfying, much to the fury of his earth mother, who would call us back from the development of personality and keep us close to the earth and its forces. The first attempted union of Eros and Psyche fails due to its infantilism. Psyche lives in a world of instant gratification and a faceless relation to Eros. Neither can grow or develop, for they are in the dark as to who they are and what their relationship is. Spurred by other parts of herself (her sisters), Psyche's cognitive powers are stirred and the adolescent fantasy love world that confused parent–child love with adult sexual love is shattered. Both Eros and Psyche must enter journeys of suffering to determine who they are before they can once again be joined. In particular Psyche must establish a relationship to the part of herself that resides beneath personal consciousness (symbolized by animals, nature, and an artifact of culture) and learn that she, as a person, has the strength to organize her multifold and chaotic "seeds," can learn to handle the violence and aggression that accompany passion, can receive lifegiving nourishment from the "higher" intellectual capacities, and can descend into the primal chaos to be reborn as an adult. The myth gives us a reason to suffer the lonely agonies of giving up childhood dependence and pursuing the journey of individuation: the joys of intimacy.[14]

The final truth in all this myth, metaphor, and literature is that persons are cultural creations. Persons are not born; they are made. Indeed, I think that the final and ultimate task of Western culture has been the production of persons who are so strongly organized and unified that they can easily function in the dynamic and multifarious world we have created. The culture has even demanded that God, above all, be a totally unified person. Personality was raised to the level of ultimate principle.

Yet something has gone awry with how Western culture makes persons. Some of our most insightful thinkers of the last hundred years have been so discouraged with the kind of persons our culture generates that they either counseled the overcoming of persons or attempted to manifest how persons weren't the final human reality. Marx's attack on private property was in essence an attack on the private, individuated person. Nietzsche ridiculed Western human beings as so banal, controlled, and mean-spirited that they had to be overcome by a higher being, the overman. Heidegger refused to acknowledge personal unity as the ground of human nature and attempted to open up that which lay beneath and beyond the personal, Dasein. Freud grasped the weakness of the person in the face of monumental biological and cultural forces, and Wittgenstein, in his demonstration that there are no private languages, found social discourse, not individuated persons, to be the basis of human life. Finally, feminist theorists such as Chodorow, Gilligan, and Jean Baker Miller have asserted that the male ideal of a person that presently dominates Western culture overemphasizes individuation and separation to such a degree that it excludes women who, through a different maturation process, need to define themselves in relationships. This has created the intolerable situation of having radically autonomous men unable to relate deeply to other human beings or nature and of having women excluded from a socioeconomic world dominated by male aggression.[15]

To grasp what has gone wrong with how the West constructs persons we need to understand the problem that called the first philosophers to thought: the problem of the one and the many. The 'one' is a unity, a sameness-through-time, offering a coherence to all that it touches. It is the order and structure of the world, the order and structure of our psyches. The 'many' is diversity, change, growth, decay, novelty. Parmenides loved the one; Heraclitus the many. As human beings we seem to revolve around these two fundamental poles. One pole is the strand of personal order that gives the psyche its unity. The other pole is that strand of occasions that is the experiential focus of the organism—the events we consciously and unconsciously (as in dreams) experience. The events in the living strand of experience are constantly fluctuating, but the personal order that accompanies them connects them and gives them stability.

It is of utmost importance to realize that being something that has life and being something that is a person are different. Life involves change, growth, novelty, decay, and historical discontinuity. Personal order involves stability, permanence, and historical continuity. Nietzsche recognized the difference more profoundly than others and counseled the overcoming of self-structures in order to live fully in the blaze of creative vitality. But the antithesis of the many and the one, of self and life, while it embodies a truth, is too simple. Total lack of an order to a self is not creative living, but schizophrenia. Although some ways of structuring the self lead inherently to monotony of experience and repression of differences, other ways of forming the self give it the secure base from which to invite diversity, change, ambivalence, surprise, and originality into life. Hence, the issue is not a matter of life versus self, or too much self versus too little self, but how to foster self-structures that allow for spontaneity, complexity, and diversity.

For Kohut and self-psychology, the key to building a strong, vibrant person is the construction of a firm nuclear self. When the unconscious nuclear self is coherent and unified, we can have spontaneity and liveliness in our conscious ego experiences. On the other hand, if chaos reigns in the nuclear self, then our narrative and ego syntheses must be tight, repressive, and defensive in order to keep our personal identities from falling into the archaic abyss of childhood that was never resolved. A strong nuclear self with an intact unification of a feeling of self-worth, ideals, and ambitions is the basis of a person's handling ambivalent feelings without repression and pursuing the many possibilities of life. But a weak nuclear self requires that later unifications be used to repress the inner chaos and injury suffered through lack of empathic mirroring or lack of a parent-imago. These later unifications are, then, the major mechanisms for holding the self together. To change the ego or narrative structures is to threaten the very stability of the self.

These defensive ego and narrative structures can be remarkably successful in interacting with the world to satisfy some needs, but they can never replace a nuclear self in three ways. First, defensive structures lack flexibility. They must be rigid (compulsive) in order to keep the injured sector of the self protected. Second, persons without firm nuclear selves are never grounded and thus never fully at ease with the world or themselves. Experience has a tinge of anxiety, of compulsiveness. Something is rotten and it can't be found, for it is at the very core of who we are, and its exposure threatens our very existence. Finally, we can never feel the full glow of happiness, regardless of what we accomplish, for part of the essential feeling of an injured or ill-formed nuclear self is a sense of worthlessness. Since we do not deserve to feel happy, we can't feel happy. Persons with weak or injured nuclear selves then take on various forms of narcissism: attempts to compensate for the lack of self-worth by artificially aggrandizing the self.

When experience becomes bonded to an overly structured narcissistic personal order, all the parts of the psyche that do not fit that order, be they needs, emotions, or cognitive faculties, are either repressed or left unrecognized and undernourished. The organism then becomes a land in which a self-aware, conscious person is ruler in its own tidy little empire surrounded by seditious rebels who are always hiding in dark recesses, always escaping just beyond the reach of the ruler's autocratic power, and always making guerrilla attacks on the main citadel. The castle's walls must be bolstered; more resources and energy must be poured into defenses to keep the ruler on his throne and the empire safe. The ruler becomes increasingly isolated from himself and the world, and feelings of alienation, disconnectedness, meaninglessness, and boredom set in. Whatever the problems the Greeks had with self (perhaps too little ego unification to deal with the complex socioeconomic world they created), they did not complain of boredom. The situation is different for us who have so much ego structure that we cannot know the power of the gods. Boredom is our chief fear.

Kohut locates the source of weak nuclear selves in sporadic failures of early childrearing. However, it is the contention of this book that these failures are systematically built into Western culture through its excessive emphasis on ego unification and its values of hierarchy and analyticity, the limitation of narratives (for the middle and upper classes) to the quest for economic and professional status, and the domination of building and forging metaphors over those of journey, weaving, art, and love. All of these values have negative effects for the formation of a nuclear self in particular and a fully integrated self in general.

The most important psychic unity for the West is the structural ego. It is this ego, with its power of understanding and will for domination, that has transformed the planet. The development of a strong ego structure is a necessity for anyone who wishes to engage in the vast complexities of our present socioeconomic system. Without a developed ego structure, it is impossible to function in the only acceptable narrative structures for the upper-middle classes—those that lead to professional and economic success. Hence, it is of utmost concern to parents in these classes that the structural ego start being built as soon as possible, often in forgetfulness of the needs of the small child and its nuclear self.

The keys to the power of the ego are its hierarchical normative system and its analytical epistemic system. A hierarchical normative system is organized to have one value designated as highest, with all other values derived from this. In such a system there can be no significant conflict of values, for the dominant value acts as arbiter in all disputes. There can be little doubt that hierarchy is the most efficient way of achieving unity, and little wonder why monarchies developed as soon as societies achieved a significant division of labor and complex economies. Many voices are anarchy and chaos; one voice is order. The idea that unity is to be achieved through a hierarchical structuring is so pervasive in our culture that we find it in every Western government, in the "great chain of being" that grounds Western cosmologies from Plato and Aristotle through Hegel, in traditional family organization where every household needs a head, in every kind of institution from economic multinationals to bridge clubs. The words Odysseus spoke at the dawn of our culture have guided it ever since: "The rule of the many is not good; one ruler let there be."[16]

The second great pillar of the structural ego in modern Western culture is an analytical epistemology. First elaborated in Plato's *Sophist*, analysis attempts to know something by breaking it down into its constituent components. These components are then seen as more basic or more real than the things they make up. If we want to know about a piece of stuff scientifically, we determine its molecular structure, which can be further analyzed in terms of atoms, which can be further analyzed in terms of protons and electrons. When we walk into a room, we rarely dwell in the experience of the whole, but notice the individual parts—the persons present, the furniture, and the decorations. When I attempted to "know" the psyche in chapters 5 and 6, I analyzed it in terms of its component needs, emotions, and capacities. When Descartes wanted to know something, he looked for clear and distinct ideas—ideas separated from all other ideas. Hume, Locke, and Berkeley looked for discrete sense data to ground knowledge. Contemporary behavioral scientists attempt to locate isolated pieces of behavior and study them with reinforcement techniques. Military commanders are not the only ones who "divide and conquer."

When analysis is applied to social life, it gives rise to democratic individualism, for individuals are the basic irreducible units of society. Thus, when analysis finally gains a complete hold on epistemology in the Enlightenment, we also get the rise of democratic politics, an ethics stressing individual autonomy, and an economics based in individual entrepreneurship. When analysis and hierarchy are combined as the fundamental categories of the psyche, then we are driven to ask which individual in the social order counts the most. This will lead politically to some form of presidency and ethically to some form of egoism—to making oneself the most important individual in the world. It is little wonder that the final products of the psyche governed by hierarchy and analysis are capitalism and Darwinism, both of which see the world as consisting of individuals out only for themselves in a dire competition for limited resources.[17] It is also little wonder that narcissism is rampant in the culture.

Another necessary product of the union of analyticity and hierarchy is specialization. Our analytical epistemologies separate tasks from one another in a seemingly endless division, and our hierarchical normative systems demand that we choose one task and make it our highest. As much as any factor, specialization has moved us from an economy in the Middle Ages where each home was more or less self-sufficient and trade was primarily in luxuries for nobles, to modern capitalism in which few individual units are self-sufficient and most of us depend upon the complex trade of goods. Plato's dream for his ideal state has been realized, for in our specialized economy, "one man performs one task according to his nature, at the right moment, and at leisure from other occupations.[18] Specialization has made our economy productive beyond the imagination of ancient minds and has radically transformed every aspect of our culture, from family life to the way we construct our cities. On the basis of the structural ego is founded the modern world.

In specialization we see the fusion of the ego and narrative syntheses that is the core of personal identity for many people in the contemporary world. The stock of legitimate narratives, at least for the middle and upper classes, has become increasingly limited to the narrative of a business or professional career. Since such narratives demand a high level of ego functioning, the narrative synthesis comes to presuppose the development of the ego synthesis. But in turn the ego synthesis presupposes the professional narrative synthesis because this is where the ego can most readily exercise its powers. That is, the highly developed powers of analysis and hierarchical organization that we attain in ego synthesis require a very specialized environment for their use. This environment can be entered only by assuming a narrative of professional success.

The union of the professional narrative with the ego synthesis is the heart of how the West has made persons over the past several centuries. While this union has been the most powerful organization of the psyche ever invented for the achievement of political power and economic productivity, it has had severe costs in terms of the well-being of individual persons and the social order.

The first indictment to be made against the hierarchical ego and the hierarchical systems it fosters in social and political life is that by necessity they generate class systems, repression, and domination. If something is higher and more important, then other things must be lower and less important. Hence, in hierarchical societies we have lower classes, a lower sex, and dispossessed people; and in the hierarchical psyche, "lowly" or "forgotten" parts—usually whatever is least like the structural ego: emotions, sex, intimacy, sacredness, beauty, and so forth. The lower parts are either dominated, repressed, or, minimally, not allowed equal access to the goods of the system. These parts are, by necessity, much more numerous than the parts occupying the upper niches of the hierarchies. When one perfect God reigns, innumerable sinners must be cast into darkness.

The second problem with the structural ego is that when analysis is applied to comprehending our particular lives, we get the modern peculiarity of dividing up kinds of experiences and isolating them from one another. We talk, for instance, of our sexual lives, our professional lives, and our home lives, as though these could and should be separated from one another. Since the Enlightenment we have also spoken of the ethical experience, the aesthetic experience, the religious experience, and others, as if these experiences could be had in some purified form, uncontaminated by the rest of lived experience. Perhaps this division of experience can best be seen in modern art, which, since Kant proclaimed the doctrine of art for art's sake at the end of the eighteenth century, has tried to provide us with pure aesthetic enjoyment without reference to ethics, religion, or politics. Pure light or color or shape. And what could this sculpture of three metal beams mean? It means nothing: just have a pure aesthetic experience of the forms. With the analytical separation of experiences, not only is intensity lost, but so is meaning. Pure sex, pure art, pure sacredness, pure business mean little because they lack that which provides meaning: an integration into the fullness of lived experience.

Third, and most important, when so much emphasis is placed on the development of the structural ego and the attainment of a professional narrative, the nuclear self is deeply injured. A nuclear self is developed through mirroring and total affirmation; a structural ego, through training in analytical tasks and organizational skills, a training most commonly done with reinforcement techniques that distinguish correct from incorrect behavior. The most powerful reinforcer, and the one closest at hand, is affirmative love. When training starts too early, as it usually does in our competitive world in which everyone must get a head start to succeed, total affirmation and mirroring are abandoned and replaced with selective love.

Selective love does not affirm the whole child but only parts of the child, or isolated acts of the child. Hence, a sense of worth as a whole self is not given. The child feels unwelcome and unworthy except insofar as she conforms to a certain model (a model that produces a highly effective ego structure). Also, the calm omnipotent parent is increasingly absent—both physically and psychologically as anxieties about the progress of the child and complexities of the world take away ease.

The parents are not to be blamed for the failure to develop the nuclear self, because they are acting out of the categories and values given to them by the culture. They are acting for the betterment of their children. How can they be at ease with a newborn, accept it just as it is in its total dependency, affirm its every moan and frolic, when they "know" this child will enter a world of stiff competition for scarce resources and statuses, competition that demands a fully developed ego structure to be successful. They must worry about the adequacy of their child to meet the challenge of the world. A functioning adult must be formed from the infant by hammering out of the psyche all the needs, emotions, and capacities that do not fit into hierarchical or analytical schemes and by building the person from the ground up to have the requisite skills and character traits to function in the competitive socioeconomic world. The ideas of weaving the threads of the person together into a rich fabric or artistically letting the person participate in her own creation are forgotten. The great journey of Odysseus becomes going to school and learning ever more complex methodologies. Falling in love is at best a sideshow. The metaphorical web of the culture is skewed: forging and building dominate.

There are, of course, other factors that either alleviate the damage to the nuclear self or increase it, and the results can vary from psychosis and childhood suicide to mild forms of feeling worthless, depression, and compulsive aggressiveness. Intimacy, which requires a secure sense of archaic self-worth, is elusive and difficult. But the general point remains: in order to make persons capable of running a highly complex socioeconomic system in a world seen as highly competitive and in which the attainment of affluent lifestyles governs narrative values, we must be so overly concerned with the production of ego structures that we neglect the deepest, most important part of the self. That is, the narcissistic personality and behavior disorders so prevalent in today's social world are not a contingent part of that world but generated by its deepest values and categories.

These personal costs are too high, for when a self becomes this diseased, emotions get repressed by compulsive character traits, thinking becomes intellectualized abstraction, and many needs go unmet or unrecognized. We are, then, left with a dominant structural ego that organizes experience tightly into its hierarchical and analytical schemes. The nuclear self falls into shambles, and the narrative self is left with an emaciated and unfulfilling story. The ego becomes so overpresent in experience that surprise is lost, and no matter where we go or what we encounter, the result is always the same: we meet only ourselves. Hence, we encounter the paradox that our structural egos have created the wealthiest and most dynamic world possible but are unable to enjoy the land of riches they created.

It is time to reconceive the self in a way that will allow the nuclear self to develop fully and to integrate all the aspects of the psyche. For this we need a new model of the self. This new self is not a structure dominating experience, but a language we speak to ourselves, a pattern of how the various psychic parts move and flow together in a dance of stable interdependencies. This new self is not a ruler commanding the rest of the psyche, but a jester humoring the psychic parts to negotiate with one another, a fragile mediator in the heart of internecine battles of the strong and varied interests of the psyche. The new self is not constructed layer by layer as is a building, nor is it forged from amorphous material into something with just this shape and no other. Rather, this self is a weaving and a weaver. It is a self that is not always at center stage, but one that resides in the background of events, communication, laughter, memory. And with the coming of this new self will be born the ecological psyche.

The ecological psyche will differ in a number of ways from the psyche dominated by a hierarchical, analytical ego. No longer will some parts (usually reason) gain a constant priority over less-valued parts, with the least valuable parts being candidates for systematic extirpation. The ecological psyche understands that every part of the psyche has a necessary function, and that every function is essential to the psyche. Each need, emotion, capacity, and character trait needs to have its say. There are no bad emotions or needs or ways of knowing that need to be repressed. In a healthy psyche each part performs its proper function in a network of interdependent relations.

The analytic structure that divided the psyche into fragmented parts, experiences, and roles will be replaced in the ecological psyche by an epistemology grounded in the truth that everything is intrinsically interrelated with every other thing and these relationships in part determine what the thing is. Everything must be grasped in its environment and with an understanding of environmental relationships. For instance, our need for sexual fitness, isolated from other needs, merely demands sexual status and physiological consummation. One-night stands or sex in a long-term committed relationship are indistinguishable in their abilities to satisfy this need.[19] But when we remember that our need for sex occurs in a being that also has needs for survival, social recognition, order, adventure, intimacy, autonomy, knowledge, beauty, and sacredness, it becomes a very different matter. Sex for this kind of complex, interconnected being might only be satisfying with a certain person, in a certain relationship, in a certain kind of way, at a certain time, in a certain frame of mind, and in a certain kind of place. In an ecologically interrelated psyche, the whole person is present in each experience, and the sexual event can touch every other need and part of the psyche. These other parts in turn give feedback to our sexual nature, enriching it with meaning and depth, and it, in turn, sends further messages back to them. The ecological psyche is a pool in which a thrown pebble can create a world of resonated meaning and intensity.

The ecological psyche also understands that the psyche as a whole is intrinsically related to its external environments. We become different persons depending on who our friends are, what our homes are like, how we relate to the natural world, how the institutions we belong to are organized, what kind of economic system we operate in, the richness of our historical culture, and so on. Choices of what to do, who to be with, and where to go all partially define how we create our psyches.

The hierarchical ego sought permanence; the ecological psyche dwells in time. The hierarchical ego demanded eternal values to support its hierarchy and rigid analytical divisions, but the ecological psyche accepts life as development and decay. In particular, the ecological psyche recognizes the need for the development of the nuclear self of the small child before training turns to any of the structures of ego or narrative formation. Affirming the child's grandiose sense of being and allowing an idealized merger of the child with the adult are seen as the first priorities. Only when the nuclear self is firmly in place do parents then proceed to the processes of separation, demand for rudimentary self-control, and optimal frustration for the production of growth which ground the narrative and ego syntheses.

Thus, values that are crucial at one stage of life may have little worth or even negative worth at a later stage. Children seem not to need sacredness in the way that older people do. Genital sexuality bursts upon us with a fury at puberty, but it is just one of a number of needs and often quite secondary in middle age. Children demand order; youth craves adventure. A young adolescent needs to be recognized by a group outside the family; a young adult needs to break from the group to explore the possibility of autonomy. There can be no final structure of values, no final list of priorities. There is only the suffering of deaths and rejoicing in new births as we grow and decay through life.

The hierarchical, analytical self was a chain of command. The ego dictated what it wanted and passed the commands down through organized channels to the rest of the psyche. In contrast, the ecological psyche seems a mad tea party of communication. Every part has to talk with every other part. The need for beauty must get along with needs for survival and social recognition, even though they have sharp differences about what ought to be done. Order and adventure usually bicker, with the need for knowledge usually taking the side of order, while autonomy is a good friend of adventure. The emotions are constantly surveying the environment and reporting their findings, much to the pleasure of some needs and the chagrin of others. Amidst this constant chaos of communication is the person. As Hermes brought Priam and Achilles to common speech, so the self gives a common language to the needs, emotions, and capacities. It listens, suggests, gets a couple of needs together that weren't talking before, laughs at the impossibility of the whole mess, and in laughing makes it all possible. The self, like Hermes, must go between Olympus and the underworld, between the conscious rational powers and the unconscious realm of dreams, images, and irrational understandings. Dreams enter the meaning of our waking life, and our conscious hopes and desires penetrate into an unconscious synthesis.

In sum, the old psyche worked according to hierarchical values, analytical divisions, timeless structures, and limited-access communication patterns. The new ecological psyche is organized according to function, environmental relations, the flux of time, and the most extensive communication network possible.

Is it possible to transform the psyche from one dominated by a hierarchical, analytical ego to an ecological psyche? Let us not underestimate the difficulties, for the whole culture conspires against such a transformation. But the most powerful of all agencies calls for such a change: a psyche suffering in its disunities and dullness of experience, a psyche longing for an intensity and joy in experience that its present structure cannot give. These conditions have dismantled numerous previous cultures and will dismantle ours.

The transformation to a new ecological age begins with the creation of an ideal of human excellence that can lure the psyche into change. For the ecological psyche, human excellence consists in the full and harmonious functioning of all the parts of the psyche in such a way that the needs are as deeply satisfied as they can be. Living well as a human being is a complex affair, for it involves coming to terms with mortality, achieving a sexual identity, finding a satisfying place in the realm of social recognition, developing stable structures of meaning and ideals, having enough chaos and adventure to stay vibrant and grow, loving other human beings intimately, becoming autonomous, transforming the world into a home through knowledge, dwelling in the sacred, responding to and creating beauty. There are profound conflicts among these needs, and they pull in vastly different directions. Allowing ourselves to hear all their voices and to attempt, as best we can, to weave them into a balanced harmony is what constitutes excellence. If we are able to satisfy all of the needs, then happiness will ensue, and a sense of fullness and well-being will fill us like the burst of flowers fills the mountain meadow in spring. Of course, not all these needs will be satisfied equally, nor will they have the same importance for all individuals, in all circumstances, at all stages of life. But if any of them remains chronically unfulfilled, an emptiness and restlessness will slowly gnaw at us until either the need is recognized or the happiness becomes irrevocably marred.

As we have found, the needs cannot be fulfilled unless the other systems of the psyche—emotions, cognitive capacities, character traits, and personal unifications—are mutually enhancing. Excellence is achieved, then, when all the parts of the psyche are functioning in an interconnected, mutually supportive way, as in an undisturbed ecosystem. Nothing is out of balance. This does not mean that there are no intrapsychic conflicts, for conflict is at the very heart of the psyche and is what ultimately thrusts us into consciousness. In a healthy psyche the conflicts are handled with communication, negotiation, and an attempt to justly weigh the claims of the various psychic components. In an unhealthy psyche, communication breaks down; negotiations are sundered. The organism attempts to solve its tensions by having one part dominate others, by creating rigid defensive boundaries that isolate unwanted psychic parts from the mainstream of conscious experience. The psychic constituents then war against each other with no hope of a negotiated settlement and no genuine satisfactions for the psyche. The problem of integration for the self, as well as society, is the deepest, most difficult problem of health and well-being.

A harmonious and full functioning of the psyche does not simply evolve. Indeed, with social forces and practices pushing us so strongly toward partiality and specialization, it is doubtful that a person could achieve full psychic integration without making some profound ruptures with ordinary modes of thinking, speaking, and acting. Our thinking must keep present all of our needs and aspects of human nature and not forget them in an overly analytic and hierarchically focused consciousness. Our language must listen and understand a multiplicity of tongues; it must not leave parts of ourselves without voice, inarticulate and undeveloped. Our character traits must foster balance, openness, and connectedness and avoid those tendencies that create structural imbalances and isolated fragments of the psyche. And we must learn to live in the world as our home rather than as a field of personal exploitation. That is, to achieve the balance and fullness of psychic functioning needed for excellence, we must learn to think, speak, and dwell, both in ourselves and the world, ecologically.

PART III

EXCELLENCE

CHAPTER 8

ECOLOGICAL THINKING

Traditionally, thinking has been for the sake of knowledge of the way things are rather than opinions of how they appear. In line with this end, the crucial concern with thinking has been to define a methodology that would produce knowledge of how things are. However, since the late nineteenth century there have been substantial attacks on this notion of what constitutes thinking. For the pragmatists, the end of thinking is to bring us into a more satisfactory relation with our environment. An idea is true if it "works." For Wittgenstein, there is no ideal methodology of thinking; each context or language game has its own use for a particular kind of thinking. In some contexts thought can attempt to discover what things really are, but in others it will be learning how to do a task, mapping a strategy, and so forth. Finally, for Heidegger, thinking is its own end. We do not think to attain a product, knowledge, but think for the sake of thinking. Such thinking, for Heidegger, is the path on which Being appears. Ecological thinking incorporates and interweaves each of these positions into a still more fundamental theory of what constitutes thinking in human life.

Ecological thinking is, first of all, pragmatic thinking—thinking whose primary goal is the satisfaction of the needs. As such, it has two initial aims: to know what the needs are and to know what activities will best satisfy them. We do not determine our needs a priori and then seek activities to satisfy them. Rather we find our needs emerging in interactional activities. Thus, thinking commences in particular problems in specific activities.

Each activity has its own peculiar kind of thinking, and in order to participate in an activity and reap its satisfactions, we must obey the patterns of thinking it requires. If we are playing chess, then we must think like a strategist; if we are healing a patient, then we must think like a physician. Hence, ecological thinking takes many different forms, depending on what contexts we find ourselves in and what we want to achieve. Precise computation, loose estimates, simple practical reasoning, complex deliberation about the whole pattern of one's life, careful aesthetic attention, empathic responses, abstract theorizing—all can be functional ways of thinking. Ecological thinkers respond to their immediate environments and immediate problems by determining the appropriate contextual patterns of thought.

But although ecological thinkers follow focused modes of thought in specific contexts, they also understand that every context is an ecosystem with complex webs of relationships within it and tendrils stretching out from it into the dark backgrounds of experience, tendrils that make each context a vortex where the individual, the community, the culture, and nature spin their forces. Ecological thinking dwells in these relations because it is only in being present to this complexity that human beings can find what their needs are and how contexts relate to the needs. We are webs—networks of interrelated needs, emotions, capacities, and character traits—and are inextricably interwoven with the networks of society, culture, and nature. The only kind of thinking that can penetrate these webs and understand them is thinking that is itself webbed, thinking that can weave synchronic nets into the environment and diachronic nets through time.

Nonecological thinkers lose themselves in the isolated focus of a specific context. They are only chess players while playing chess or doctors while curing patients. Ecological thinkers keep present the fullness of relationships and the fullness of background. The chess player recalls his daughter's growth in learning the complexities of chess, empathizes with some unfortunate setbacks she has recently received from the world, sees how intensely she is playing, and carefully loses the game. The doctor, while anticipating the complex details of an imminent surgery, recalls her own humanness in responding to her patient's fears and hopes.

In seeing relationships as webs, ecological thinking differs markedly from traditional thought whose model for understanding causal relations is linear and whose organizational structures are hierarchical. In distinction from linear thinking, which has as a model "*A* causes *B* causes *C*" and so on, ecological thinking sees reverberations, feedback mechanisms, and secondary consequences. If A causes B, the creation of B will affect the ecosystem that contains both A and B, and thus will have a causal effect on A. Ordinary relational thinking saw that DDT exterminated harmful insects; ecological thinking followed the effects further and found that the poisoned insects were part of the food chain of birds and fish, devastated these natural predators of insects, and therefore had the "side" effect of increasing the insect population.

Ecological thinkers not only see and understand webs of relationships, they locate themselves in these networks. They accept Heisenberg's discovery that observers affect the world they are observing: the observer is an integral part of the observed, and the observed is an integral part of the observer. In its interweaving of the known and the knower and its placing of the epistemological enterprise in the middle of webbed relationships, ecological thinking is aligned with the hermeneutical thinking developed by Heidegger and Gadamer. In hermeneutics, all thinking is interpretation. We are able to interpret texts, events, or objects because we belong to a culture that gives us the tools of interpretation: language and categorical structures. Yet interpretation is not simply the application of cultural schemes of understanding to objects, for in this case all we ever encounter are our own biases. Rather the event of interpretation is an interplay between ourselves and the foreign (the object we want to know, but don't), in which our belonging to a tradition gives us inroads into the understanding of the foreign and the foreign acts as a challenge to our categorical systems. Thus, thinking is a dynamic interaction between knower and known in which these are not set final truths. Both subject and object can change, develop, enter richer fields of connections and wider schemes of meaning.

But the great thinkers of the Enlightenment would counter that cultural categories are always prejudiced. We do not want interpretations; we want the truth. The only way to get the truth, they would claim, is to break away from the biases of culture, clear one's head of preconceptions, negate all emotional involvement with the objects to be known, and approach them with a methodology that is public, verifiable, and hence objective. Hermeneutics would reply that scientific methodology is not objective but a prejudice of the culture that comes with a highly dubious metaphysics, which separates mind from matter, and a questionable ethic, which seeks domination as a final goal. We have only begun to penetrate the consequences of this bias, but we can already understand that, along with giving us immense control over natural processes and a cornucopia of material goods, it has isolated us from nature, condemned hundreds of species of plants and animals to extinction, bifurcated our cognitive powers from our emotions, reduced experience to an uninvolved analysis of objects, and spawned weapons that threaten to bring life on our globe to a fiery end. And why not end it? Experience has lost so much meaning and vitality of involvement that, for many, ultimate annihilation seems hardly a problem worth considering.

Ecological and hermeneutical thinking reconnects us to world we are trying to know and enmeshes us once again with its webs. It does not try to overcome cultural prejudices by completely isolating an abstract cognitive part of the psyche from all else in the psyche and the world, but by asking the knower to go through a hermeneutical process that constantly challenges our visions and expands the scope of our understandings.

What does it mean to be connected to what we are knowing? What constitutes a connection? In one sense we are always connected within the webs of nature and culture, whether we know it or not. To be is to be connected. But even though we are in fact connected to the world, we can be unaware of the connections and so feel isolated and disconnected. This state occurs when thought separates itself from emotion. It is the emotions that connect us to the world, for they are the primary system for monitoring the relation of the needs to the environment. When an event saddens us, or excites or scares or disgusts us, we feel directly related to it. Emotions are bonds; reason is separation. Reason, by itself, abstracts the mind from the world in order to see it clearly and distinctly. Reason might know what the world is, but emotions know what it means for us. When reason and emotion are integrated in thinking, not only does the world gain a depth of meaning for us, but we become more attuned to what our needs are and how we are relating to the world. Ecological thinking as the interweaving of reason and emotion integrates our psyches with the world, and provides the knowledge that allows us the fullest satisfaction of the needs.

In requiring us to be aware of our emotional, natural, historical, and cultural roots, ecological thinking is only asking us to make conscious what is unconscious. We created a myth that the mind could extricate itself from the world and objectively observe it, a myth that was astonishingly productive but that has become too dangerous and too impoverished to continue. Objective, disconnected reasoning needs to be replaced by webbed thought. Above all, ecological thinking is webbed thinking.

Yet analytical reasoning cannot be fully abandoned. All relational thinking depends at base on locating and analyzing the individual items of a context. Relationships are among relata. Without an analytical description of the needs, emotions, and cognitive capacities, such as that found in chapters 5 and 6, we could not understand the psyche. What analytical thought discovers, however, are fictions—necessary fictions, important fictions, but fictions nonetheless. For instance, analytical thinking discovers a need to survive, but there is no need for survival. Rather there is a need for survival in relation to needs for sexual fitness, beauty, knowledge, order, and the like, in relation to a particular constellation of emotions, character traits, and cognitive abilities, and in relation to certain social and natural environments. All of these relations affect the need for survival and at least partially transform it. Without this relational understanding, it is impossible to grasp why human beings willfully choose to die, or lower their survival potential by placing themselves in dangerous situations, as the martyr and soldier do. We can sacrifice our lives for those we love or a way of life we love. We can die for honor (social esteem). We can develop such powerful forms of self-hatred that we must annihilate ourselves. It is wrong to say that we always desire to survive; rather, certain of us, under certain conditions, at certain times, wish to survive. Individual needs are abstractions; the reality is a complex organism in a set of Chinese-box environments, a reality that demands both keen analytical thought and complex relational understanding.

In its dual demands for webbed understanding and focused analysis, ecological thinking creates a profound tension, a tension that should not be broken. Focused analytical thought hates roots, to be tied to complexities, to feel connected. It wants to break things out of their backgrounds to see them clearly, to give them definition, to be resolved about them. Heraclitean change, labyrinths, and feedback relations are its sworn enemies. On the other hand, relational thought despises focus, despises the world broken into isolated individuals. It dwells in swamps and wants nothing to leave its murky bogs and captivating smells. To think ecologically is to be both analytically focused and webbed. It is to have the sparkling diamond of clear analysis set in the rich bonds of memory.

Finally, ecological thinking is temporal thinking, a thinking attuned to time and the relationship of beings to time. All things change, and hence, to know something requires that we know where it is in its history or how it is located in time. The newborn baby, toddler, seven-year-old, adolescent, youth, adult, and geriatric are all humans; yet they have such different ascendant needs as to be very different beings. The babe needs basic trust, care, nourishment, safety; the youth, adventures into the unknown—a testing of character; the adult, a fullness of functioning; the old, meaning, sacredness, knowledge. Not only does the arrangement of needs change over time, but so do the needs themselves. What was sexually satisfying at two is not so at thirteen or forty. The kind of order that sustains us as adolescents does not sustain us as adults. Knowing where we and others are in life's journey, what we need to be accomplishing now and what we need to be renouncing, is a wisdom as precious as it is rare. "To every thing there is a season, and a time to every purpose under the heaven: a time to be born and a time to die."

Thinking that dwells in time is a suffering. The passage of time always brings loss, death. The one-year-old who delighted us so much that we hoped she would never change dies and becomes transformed into the two-year-old with such charming assertiveness we wish she would never change. The virgin forest we played in as children becomes the housing development of the next generation. The mother who so mysteriously gave birth, dies in an equally incomprehensible mystery. Time sows the seeds of all beings and reaps them in a harvest that nothing escapes.

We suffer time as limitation. We want to plant, but it is winter. We want to feel nourished and completely safe, but we have grown and childhood is forever past. We crave wisdom, but we are young. Neurotics are people who refuse to live in the flux of time. They remain fixated at a certain stage of growth, in a certain structure of behavior that is impervious to time. They attempt to continually repeat in the present what didn't get solved in the past, and all for nought, for time has passed. The victory can no longer be won.

As temporal thinkers we know and dwell in a reality that is process, a process that always involves connectedness and rupture, inheritance and loss. In our webbed thinking we locate ourselves in the connections, nets, and togethernesses of time. In connectedness we have a home, joyously dance in the relatedness of all beings, but are bound by chains and feel stifled. In our temporal thinking we find ruptures, seams, births, deaths. Here we are frightened, excited, angry, sad. There is the joy of a new vista opening and the sadness of the loss of the old. What was will no longer be. The two modes of thinking are intertwined, for we cannot experience the ruptures without first knowing the connectedness. But to feel the meaningfulness of connections, to know their worth, to feel them as integral to oneself, and then to encounter the rupture, the death, is to dwell in tragedy. Hence, ecological thinking is never far from sadness; our deepest thoughts always seem to generate in a realm of tears. "The heart of the wise is in the house of sorrow" (Eccles. 7:4).

Our portrait of the ecological thinker is now fully sketched. Thinking for the ecologist is not an abstract methodology for solving problems, but a way of gathering oneself and the world into a fullness of experience. Pragmatically seeking goals, thoroughly engaging in specific activities, minutely analyzing details, grasping complex connections, delving into past roots, imagining future consequences and ideals, and sensing the flux of time are all essential parts of this gathering. Initially, we learn and perform these epistemological enterprises in separate moments, for each mode of thought requires much training and concentration to do well. Yet we do not become full ecological thinkers until these ways of thinking are more or less always present and constantly penetrating one another. When this interpenetration occurs, our thinking becomes thoughtful.

How can we become thoughtful thinkers? How can we hold together so many complex and conflicting processes? This kind of thinking can occur only when we learn how to think within the presence of memory. "To think within the presence of memory" sounds to our ears like a foreign language, for we live in a culture that trains its members to lose memory. Our world demands that we have clearly focused goals and that we concentrate on analytically solving the problems of the moment. Other times, feelings, and darker connections are at best irrelevant and at worst hindrances to the workings of our methodologies. Once people knew the *Iliad* and *Odyssey* by heart; they retained complex memories of their lives, tribe, family, and culture. Now memory is a matter for libraries and databanks. We live in forgetfulness of everything except the methodologies to retrieve the information we need for our present tasks. In our loss of memory, we have lost our ability to think ecologically and to become whole.

This thought, that memory has been lost and must return for human beings in the West to achieve wholeness, has been spoken by profound thinkers in our century. Proust, in his monumental *Remembrance of Things Past*, gives us a literary portrait of how a fragmented, isolated person restores himself through the recovery of memory. Freud explicitly states that health returns to the psyche only with the restoration of a certain kind of memory. And Heidegger writes:

> Memory is the gathering and convergence of thought upon what everywhere demands to be thought about first of all. Memory is the gathering of recollection, thinking back. It safely keeps and keeps

concealed within it that to which at each given time thought must be given before all else, in everything that essentially is, everything that appeals to us as what has being and been in being.[1]

How can memory restore a fragmented person to wholeness and gather thought so that it always thinks what needs to be thought? What always needs to be thought? We can grasp memory only by remembering what memory is. 'Memory' derives from the Latin *memoria*, which means "mindful." This connection is also found in Greek, where the word for memory, *mnemosyne*, literally means "full of mind."[2] To have memory, then, is to have a fullness of mind, to be great-minded. When we are full of mind or mindful, we take care not to isolate ourselves in the particular focus of a present situation, but remain in constant recall of the wider meanings of events, meanings that give both preciousness and perspective to the present. Mindfulness has the tempo of a largo or andante. When we are overly focused on the present or thoroughly engaged in the achievement of a task, we live at the pace of an allegro vivace or a scherzo. These quicker tempos can also characterize a person of memory who recalls that life must have many rhythms, but there is always a return to slowness, to a quiet gathering in the background. Even that thinker of dazzling quickness, Nietzsche, writes:

> How does one become stronger?—By coming to decisions slowly; and by clinging tenaciously to what one has decided. Everything else follows. The sudden and the changeable; the two species of weakness. Not to mistake oneself for one of them; to feel the distance before it is too late.[3]

How can we come to this mindfulness, this fullness of memory? Here I turn to mythology, for I find in myths a path to first truths that is not known in discursive language. In myths truth is so irrevocably implanted in a web of symbols that we must respond to it with our whole psyches, not just our minds, and in so responding we recall more fully who we are. Myths gather both our thoughts and our selves, and in this gathering restore memory. Mythology represents the first attempt of language to speak the truth of the psyche. Here experience is fresh and forgetfulness absent. Later philosophers and scientists derided myth as fiction, for they needed to create clearer, more rational discourses to push the psyche into new realms of understanding and power. But myth is the first word (*mythos* means "word"), and to it we must turn to discover what later languages forgot.

Hesiod said that memory (*Mnemosyne*) was a Titan, the daughter of the first god and goddess, Ouranos (sky) and Gaia (earth). Ouranos and Gaia had a number of other children: eleven or twelve other Titans, three huge sons each of whom had fifty heads and a hundred arms (hence their name, Hecatoncheires), and another three sons, the Cyclopes, each of whom had one eye and the power of making thunder and lightning. Ouranos was upset by the unruly behavior of the Hecatoncheires and Cyclopes and threw them into Tartaros. Displeased with this imprisoning of her children, Gaia convinced Kronos to lead the Titans in rebellion against Ouranos and gave him a sickle for a weapon. Kronos castrated his father (whose semen fell on the sea, to produce Aphrodite, and whose blood fell on the earth, to produce the Giants), became ruler, married his sister Rhea, but kept the Hecatoncheires and Cyclopes in Tartaros. Since it had been prophesied by Gaia that Kronos would be overthrown in turn by one of his own children, Kronos ate his children as soon as they were born. Finally, unhappy Rhea hid her birth of Zeus in a cave on Crete and gave Kronos a stone to eat in his place. Zeus grew up, gave Kronos a potion that made him regurgitate the swallowed children (Hestia, Hera, Demeter, Poseidon, and Hades), gained their support as leader through promises of positions and rewards, and entered into a ten-year war against Kronos and the Titans. Zeus and the gods finally won when Zeus freed the Cyclopes and Hecatoncheires from Tartaros and used their natural powers to overcome the Titans. The Titans were then hurled into an abyss below Tartaros, and the Hecatoncheires were given the political plum of guarding them.

Surprisingly, we later find that Zeus has become the lover to two Titans: Mnemosyne, who bore him the Muses,[4] and Themis, who bore him the Seasons, Lawfulness, Justice, prospering Peacetime, and the Fates. In other stories of the Titans we find that one of them fathers forethought (Prometheus) and one afterthought (Epimetheus), and that Prometheus in turn fathers Deucalion, who alone with his wife survives the great deluge and restarts human life. Finally, Hesiod locates the golden age as having occurred during the reign of Kronos. These myths concerning the Titans seem to recall a moment in human evolution when there was some emergence of consciousness so profound that it appeared both as a deluge and a rebirth.

This history of the gods is a metaphorical expression of the history of the psyche. What does it mean that memory is a Titan? Why does the reign of the Titans come after that of Ouranos and Gaia and before that of Zeus? Why does Zeus mate with two Titans whom he had previously thrown into Tartaros? Ouranos and Gaia are nature gods, and their world is one of natural forces—a world without intelligence, political order, or personal order. It seems to be the world of the hunter-gatherer tribe in which everything is close to nature. But something is unstable in the realm: the Cyclopes seem to be banished because they are not capable of living with law, and the Hecatoncheires (who have enough heads and arms to represent a typically sized hunter-gatherer tribe) are such a condensed communal oneness that there is no individuation. On the other hand, Zeus and the Olympians are very distinct individuals, and Olympus is a political realm. Zeus reigns not because he is the oldest son or the strongest (natural criteria), but because he is able to form political alliances and organize the gods with craft and intelligence. The order of Olympus is not based upon cycles of nature or an attempted mimesis of natural events: it is the arbitrary invention of a creative, personal intelligence.

Between the inchoate realm of nature and the conscious, intelligent, political world of the Olympians is stretched the realm of Kronos and the Titans. Indeed, to be a Titan is literally to be stretched like a bow or to strain at a task (*titaino*). The Titans are stretched between earth and sky, nature and intelligence, communal ritual life and the political state. That the Titans have relations to both worlds is further present in the language. *Titaia* was a title of earth, and *titan* means "white earth"—a connection to the powers of the earth and ritual, for persons wearing white earth (gypsum) conducted ritual ceremonies as daimons (ancestor earth spirits). But the realm of ether is also called "the Titan," and there is a tradition that sees the Titans as sky gods, for they ousted their father, the sky, and took his place.[5]

Thus, to be a Titan is to be stretched between the forces of nature and the organization of the intellect, between the communal and the personal, between the urges of the basic needs and emotions and the counsels of the ego. It is in this stretching where memory is located, for memory, as a Titan, is a stretching. At the most basic level, memory stretches over time and gathers disparate events into patterns. From the patterns gathered in memory we can see through time, back into the past and forward into the future. It is memory of patterns through time that allows for the creation of agricultural life. Kronos's name means "harvest," and his symbol is a sickle. With agricultural life comes division of labor and the roots of individuation. The Titans are the first individuated gods.

But they were not individuated enough. Their connections to the past, nature, emotion, and ritual hindered the growth of intelligence, personality, and the development of a complex socioeconomic political order. Zeus had to get rid of them. Yet something is wrong with Zeus's bright new world. The gods are frivolous little egos bent on their own self-aggrandizement, ungrounded in either nature or an ethical universal. The gods reach full consciousness, but the price they pay for this goal is a further separation of the conscious from the unconscious, as the Titans must be banished to the underworld. Although Zeus raised the Cyclopes and Hecatoncheires from Tartaros, he then used them for defensive purposes against the Titans. They were hardly integrated into the new world. In this new realm of private individuated intelligence, both the psyche and the community become fragmented. This is why Zeus recalls the Titans Mnemosyne and Themis, for memory restores the psyche to wholeness, and the spirit of the communal order (it is Themis who calls the gods to assembly)[6] renews the sense of community.

Memory resides at a level of psychic functioning that precedes and develops into individuation and consciously ordered experience. Memory's relation to both the preconscious and the individuated consciousness is not accidental, for memory is a Titan, not an earth mother or an Olympian goddess. To have memory is to dwell in the region between the conscious and the unconscious, the personal and the nonpersonal, with connections into both worlds. With memory we transcend the narrow realm of the personal ego and become full human beings.

How does one dwell between the conscious and unconscious, between the personal and nonpersonal? We in the West have little problem with attending to conscious, personal functions. It is what resides outside the clear forms of consciousness that bothers us and that we need to incorporate in our memories. When we turn to dreams, mistakes, slips, symbols, peripheral feelings, and thoughts that come from free association rather than a logical sequence, we come in contact with what lies outside the usual boundaries of ego consciousness. When we are able to interweave this material with that of consciousness, we perform what Jung calls "the transcendent function."[7] This is hardly an easy task, for consciousness, like Zeus, is definite, directive, and highly organized, while the unconscious, like Gaia and Ouranos, can produce monstrous offspring, be diffuse and dark, love repetition, but also, can give life vitality and meaning. When we develop memory, we are able to unite the two realms for a fuller, richer life than either alone could produce.

When our intelligent personal egos rediscover the memory they once cast aside as a hindrance, the Muses are born. With the birth of the Muses we learn how to dwell poetically, narratively, musically, as members of a historical culture, and as engaged in a scientific understanding of ourselves and the world. In their inspiring of these languages or ways of articulating ourselves, the Muses open up our potentialities for rich and variegated living and thinking. But even more important than the different facets of thought that we must keep in memory is that which all the Muses have in common: music. Music—rhythm, meter, harmony—this is the language beneath other languages, the language that tells us how we are with ourselves and the world. Music embodied is dance. For all cultures, except those that have become the most forgetful, the essential communal activity is dance. In dancing we recall the god of dance, Dionysos. This agrees with the myths older than Hesiod in which the Muses are not named and do not represent modes of articulated thought. They are nymphs of springs who inspire whose who drink from them. As nymphs, they live in the realm of Dionysos.

The gift of memory is the birth of Dionysos in the psyche. Who is Dionysos? He was conceived in a mating between Zeus and a mortal woman, Semele. When Semele asked to see Zeus as he really was, the subsequent bolt of lightning consumed her. Zeus then put the fetus Dionysos in his thigh to complete the pregnancy. There are other variations of this story, but all have a common theme: Dionysos is the double-born.

As the son of Zeus and the double-born, Dionysos is a paradox. We would expect the next generation of gods to be even more personified and more intelligent than Zeus, but Dionysos is not concerned with the intelligence that builds political orders, nor does he have a clearly delineated personality structure. Like his mother, he is tied to the earth; like his father, he has a recognizable personality, is full of cunning, and is immortal. But he dies and is reborn. Who is this Dionysos? Here is what characters in Euripides' *Bacchae* say: "god of laughter," "spirit of revel and rapture," "god of joy," "a prophet," "his dear love is Peace. . . . In wine, his gift that charms all griefs away, alike both rich and poor may have their part," "Dionysos, son of Zeus, in his full nature God, most terrible, although most gentle to mankind," "Come Dionysos! Come, and appear to us! Come like a bull or a hundred-headed serpent, come like a lion snorting."

Dionysos is a boundary figure and a breaker of boundaries. In laughter, revel, and wine he comes to smash the overserious plans and structures of the rational ego. He recalls us to the chaos of life, for he is constantly dying and being reborn. He dies as a woman's child and is reborn in the male community—but he retains a female *thiasos* (group of followers). He is a man but looks like a woman with long flowing golden locks. He is welcome in Olympus, but is not part of the official pantheon. He is an older nature god—a bull, a hundred-headed serpent, a lion—connected with death, rebirth, and communal ritual, but has too much personality to be just a force of nature. He has no home, but wanders over the boundaries of countries through Asia and Greece, sometimes bringing the grape and joy; other times death and destruction.

Thus Dionysos, like the Titans, is stretched: between male and female, Zeus and nature, the ordering systems of the psyche and the chaos of the emotions and needs. He seems to exist in the boundaries between the psychic components, relating personal order to subpersonal forces. He lives neither in ego structures, like his nemesis, Pentheus, nor in the blind forces of nature, like the Giants or Cyclopes. When he lives in the interstices of the psyche, we fill with joy and sorrow, we revel in the mystery of creation, we live in the memory of the sacredness of life—its meaning beyond any limited contextual meaning. Dionysos joins all the psychic components in a swirling communal round-dance that restores our wholeness. Nietzsche understood this gift of Dionysos that memory gives:

> The word "Dionysian" means: an urge to unity, a reaching out beyond personality, the everyday, society, reality, across the abyss of transitoriness: a passionate-painful overflowing into darker, fuller, more floating states; an ecstatic affirmation of the total character of life as that which remains the same, just as powerful, just as blissful, sorrow that sanctifies and calls good even the most terrible and questionable qualities of life; the eternal will to procreation, to fruitfulness, to recurrence; the feeling of the necessary unity of creation and destruction.[8]

When memory is present, then, we become stretched, like Dionysos and the Titans, between all the competing factions of the psyche. In our stretching we remember our connections to mortality, sexuality, chaos, the emotions, the sacredness of the harvest, and the cyclical patterns of time. We hear the calls to adventure, beauty, knowledge, and autonomy. We remember our groundedness in a common language, values, institutions, economies, and the recognition of others. In the midst of this remembering and at its heart lies a yet deeper memory, a memory that gathers all the above memories and keeps them present at the center. It is the memory that these life-giving grounds are gifts that are not our creations but that create us. Heidegger understands this when he ties memory to thinking, and thinking to thanking.

What is it that is named with the words "think," "thinking," "thought?" Toward what sphere of the spoken word do they direct us? A thought—where is it, where does it go? Thought is in need of memory, the gatherer of thought. The Old English 'thencan,' and 'thancian,' to thank, are closely related; the Old English noun for thought is 'thanc' or 'thonc'—a thought, a grateful thought, and the expression of such a thought; today it survives in the plural 'thanks'. The "thanc," that which is thought, the thought, implies the thanks . . .the 'thanc' means man's inmost mind, the heart, the heart's core, that innermost essence of man which reaches outward most fully and to the outermost limits, and so decisively that, rightly considered, the idea of an inner and outer world does not arise.

When we listen to the work 'thanc' in its basic meaning, we hear at once the essence of the two words: thinking and memory, thinking and thanks, which readily suggest themselves in the verb, "to think."

The 'thanc,' the heart's core, is the gathering of all that concerns us, all that we care for, all that touches us insofar as we are, as human beings.[9]

We come to this state of thankfulness most fully when we learn to think on our thinking. Thinking on thinking is not the same as the self-consciousness in which we attempt to examine our thoughts concerning a certain matter, for these thoughts are entertained as objects. The thinking on thinking that issues into thankfulness is a thinking that immediately apprehends itself in its activity. There is no object; just thinking aware of itself. In this experience, thinking is not felt as "my" thinking, for no subjective ground for the thought appears. Descartes was wrong: "I think" is not the base; thinking is. Nor can we discover any theoretical ground for thinking, because all theories about the origin of thinking—be they biological, sociological, or psychological—already presuppose our ability to think. The ground of all experience, of all theories, of all living is: thinking. This is memory's first truth. For Aristotle, the ability to think upon thinking is the final mystery of the universe, the ultimate beyond which nothing can go and upon which all else depends. In this state of thought thinking upon itself, the feeling of thankfulness comes, for we grasp that we are not responsible for our thought or our lives. These are gifts, and we are all gifted. Personal possessiveness is foregone; the "I," overcome; and the essential memory of what lies beyond the personal, restored.

Our thankfully recalling the fullness of who we are is, at first, an activity, one that can be worked on and developed. We learn how to think thoughtfully by thinking thoughtfully, and to sexually feel our sexuality by sexually feeling our sexuality. In these moments we develop memory. The more we remember who we are, the more we begin to be persons of memory who carry their fullness with them. We do not have to try to remember who and what we are, because our memory has become part of the process of perception and is present in all of our experiences. We have become ecological thinkers.

Ecological thinking is not simply a matter of mastering some new methods of reasoning—methods of finding connections, analyzing functional particulars, noting developmental sequences, or seeing feedback relations. Rather, ecological thinking is the kind of thinking done by a person of memory. Such a person comes to experience not as an isolated consciousness examining the world with a set of techniques, but as an integrated organism whose consciousness of the world is grounded in a psychic fullness. We can throw diachronic webs into time and synchronic nets into the world, because we, like the Titans, have become stretched into ecological webs, and like Dionysos, revel in both the light and dark, the boundaries and highly focused centers. Our minds, rather than being empty receptacles ready to impose methods on the world, are now full, and we have become mindful. In this mindfulness we become slower, more deliberate persons, persons whose activities have a greater depth of satisfaction because we participate in them as fuller, richer people. The constant restlessness that characterizes so much modern activity disappears as memory by itself makes us full.

But we are not yet persons of memory. Our overly structured consciousnesses do not welcome memory into their beds, do not stretch deeply into the emotions, needs, and connections to the earth. The Muses have left, and our powers of articulation have become uninspired technical exercises. Dionysos no longer dances in the interstices of the psyche; mediocre feelings have come to replace great joy and sorrow. How can memory be restored? How can Dionysos be recalled?

Anthropology and myth tell us that Dionysos returns in communal rituals that celebrate death and rebirth. Dionysos is found in ritual dance, in ritual sacrifice, and the eating of the sacrament. The final way in which Dionysos is stretched is as a goat or a bull on a skewer. Christ knew the relation of memory to sacrament when at the last supper he said, "This is my body which is given for you; do this in remembrance of me." But transubstantialism is rarely believed in our rational culture; communion is at best only a symbolic act. For the upper and middle classes of the West, ritual is dead. Our individuated personalities are too strong to fully join in a Dionysian ritual of community and sacrament. God himself became too personal, too eternal, too rational, to be eaten and drunk. Christ is only symbolically the lamb; the full Dionysian transformation does not occur for us. If God cannot become a goat or lamb or roaring bull, how can we ingest him?

Is Dionysos irrevocably lost with the loss of ritual community? Are there other ways to Dionysos? The ancient communal ritual has been replaced by the contemporary "vacation." Vacations are our holidays—holy days—in which we vacate our ordinary modes of living in order to find the god. It is no wonder that when we ponder where to spend our holidays, we think of places of natural beauty and power—the ocean, lakes, the mountains—the very haunts of Dionysos and the Titans. We vacate our indoor selves and rush to air, earth, fire, and water. In recreation we seek to re-create ourselves, to be reborn like Dionysos. We give our bodies to Helios and leap into Poseidon. We climb mountains like Titans and strain against the sky. We engage in great combats of tennis, golf, baseball, football, and track, and in so doing recall the contests between the gods and the Titans, the gods and the Giants, Hercules and the monsters, Theseus and the minotaur. Sexuality returns. We laugh and drink the wine of Dionysos.

Vacations can be profoundly restorative, but usually they, like the mini-Dionysian event of "the party," either fail to break the bonds of our personal orders or soon get reduced to isolated experiences, cut off from the rest of life. Memory might be restored for the moment, but then we plunge into forgetfulness as we go about our daily business. To recall memory we need to find restorative activities located not at the periphery of life, but at its heart, activities that demand our stretching into the earth and sky, into others and ourselves, into our deepest needs, emotions, and ideas. There is such an activity. It is one that has never been recommended by any major philosopher. Yet it is the activity sought more intensely by more people than any other: sexual intimacy.

Sexual intimacy not only sends tentacles into the farthest reaches of our needs and emotions; it also reaches out to those in another human being. Almost every activity other than intimacy demands that we play a specific role, follow a certain script, and, hence, be conscripted. These contexts do not invite us to stretch ourselves in our full human nature; they want us to be a chemist doing an experiment, a driver concentrating on the road, a professor meeting the standards of excellence in her field, standards that have nothing to do with sexuality, sacredness, beauty, personal autonomy, or the emotions. As human beings, we must live in these contexts with specialized goals and rules, and thus, as human beings, we are constantly called to forgetfulness. Against this ever-present and pressing contextual invitation to forgetfulness stands intimacy's invitation to be whole human beings, to present ourselves in our entireties, for better or worse, in the relation. When we consciously or unconsciously withhold a portion of ourselves from the relation (we may also be withholding from ourselves), the intimacy is marred, lessened. Trust is violated. A human being only partially in a relation is not being intimate. In demanding that we be whole persons, intimacy lures us to stretch into unknown parts of ourselves and to restore our memories.

It is heresy to suggest that thinking and sexual intimacy are intertwined partners, that thinking and loving require one another. The West has long separated them, asserting that one could think well without being a good lover or could love well without being a good thinker. Although there is a problematical connection between love and thinking in that dark dialogue of Plato's, the *Symposium* (do we have to abandon sexual love to climb the ladder of love to finally think the forms, or are the bottom rungs to be retained in every successive step?), it is only when we get to Freud that we start to understand how memory, emotion, sex, and thought are inherently intertwined.

What Freud discovered in his patients were people who had developed structural habits to insure that a part of themselves remained in dark forgetfulness, the part usually being a strong sexual drive, wish, or emotion that conflicted with another drive, wish, emotion, or certain ingrained moral dictates. The conflict provoked an unbearable anxiety that was then, along with the conflicting emotions, hurled into the Tartaros of the unconscious, there to be guarded by such monsters as intellectualization, dissociation, denial, projection, and depression. But the forgetfulness of these conflicts did not make them disappear. Just as Dionysos returns to destroy a forgetful, overly rational Pentheus, so our repressed libidinal and aggressive urges come back to haunt the psyche, injuring it with uncontrollable compulsions, unrealistic fantasies, and self-destructive behavior.

Freud found that, through hypnotic techniques and questioning certain involved parties, he could determine in many cases the nature of the original trauma and tell the patient. But the recovery of this kind of memory did not alleviate the symptoms or restore the patient to health. It was a kind of "knowing that was not knowing." That is, the act of intellectually recalling the facts of the case was not itself an integrative act, for the subject was only partially present in the act of knowing, present only as a disembodied consciousness. Further, the objective facts of what actually happened were found to be almost irrelevant for the restoration of memory: what mattered was whether the subject could emotionally reexperience in the present the emotional psychic content of the repressed situation of the past. Thus the question for Freud was: If a patient is now in a state of forgetfulness and nonintegration, and no outside objective forces can alleviate this state, how can the patient ever move to a state of memory and integration?

In answering this question, Freud revealed the depth of his genius, for the process he invented to restore memory was none other than a Dionysian ritual reinterpreted for the death and rebirth of an individual person rather than a community. Like all rituals, therapy has a sacred time and a sacred space. In this sacred space, at the sacred time, there is an epiphany of the god—Dionysos himself—in the guise of the therapist. Like Dionysos, the therapist does not reveal his personal life or background or show a fully developed personality. The analyst greets the patient with an "otherworldly" glance, a look that appears to pierce through the patient and go to his most secret inner realms. Ordinary modes of discourse are disallowed. The therapist refuses to chitchat, directly answer questions, or interpret events and words in ordinary ways. Like Dionysos, the therapist loves darkness and the events of darkness: dreams, mistakes, irrational behavior patterns, things the patient wishes to keep hidden. The experience of the therapist as god is further enhanced by the process of transference, in which the feelings the patient had for his godlike parents in childhood become centered on the analyst.

These reversals of ordinary life throw the patient into chaos. The Bacchic dance of disintegration begins, for the only path from nonintegration to integration is through disintegration. Only when defensive structures come crashing down can the fullness of psychic realities be recalled. How can the therapist lead the patient into the underworld? Because she is the double-born; she herself has been torn apart by the white-faced Titans and been reborn. She can guide the patient through the Inferno because she has been there herself and come back out. The therapist is loved as this guide, but also hated as a devastating monster, who rips the defensive, but life-preserving, structures of the individual to pieces. "Dionysos, most terrible, although most gentle, to mankind." The end of therapy is not the transformation of the patient into a god of invulnerable strength, but the creation of a human being, who can suffer and enjoy more fully what it means to be a human being. Before the therapeutic ritual, the patient was held together by an exoderm of rigid beliefs and habits; now a new center appears: memory.

Freud described this ritual for the restoration of memory as the "talking cure," for he understood (at some level) that the fragmentations of neurosis and the loss of memory were, at bottom, problems of language. Loss of memory is equivalent to the inability to articulate what has been forgotten. These inarticulate parts then get broken off from the conversational matrix of personal consciousness. There is no exchange of information between the fragmented parts and personal consciousness; the parts no longer speak the same language and do not communicate with one another. Without a common language for the settlement of intrapsychic disputes, the parts of the psyche become like autonomous nations, each speaking its own language and without concern for the well-being of the other countries. Thus, our question of how to restore memory has transformed itself into the question of how to establish a communicative system within the psyche such that all the parts of the psyche can enter a common set of negotiations. And our question of how to think ecologically has transformed itself into the question of how to speak ecologically.

CHAPTER 9

ECOLOGICAL SPEAKING

Communication is not a secondary by-product of the primary processes of the psyche; it is an essential part of them. Human beings must express themselves; they must "press out" what happens within the psyche to complete its activity and feel fulfilled. This "need" for expression and communication is not another need like those for survival and reproduction, for it encompasses all the needs, emotions, capacities—indeed, every psychic component. There would not be anything to express without these psychic elements, but they, on the other hand, would remain unfulfilled, undeveloped, and inchoate without expression. Unless we have systems of communication, we cannot think or organize ourselves socially, economically, politically, or psychologically.

It took Western thinkers a long time to realize the primacy of expression in human life. The most influential thinker of the seventeenth century, Descartes, could still claim that the primary knowledge of the psyche was given in an immediate intuition, the *ego cogito.* But by the nineteenth century, theoreticians of all stripes were claiming that Descartes's interior intuition was not the ground of the self. Humans were most fully revealed in their expressive productions. Romanticists crowned artists as the most profound purveyors of truth because they created works that expressed human nature more fully than scientists, philosophers, or theologians. The self did not lie waiting to be discovered by contemplation, but needed to be created in fundamental acts of self-expression. Hegel took this idea and constructed an entire theological metaphysic around it: the Geist must express itself in particular concrete productions, and thus has to enter

nature, culture, and history. Feuerbach took the idea in just the opposite direction, claiming that all theologies were nothing but expressions of what we find to be most important in ourselves. The Enlightenment's conception of God as one, rational, and dominating was
merely an expression of what Enlightenment psyches had become.

The primacy of expression is also at the root of Marx's philosophy,
for the product of a person's labor is the objective expression of his
nature—to be alienated from one's productions (as one is in industrial
capitalism) is to be alienated from oneself. The theory is likewise the
cornerstone for the foundation of archeology, which attempts to gather
from artifacts the lived experience of a people. With this kind of
nineteenth-century background, it is little wonder that Freud conceived the cause of neurosis not as the malfunctioning of basic
biological drives or emotions, nor as unavoidable conflicts, but rather
as the inadequate expression of these drives, emotions, and conflicts.
Blocked expression of the psychic forces dammed natural energy paths
through the psyche, creating isolated pools of pent-up energy, which,
because they were cut off from the main communicative stream of
consciousness, could wreak havoc on the person. The major task of
psychoanalysis was seen as bringing repressed, inarticulate elements
to articulation and integration with the main communicative system
of the patient.

Since Freud, the expressive and communicative systems of the
psyche have achieved such importance that a number of contemporary
theories equate them with the whole functioning of the psyche.
According to these theories, emotions, needs, and capacities are
generated by the learning of certain sign systems and would not exist
without them. If our culture has a language for the emotion of anger,
then we can feel anger; otherwise it does not exist for us. If our culture
has expressions for the need for adventure, then we feel the need for
adventure; otherwise we have no such need. The position of this book
is in sharp contrast to these theories, for it claims that the needs,
emotions, and capacities exist regardless of the semiotic systems of
a society, and that if a society does not develop adequate modes of
expression for the psyche, then psychic malfunctioning occurs. However, the two positions agree that no psychic component can be consciously articulated, developed, or integrated unless the subject has
an adequate way of expressing that element.

The general truth in all the above positions is clear: the psyche
is not an isolated inner temple whose secrets can be hidden forever.
What is inner must become outer. If a psyche is to be rich, its modes
of expression must be complex and full. If a psyche is to be profound,

then its expressions must be profound. If a psyche is to be ecological, then it must express itself ecologically. But what are ecological expression and communication? How do they differ from the ways we ordinarily express ourselves?

We express or communicate something through signs, a sign being any physical event or object that can be interpreted as having meaning. According to Habermas, human beings have three basic sign systems: actions, gestures, and language.[1] A psychic event is completely expressed only when it is congruently articulated in all of these sign systems—when our language, body, and actions say the same thing. Perhaps the clearest symptom of psychic disturbance occurs when these sign systems are not aligned, as when someone says "I love you" but has a worried, uncertain facial expression and acts in ways that "unintentionally" hurt the beloved. Such a nonalignment indicates that parts of the psyche are not in communication with one another, that the interior conversation is a fragmented one, with parts constantly "talking by" one another or engaged in different stories. When the psyche is functioning in an ecologically integrated way, the sign systems are congruent: they all give the same message.

In the West, we have enthroned language as the chief form of communication, often to the detriment of actions and gestures. Aside from the vast importance the written word has achieved in our culture (and the importance of this factor is never to be underestimated), there are a number of reasons for this dominance. Language seems to have much more depth, flexibility, and possibilities for communication than the other sign systems. When anger is expressed in violent acts and gestures, it rips the social fabric and remains unintegrated with other needs, emotions, personal history, and future expectations. Anger in acts and gestures is often brute, sudden, and irredeemable: a punch breaks a tooth and that is that; the damage cannot be undone. But the words "I hate you" can later be modified, withdrawn, explained, or excused. Here the social fabric can be restored, and the psyche has articulate material to work through and integrate. Also, the language of theory seems to have no corresponding gestures or actions. How does a person gesture or act the propositions of physics? What are the gestures that express a mathematical theorem? The language of theory seems to break from practical life and form a world of its own. This is expressed by Plato with his theory of Forms and by Aristotle with his contention that theory only addresses that which is unchanging.

But ecologically minded persons know that in lived experience the primacy of language is not to be overemphasized in forgetfulness of gestures and actions, for when language is unconnected to gestures and actions, there is a noncongruence of the sign systems. Despite the recent discovery by analytic philosophers that some linguistic utterances constitute acts, words cannot do everything. It is not enough to say "I love you" and write poems of love, if the love felt is sexual and intimate. There must also be the gaze of love, gestures of affection, acts of physical communion for the words to have embodied, concrete meaning. Language becomes abstract when it is not grounded at some point in gestures and actions. In our culture anyone can write any words that come to them, but in other cultures, words carry little weight unless they are associated with persons whose actions and gestures allow them to write the words. One cannot write about Zen meditation without having had a long practice of such meditation.

Consider the following passage from Shunryu Suzuki, who is concerned with not just how words can express an ultimate truth, but how our bodies can express that truth in gesture and act:

> Now I would like to talk about our zazen posture. When you sit in the full lotus position, your left foot is on your right thigh, and your right foot is on your left thigh. When we cross our legs like this, even though we have a right leg and a left leg, they have become one. The position expresses the oneness of duality: not two, and not one. This is the most important teaching: not two, and not one. Our body and mind are not two and not one. If you think your body and mind are two, that is wrong; if you think they are one, that is also wrong. Our body and mind are both two and one.[2]

In sum, our first task in becoming persons who express themselves ecologically is to be aware of how our three systems for giving signs are functioning in relation to one another and to work to bring them into a coherence. Crucial to a successful undertaking of this task is acceptance of the belief that everything human beings do or say is a sign. It was this belief that allowed Freud to find meaning in human events that others had declared meaningless—such as dreams, sudden images, slips of the tongue, mistakes, and hysterical actions. If we find that we cannot interpret an action, gesture, or linguistic event in our lives, this should be an impetus not to disregard it as trivial, but to deepen our system for the interpretation of signs. These incoherent moments that transcend the boundaries of our ordinary systems of interpretation are the passageways into the dark recesses of the psyche, into the inner workings of the psyche below the levels of conscious order. When we warily enter them and seek to know how a mistake, strange feeling, or dream could have been produced by us and how it fits the rest of our life patterns, we begin not only to explore the deeper levels of expression in ourselves but also to break limiting structures of consciousness. Perhaps more than any other path, attempting to find ways to interpret our prima facie incomprehensible signs is the most direct way to restore lost memories and achieve a fuller conception of ourselves.

Take the (actual) case of Bill, who verbally said he had no prejudices against women, loved them, always acted in the most chivalric manner toward them, but who had the following dream:

> I am a little boy being tossed over the ocean into a net by a motherly woman. There are many snakes on the beach which other people seem to pick up. Then, numerous huge rattlesnakes start down the beach toward me. I run, but alligators start coming out of the ocean toward me. The only place to escape them is back with the rattlesnakes. The dream wakes me up.

How can one interpret such a psychic production? How can such a sign be made coherent with the rest of Bill's language, gestures, and actions? The dream evoked memories of Bill's being almost "drowned" by his mother's needs, caught in the net of her impossible problems, and feeling an almost unbearable fear of her sudden and inexplicable fits of anger that seemed to come at him from all directions. Later dreams revealed not only a fear of women but a massive rage at them. How can these dreams fit the language and actions of respect toward women? Bill found that his language and chivalry were defenses to appease women and protect himself, and further, that the chivalry was a way of negating women by manifesting to them how dependent and incapable of autonomy they were. This insight did not condemn Bill to remain in this attitude, for once the feelings were in the open, they could be worked through and overcome. The pursuit of the incongruity thus led to both a more coherent use of signs and a more coherent psychological ecosystem.

The second task in learning to express ourselves ecologically is to explore in depth the languages of the psyche. Each need, emotion, cognitive capacity, and psychic system (e.g., archaic self, narrative self, structured ego) has its own peculiar set of signs. This is a necessity, for if there were no difference in how any two psychic components articulated themselves, they would be indistinguishable. For two things to be different they must express themselves by different actions, behavior, language, or gestures (this is true for all entities, be they subatomic particles or human beings).

The psyche grows in its depths and powers only as it enlarges its abilities to express itself in its various languages. To explore and develop the psyche involves discovering the languages of the psyche. For instance, if one wishes to be autonomous, one must know what the gestures, actions, and language of an autonomous being are. How does an independent person act? What kind of language expresses independence and inspires us to achieve it? One tries to find, as best one can, a strong model of autonomy to observe and mimic her actions, gestures, and ways of speaking. One reads the culture's greatest thinkers on autonomy and by learning their concepts and modes of expression, expands the scope of one's autonomy. Thus, being autonomous is not some strange inner capacity or state, but is being able to act, gesture, and speak as an autonomous being. To become more autonomous means learning richer, fuller ways of expressing ourselves autonomously.

As it is with autonomy, so it is with every part of the psyche: fullness and growth are directly related to the development of means of expression. This is why the poets, painters, musicians, dancers, sculptors, philosophers, theologians—artists and thinkers of all kinds—are so important to society. They teach us new and more profound ways of expressing ourselves, and in so doing give us the tools for richer, more complex psychological growth. We become philosophical beings only by mastering, to some degree, philosophical language—its questions, vocabulary, concepts, and rules. We can dwell as historical beings only by having the language of history.

The development of the many special languages of the psyche, however, presents us with an immense problem. Each special language functions well within its own context, but it has great trouble finding a common speech to solve conflicts with other languages. The language of sacredness is incommensurable with the practical efficiency of our language for survival. The role-playing language of social order is antithetical to the sign system for autonomy. With the learning of many languages, the psyche becomes a babel in which each voice can be successful in its own domain, but the whole lacks integration and a language for solving quarrels.

The major response of Western theoreticians to this problem has been to search for one single language as the most important or only language the psyche should speak. Plato was adamant in declaring the superiority of philosophical language over that of poetry and other modes of discourse. Numerous philosophers and scientists since the eighteenth century have attempted to convince us to use nothing but scientific language. Bentham and the utilitarians wished to solve

practical disputes by translating all events into a language of quantitative units of pleasure and pain, and then weighing the units. These
attempts all ended in failure, for the needs, emotions, capacities,
intricate balances, and patterns of growth can never be encompassed
by a single language. Human activities and the events of the psyche
that need expression are so diverse and multifold that no specialized
language can possibly succeed in doing all the linguistic work.

It was the tortured twentieth-century genius Wittgenstein who
saw more clearly than anyone else the impossibility of a specialized
language being the one and only language we should speak. His
answer to the problem of how to learn and integrate the many
languages of the psyche was to declare that there is no problem, for
the language we all ordinarily speak does the job superbly. Ordinary
language (an interwoven matrix of language, gestures, and actions)
is the language commonly used by the members of a culture or subculture that one learns simply by being a member of that culture.
Unlike specialized languages, it requires no special training. Ordinary
language contains both the diverse languages needed to express the
various components of the psyche and the transitional mechanisms
that allow us to flow from one context or component to another with
more or less consummate ease. We chat about politics, the weather,
our meals; we go to work, get angry, enjoy a beautiful scene, research
a problem, make love, converse with friends, talk to ourselves about
every matter in the world, listen to a sermon and pray, express joy
at coming home, get excited about a vacation—all without being
terribly bothered by the change of languages, because ordinary language is so rich and flexible that it can do all this work easily. When
we do use specialized languages (as for physics, accounting, and
theology), ordinary language not only provides the entrances and exits
to them but also remains as the background of established meaning
in terms of which the specialized discourses can be understood and
translated. Physicists cannot rest content with abstract mathematical
equations; they must hypothesize whether the equations mean that
the entities in question are behaving like balls or waves—concepts
of ordinary language.

Ordinary language is the glue of the psyche. More than any other
factor it is this speech that binds us together and gives us a sense
of continuity. When a special language cannot be integrated into
ordinary language, it also cannot be integrated into our primary
systems of understanding or action. It remains an abstraction, meaningful only in its own terms and context, but meaningless in relation
to all else. The most grievous sin of contemporary liberal education,

which ought to give the psyche a wealth of expression, is that the disciplines are usually taught as special languages, learned and then forgotten, or stored in isolated cupboards in the psyche, to be opened only in the proper contexts. It is only when the disciplines entwine with ordinary language that they become vital forms of expression for the psyche.

Ordinary language always has a communal base and an oral practice, for the sustaining lifeblood of any language is its use in a community of speakers. Without the reflection of a community, a personal language dies from lack of verification or becomes so subjectively involuted that we grow to mistrust it. As Wittgenstein said, trying to see whether one is using a private language correctly is like buying a second copy of the morning newspaper to see if the first one is correct. In the language of psychoanalysis, private languages lack reality testing: they are mere realms of fantasy.

The oral basis of ordinary language is of immense significance. In oral discourse language, gesture, and act are inherently intertwined in a way they cannot be in written language. In oral conversation words are garbed in tones of voice and tempos of speech, interspersed with meaningful silences of varying lengths, and amplified or made more complex with gestures and acts. The written "hello" says very little, but this word combined with a face beaming with excitement, a vibrant handshake, and a pause to take in the other person, can be as profound a communicative moment as there is. Here is the arena of meaning, and it is to this arena that we must bring all of our special languages if they are to enter the life and substance of our systems of meaning.

Oral discourse not only gives us our primary means of communicating with others, it is also the language with which we speak to ourselves. We can write poetry or philosophy or science in particular private moments, but we usually speak to ourselves in ordinary language. The Socratic dialogues can be read as either Socrates' talking with other Greeks or as conversations internal to himself, conversations in which various sides and voices of Socrates speak their parts and attempt to achieve a mutual resolution. If we find ourselves unable to carry on Socratic dialogues within ourselves, it is due to either a silencing of voices in our psyche or the lack of such dialogues in our conversations with others.

Yet for all its glories and powers, there are some severe problems with trying to make ordinary language the primary communicative system of the psyche. For one, ordinary language is part of a particular culture at a particular time. As such, it suffers the biases, limitations, and blindnesses of that culture. It might, like eighteenth-century Puritan culture, have a strong grammar for sacredness but an impoverished set of signs for expressing sexuality. I once stood watching a glorious sunset with a friend who could only mutter, "What an outstanding sunset," and walk away. Part of the structure of the ordinary language for his class and culture at this point in its history is the primacy of ranking and the lack of value for poetic, artistic, or meditative responses. If something is ranked, then the experience is complete. Such language serves the need for order well, but our sense of beauty and creativity is hardly nourished.

Second, the ability of ordinary language to easily transist between various special languages has the secondary consequence of preventing us from exploring and developing any particular language in depth. Ordinary language always has the tendency to stay on the surface of things. The deeper language gets into a particular subject, the harder it is to incorporate into ordinary language. We all have our "sidewalk" philosophies, but to do philosophy in the depth of a Kant or a Hegel means to leave ordinary language far behind. Ordinary language can understand that light acts as waves or balls, but cannot follow the physicist into the mathematics of the case.

Finally, ordinary language is inherently conservative. It knows the "right" way to see the world; it is comfortable, effective, and supported by a whole community. New languages threaten ordinary language and the community that is its base, and hence are to be rejected if possible.

How can we achieve a language that is both general and flexible enough to transist between the parts of the psyche and culture and yet rich and deep enough to articulate that which goes beyond the usual? Ordinary language is able to flow to the various recognized parts of the psyche, but is conservative, shallow, and blind. The special languages take us into depths beyond ordinary language and stretch us into the foreign. They give us fuller, more complete forms of expression that can overcome the biases and conservativeness of ordinary language, but they fragment the psyche and culture into a babel of voices unable to comprehend one another. The integration of the foreign and the familiar, the general and the special, the different and the same, cannot be a matter of inventing some new superlanguage, for even if we could accomplish this, it would soon become a new ordinary language with all the traditional problems of an ordinary language. Rather, this integration is a matter of taking a certain stance toward language and participating in language in a different way and at a different level than we presently do, a level that lies beneath both the conventions of ordinary language and the special languages. This way of being with language was first, and is still best, exemplified by the Greek god Hermes.[3]

The story of Hermes is perhaps the strangest of all the strange Olympian biographies. The Homeric Hymn to Hermes tells us that Hermes is the son of Zeus and the naiad Maia, who is the daughter of the Titan Atlas. (We are once again back with the Titans). Zeus was fond of visiting Maia in her dark cave in the Arcadian mountains in the black of night while Hera slept. Hermes was born in that cave and had a remarkable first day of life. He leapt from his cradle, went outside, and met a tortoise, which he proceeded to kill and whose shell he turned into the first lyre. He then sang of his glorious parents, in effect praising their offspring. After this he went out and stole fifty of Apollo's sacred cattle, marching them backward over mountain and plain so that their hoofprints appeared to be going in the opposite direction. He hid them in another Arcadian cave, where he slaughtered two of them as sacrifices to the twelve Olympian gods—including himself! He then returned to his cradle.

Apollo was furious over the theft of his cattle and even more furious when he, the far-seeing, could not find them. He soon determined that Hermes was the thief and went to his cave to accuse him. Hermes innocently replied: "Am I a cattle-lifter, a stalwart person? This is no task for me: rather I care for other things: I care for sleep, and milk of my mother's breasts, and wrappings round my shoulders, and warm baths."[4] Frustrated, Apollo hauls Hermes off to Zeus, where Hermes again proclaims his innocence and swears a great oath that he did not take the cattle to his home (and he hadn't). Zeus and Apollo both laugh at the little trickster, but Zeus demands that he show Apollo where the cattle are. While revealing the hidden cattle, Hermes also shows Apollo the lyre he invented, and so enchants him with it that Apollo agrees to trade some cattle for the lyre. Hermes further promises never again to steal from Apollo, and Apollo swears undying friendship and loyalty to Hermes. Thus, through stealth, trickery, buffoonery, and inventiveness, Hermes achieves parity with Apollo—a remarkable accomplishment, since most of Zeus's children born to non-Olympians do not become Olympians.

Hermes never loses his connection to his earth-goddess mother and her cave. He is an Arcadian nature god, a fertility daimon (often represented by a phallus) who protects herds and pastures, mates freely with the woodland nymphs, and fathers the most raucous of satyrs, Pan. His birth out of darkness enables him to guide travelers over boundaries into dangerous foreign lands (as when he leads Priam to Achilles) and lead souls to the underworld. However, unlike other, somewhat dull-witted, nature gods, Hermes is the brightest, quickest, gayest, most audacious of the gods. He is so facile with language that Zeus makes him the herald of the gods, the bearer of the divine word. He is so crafty that he is given innumerable missions of guile, as when he steals Ares out of a jar where he had been imprisoned by the giants, or puts the one-hundred-eyed Argos to sleep so that Io can escape Hera. He fathers the greatest of thieves, Autolycus, and endows Pandora with a "shameless mind and a deceitful nature." Despite his offenses, everyone, gods and humans alike, love Hermes, for he fosters fertility, travel, trade, music, laughter, and wit.

For all his light-heartedness, though, Hermes is a dark god, riddled with contradictions. How can a nature god kill a tortoise and transform it into a cultural artifact? How can the bearer of the divine word, the guardian of the most sacred language, be a liar—a destroyer of language? How can the governor of fair exchange in the marketplace be a thief? How can a jocular god have the grave duty of guiding souls to the underworld?

We can understand a number of these contradictions by examining Hermes' archaic social roots, for Hermes was first born in an age when the primary living units were the family and village. Exchanges with strangers from neighboring villages took place mainly at the intersecting boundaries of the villages, often marked with piles of rocks called "herms." Such exchanges needed some kind of ritual to lessen the possibility of pollution, peril, or just being cheated. The participants and place had to be endowed with a magical power to aid them, and the tribesmen invoked the god in the rocks that marked the boundary, Hermes. All exchanges that took place at boundaries were a kind of "thievery" because there were no institutions governing equality of worth or fair market prices. Hence, Hermes became the god who, at the herm, provided luck in exchanges. He was also a guide over boundaries, for all contact with the foreign went beyond the limits of the familiar. Since not only goods were exchanged between villages, but also women, Hermes became a god for stealth with women. Later, when the lower and middle classes, whose life was based on commerce, were seeking political parity with the landed aristocracy, Hermes became a culture hero for them. The Hymn to Hermes is a late Athenian creation and symbolizes the mercantile classes' achieving political equality with Apolline aristocrats through their inventiveness, intelligence, cunning, and ability to travel across boundaries. The old order is baffled and enraged by the new, but cannot eschew its inventions.[5]

Concomitant with change in any socioeconomic order is a change in psychic order. Hermes is not just a socioeconomic myth, but a representation of one of the most profound capacities of the psyche, which began to be fully realized in the Archaic era, the power of transformation. Hermes transforms nature (tortoise) into culture (lyre), binding language (oath) into fluid jokes, property from one owner into property of another, the words of the gods into human language, the foreign into the familiar, the living into the dead, and himself from a babe to an adult to a god and back to a babe. These transformations explain why Hermes is so full of contradictions. They also explain why Hermes is a magician, for the essence of magic is the transformation of one thing or state into another. Hermes is the archetypal trickster, the master magician.

The most magical of all acts, the ultimate transformation, is the transformation of a brute physical world into a human realm of meaning and values. What gives the world meaning, enables humans to create culture, and lures us to consciousness is language. As Aristophanes, the most Hermetic of the playwrights, says after creating the realm of *The Birds* merely through the manipulation of language, "Words are wings and wings are words." Words are what let us magically create our worlds, as they are doing right now in this very text. At Delphi, the religious center of Archaic Greece, Apollo's words were translated, "*herméneuein*," into human speech. Here is Hermes, the magician, transforming the inarticulate and the meaningless into the meaningful.

How is this possible? How do words get meaning? Hermes understands that language acquires meaning simply by the imposition of arbitrary conventions, not by some ultimate relation to a "correct" set of forms. This insight enables Hermes to play with language, challenge conventions, mock old orders, break rules. Meaning is invented, and Hermes, the archinventor and craftsman, knows how words create worlds. But Hermes is not content with language as convention, for this is the realm of ordinary language, of public institutions, of the familiar. His haunts are not the common ground, but the boundaries, the place where communication occurs without common conventions, where the foreign must magically become familiar.

How can there be communication with what is not included in a culture's structures of interpretation?[6] How can we transform what makes no sense to our categorical forms of understanding into something that makes sense? This process of interpreting the foreign is understandable only if we have hermetic powers of understanding that exist beyond the structures of ordinary language. A dream is remembered. It makes no literal sense; it corresponds to nothing in the person's ordinary way of understanding herself. The person ponders her dream, and nothing happens. It is a mysterious artifact from the unexplored realms of her psyche that seems to defy interpretation. Then suddenly an insight occurs, a connection to the previous day's events, a connection to a past trauma. The meaning starts to unfold, to make sense, but only as our categories of understanding start to shift to accommodate such a realm of meaning. How are the connections made? How are we able to decode something for which it seems we have no codes?

This, indeed, is impossible. One cannot decode a message without some kind of decoding mechanism. We can make connections between the foreign and the familiar only when some aspect of the foreign is *like* something that is familiar. The relationship of likeness is the basis for all hermeneutical interpretation of the foreign. Likeness is, however, the fundamental structure of a certain form of language, namely, symbolic language. A symbol is a sign that is like something else or shares a common characteristic with something else. While all symbols are signs, not all signs are symbols. Signs, in general, have conventional meanings; the relation between signifiers and the signified is arbitrary, one determined merely by conventional rules. For instance, there is no likeness, no concrete connection, between the phonemes in the word *crying* and the process of tears falling. Hence, the word *crying* is not a symbol for crying, but a sign used to designate this experience. For something to be a symbol of tears and sadness, it must be like them in some way. The sun shining cannot be a symbol for sadness; a rainy day can be. Hence, a symbol is not a wholly arbitrary construction; it has some likeness to that which it symbolizes.

That we have an unconscious ability both to generate and interpret symbols was a discovery that shocked Freud:

> We are faced by the fact that the dreamer has a symbolic mode of expression at his disposal which he does not know in waking life and does not recognize. This is as extraordinary as if you were to discover that your housemaid understood Sanskrit, though you know that she was born in a Bohemian village and never learnt it. It is not easy to account for this fact by the help of our psychological views. We can only say that the knowledge of symbolism is unconscious to the dreamer, that it belongs to his unconscious mental life.
>
> These symbolic relations are not something peculiar to dreamers or to the dream-work through which they come to expression. This same

symbolism, as we have seen, is employed by myths and fairy tales, by the people in their sayings and songs, by colloquial linguistic usage and by the poetic imagination. The field of symbolism is immensely wide, and dream-symbolism is only a small part of it. . . . One gets an impression that what we are faced with here is an ancient but extinct mode of expression.[7]

Jung agreed with Freud that symbolism was the most ancient mode of expression in human beings, but rather than finding it extinct or some kind of vestigial language, he found the production, reception, and interpretation of symbols to be the essential activity of the psyche:

> We should understand that dream symbols are for the most part manifestations of a psyche that is beyond the control of the conscious mind. Meaning and purposefulness are not the prerogative of the mind; they operate in the whole of living nature. . . . As a plant produces its flower, so the psyche creates its symbols. . . . Symbols are natural and spontaneous products.[8]

Symbolic activity is the primary way we obtain meanings concerning the world and ourselves, and it is the primary means by which the various parts of the psyche express themselves.[9] Our conscious world is usually a literal one in which things are just what they are (a rose is a rose, a house is a house), but our subconscious minds experience a world teeming with symbols. A rose is not just a rose to a young maiden on her first date. Its fragile petals hold all the aspirations and emotions of romantic love. A house is not just a house, it is a space that can be more or less symbolic of a psyche's inner space, as our dreams about houses often reveal. A city is not just buildings, but a symbol of the fundamental values and experiences of a culture. In the Middle Ages, no building was higher than the steeple of the church located at the center of the town. Now nothing is higher than the commercial towers spotted throughout our cities. The mountain stream cascading between giant rocks is also a symbol for the great truth of the interplay between flux and permanence. For our psyches, everything and anything can have symbolic meaning, from a snail crossing a lawn to a slum next to a high-rise luxury apartment.

This view of prereflective experience as filled with symbolic meaning is a radical departure from the two major traditions that have formed our views of what it is we experience before we bring our forms of understanding to it. Empiricism posits sense data—atoms of color, sound, taste, touch, or smell—as the fundamental units of experience.

Rationalism, on the other hand, says that experience is grounded in certain simple, a priori truths, such as "I exist" and "clearness and distinctness are the marks of knowledge." These truths are always expressed in nonsymbolic language and are meant to be self-evident, as "$1 + 1 = 2$" is. The view proposed here does not find prereflective experience to be such dry, analytical, meaningless stuff, but a complex web of symbols that can nourish, give meaning, and call us to genuine thoughtfulness. Whether these symbols are grounded in a set of genetically heritable archetypes (Jung's theory) or whether they are generated by connections in early experience is not an issue to be solved here. What is of importance is that we recognize the power of symbolic language and incorporate it into our ordinary language, which, in its quest for productive efficiency, has for the most part forgotten the power of symbols.

Like Hermes, symbols are magic. Anything that is a symbol is both what it is and not what it is. For most primitive cultures the world was full of magic because their languages were based in symbols. Birds, snakes, mountains, directions, and winds were, not what they are for us, but omens and symbols of great forces and pending fates. The Rembrandt portrait is not just a picture of an old man, but a symbol of human mortality luring us to face our own finite natures. It magically is a portrait of ourselves.

Because symbols must have a likeness to whatever it is they are symbolizing, they are always embedded in a concrete particular image or structure and have a complex web of relationships to other particular objects. Yet they call out to be interpreted, to be understood, to be freed from their embeddedness. Interpretations are given in abstract conventional language that attempts to overcome the particularity of the symbol. The Trojans see an eagle drop a snake it had caught and want to know what this omen means. "The sign means that although we have the Greeks in our hands now, we will lose them." This interpretation gives a clear and understandable meaning to the symbol, a meaning that can be debated and acted upon. But the rich particularity of the symbol is lost—the power of the eagle in flight, the snake writhing in the grasp of its sharp talons, the snake desperately lunging at the eagle's throat, the eagle deeply wounded by the viper's bite, the snake falling through the sky, thudding on the ground.

We come to a late Van Gogh landscape with a swirling sky and dancing cypress trees. We say to ourselves, "This painting is a symbol of the *élan vital* of nature, the primordial energy that underlies all structures, all forms, and that ceaselessly creates, destroys, and creates anew." We draw connections to Nietzsche, Bergson, Whitehead, and the shift in modern physics to energy as the primary concept. We recall Heraclitus. Thus, we have an interpretation. But can we replace the painting with a few sheets of paper on the wall saying "All is flux; all is ceaseless destruction and creation. See works of Nietzsche, Bergson, etc."? *No!* The painting is irreplaceable; it brings us to the meaning of process in a way entirely different from the written word— it concretely gives us the flux in its symbols. It has its own peculiar richness and depth that expresses in its concrete embodiment these final truths in a way that the abstract "All is flux" simply cannot. Like the Van Gogh painting, all symbols are ambiguous: they demand interpretations but can never be fully replaced by them.

It is this ambiguity of symbols that makes it impossible for there to be only one correct interpretation of a symbol. Symbols retain their concrete opacity and refuse to shrivel up and disappear, even when a brilliant interpretation is made of them. To become overly serious and demand the one correct interpretation is to fail to recognize the unfinished nature of symbols. How are we to know if we have interpreted the symbols of a dream correctly? How are we to know if we are right or giving a distorted interpretation to defend against what is most anxious in the dream? There might be more or less coherence between the interpretation and other events and meaning structures in one's life or a certain feeling of rightness to the interpretation; but one never knows for sure what is manipulating the interpretation. The world of symbols is not a realm for final public adjudication to see whether rules are being followed, nor a realm of truth achieved through the application of some publicly accepted methodology. Rather, this is the realm of Hermes, the trickster, the transformer. A realm of riddles, guessing, and laughter. A realm in which one abandons the notion of objective truth and gives up the quest to be right in order to explore the profound symbolic networks that lead into every cave of the psyche.

However, that there is no "right" interpretation of a symbol does not mean that the process of interpretation is frivolous or arbitrary. Contemporary French phenomenologist Paul Ricoeur posits three steps for the adequate interpretation of any symbol. First we need to explore the relation of the symbol to other symbols that form its context—the symbol system of the dream, event, painting. Next we must decide whether we believe the symbols are carriers of truth, and then attempt to live that truth, for it is only by living in the belief that the symbols are true that their full meaning and their adequacy or inadequacy will become apparent to us. This is not scientific truth or truth determined by the application of method, but existential truth. Symbolic meaning and truth are fully available only to initiates, not to observers.

> Then is discovered what may be called the circle of hermeneutics, which the simple amateur of myths unfailingly misses. The circle can be stated bluntly: "You must understand in order to believe, but must believe in order to understand." This circle is not vicious; still less is it deadly. It is quite alive and stimulating. No interpreter in fact will ever come close to what his text says if he does not live in the aura of the meaning that is sought. And yet it is only by understanding that we can believe. The second immediacy, the second naiveté that we are after, is accessible only in hermeneutics; we can believe only by interpreting[10]

That full understanding comes only with committed belief cannot be emphasized enough in our culture whose primary epistemology contends that knowledge can best be achieved through disengaged observation and objective methodologies. Hermeneutical interpretation is dangerous for it requires us to believe in a set of symbols before we have a full revelation of its meaning and consequences.

But living the meaning of symbols is not the final step of interpretation, for we must critically reflect on the symbols and test them for their conceptual coherence, experiential verifiability, and ability to cohere with our other symbol systems. Without this moment of philosophical reflection, various symbol systems can remain isolated fiefdoms within the psyche. Reflective thought opens up wider realms of connectedness among symbol systems or else reveals fundamental inconsistencies that require critical adjustment of the symbols. A striking example of the latter case occurred in the nineteenth century when persons who believed fully in both Christianity and modern science were faced with the theory of evolution. Symbol systems that had previously cohered now became inconsistent: one or the other had to be abandoned or adjusted in some excruciating ways.

Like all inconsistencies, symbolic fragmentation weakens the psyche and deadens experience. When the symbol system we use to make sense of our religious life contradicts the symbol system governing our secular life, the two become isolated from one another, unable to merge into a flowing river that would be stronger and more vital than either of the streams. Without a religious component, secular life always verges on becoming a meaningless accumulation of trivial goods, and a religious life that has no grounding in daily material activity typically descends into impotent abstraction.

Insofar as philosophy is the discipline that most thoroughly critiques the symbol systems by which we organize our lives, and whose goal is to form a completely coherent set of beliefs, it is a vital activity of the culture, an activity ceaselessly driving us to rid ourselves of enervating symbolic fragmentations. But philosophy's search for coherence has to negotiate a veritable Charybdis and Scylla in order to be successful. One danger is the reduction of symbols to abstract concepts. Concepts are easier to systematize into logical schemes than symbols, but they lose the concrete grounding and rich reservoir of meaning of the symbols. Philosophy that succumbs to this nemesis has the sense of being so abstract that it has little relevance to life as we live it. Philosophy appears to be a great epiphenomenal balloon, inflated with empty concepts, floating above the lived vital experiences of everyday life.

The opposite danger from abstraction, the one on which most dogmatic theology founders, is to simply repeat the "truth" of the symbol in a disguised form. We never really get beyond the symbol: Christ on the cross is the truth, and that is the end of the matter. Here critical rationality is bypassed, and we remain embedded in the symbol. Connections are not stimulated, growth is stifled, the psyche is suffocated in its quest for fullness.

The hermeneutic path between abstract conceptual analysis and dogmatic attachment to symbols seems the only way to a postreflective state in which we can both dwell in the depth of concrete symbolic meaning and yet be free to explore richer, fuller ideational systems. This path, in fact, happens to be a complex network of roads connecting the myriads of symbol systems of the psyche, a network that seems like the maze of streets in the ancient sections of Near Eastern cities. The temptation to broad boulevards and geometric grids is a product of the French Enlightenment, which wanted purely rational cities and psyches. Such arrangements are humorless, without stealth, and without need of a guide. Hermes is not wanted in such a world. But when these overly organized and dominating structures are quitted and all the voices of the psyche are allowed to speak—all the emotions, needs, capacities, and layers of self—then the psyche becomes an oriental bazaar, and we need Hermes to translate, negotiate, and guide us through the intricacies of our inner worlds.

Hermes could not perform these functions were he not amoral. Unlike the other gods, who would have us be powerful, or brave, or sexually potent, or just, Hermes does not have a particular way of life or set of values to peddle. Like his sons, Pan and Autolycus, he exists in a realm beyond good and evil, beyond judgments of worth and worthlessness. He explores lands, an activity that cannot occur if one always needs to be in the right land or the good land. How can we explore a dark oedipal dream from the land of right and wrong? If we admit we have incestuous desires, then by morals we are immoral. But Hermes is amoral. He can plunge into incestuous desires, explore them, relish their lurid immoral fantasies, and then return from the underworld to Olympus.

To nourish the Hermetic in ourselves, we too must learn to be amoral. Yet to act, to live in a community, and to have a personal identity requires that we have determinate values, that we have tablets of good and evil, right and wrong. Without these life has no stability and no purpose. So, the self must be moral and amoral. Here there is dynamic tension, but not contradiction. The moral and the amoral can form a bond, which, like the friendship of Hermes and Apollo, is always a bit uneasy, but which is better than one achieving domination over the other. To be fully moral is to imprison oneself in the realm of truth and goodness and prevent necessary explorations of the foreign within oneself. When we are overly Hermetic, we are so evasive and exploratory that we fail to achieve a strong identity or make a commitment to a purpose, which is as crucial to development as exploration. Apollo allows Hermes to leave his dark haunts and come into the light. Without this legitimation, Hermes would have remained a dull, earthbound nature god. In turn, Hermes brings laughter, music, and depth to Apollo's overstructured, oversimplistic world of light.

What holds the friendship together? Not some third entity (a transcendental ego) or preordained structure. The friendship is held together because the interaction between Apollo and Hermes is more intense and more satisfying than the experience of either of them alone. They need one another and like one another; they complete and complement each other. Here, then, is another metaphor for how to achieve a unity of the self without imposing a rigid personal structure. The model of unity is not that of an entity, but that of a friendship. Is this too precarious? Are friendships more liable to "break up" than hierarchical structures? It might seem this way because the friendships (including marriages) we make in today's mobile, competitive world can be shallow, unrooted affairs. They reflect our inability to make profound friendships among the diverse parts of our psyches. As Aristotle said, "Friendly relations with one's neighbors, and the marks by which friendships are defined, seem to have proceeded from a man's relations to himself."[11]

The two keys to establishing and maintaining friendships, be they between the various parts of the psyche or with other people, are the development of a full, rich, communicative interaction, on the one hand, and the ability of the friends "to stay in touch" on the other. Communication is fostered by the hermetic side of ourselves, while staying in touch is a function of memory. The two are intrinsically interwoven, for it is through symbols that memory articulates itself, and it is by memory that symbols are able to be interpreted. There is little wonder why Hermes sings of Mnemosyne as the "first among gods." To the forgetful, a teacup is an item to be used for the transportation of tea to the mouth when desired, but for Proust the teacup, as symbol, could gather a universe of meaning. To those whose speech is limited to the literal or conceptual, a dream is at best a crazy story, but for the hermetically inclined it is a symbolic production whose interpretation can restore memory. We can now understand why the hero who retains his memory best, Odysseus, is also the hero who is the master of ambiguous, symbolic language.

The loss of memory in contemporary living is, then, partially to be explained by our loss of symbolic language. The ordinary language of the contemporary world—at least in its professional classes—is almost fanatically literal. Clarity, logic, efficiency, singleness of interpretation are all favored. Poetic nuance, well-turned phrases, metaphors, similes, dark symbolic readings of events that have decent literal interpretations are shunned. This literalness has roots extending back to the very foundations of the culture—to Lydia, where Croesus and literalness were kings. Croesus thought he was rich because he had riches. He couldn't comprehend why the greatest gift that Cleobis and Biton could receive for their heroic deed was death. He lost his son because he failed to interpret the symbols of a dream correctly and lost his kingdom because he misinterpreted an oracle. Others in Herodotus's history who cannot work with symbols— Astyages, Cyrus, Cambyses, Xerxes, and Darius—all meet with doom, while those who understand this language—Solon, Artabanus, and Themistocles—are successful and happy. Herodotus lived during the time when an ancient ritual culture was in the final stages of death, and was being replaced by the city-state, secular politics, and conventional language. In this time of great forgetting and transformation he, like the dramatists, tried to recall the Athenians to their older traditions and language, but social and economic forces were against him and his message was forgotten.

The Enlightenment, which saw as its major task the demystification of the world, provided the final, fatal blow to symbolic language in the West. Only the language of empirical observation and quantitative measurement could be used by a mind intent on discovering truth. The gods retired; myths and symbols died, leaving in their places a meaningless, dreary world of objects, known by science and manipulated by technology. An unprecedented wealth was produced in this demystified world, and the psyche became fully impoverished. Solon would have understood.

To become rich in its own realm, the psyche must begin, once again, to speak the language of symbols. We begin this speaking by honoring symbolic activity—by placing paintings, sculptures, and other symbols in our homes rather than mere decoration, by performing symbolic acts rather than just efficient deeds, by using metaphors, images, and other symbols in our speech, by being present to our dreams. Each of these acts is a worship of Hermes and brings us closer to the god who carries the caduceus, symbol of wealth. With our new speaking, our homes become filled with truths rather than furniture, and our worlds become filled with signs rather than stuff.

But let us not overromanticize. We cannot become ritual tribespeople again, dwelling in a full but unprogressive matrix of symbols. Conventional language in the arts and sciences not only has opened up a world of material plenty by giving us increased flexibility and power, but has also given the psyche many more languages than ever before by which to express and create itself. The cost of developing these powerful tools was the loss of a religious/symbolic language, one that was not as flexible or utilitarian, but that could give meaning, groundedness, and integration to its speakers. It is now time to reclaim our losses and live in a more bountiful world than was available in either tribal life or secular economic existence. This fullness will come when we are able to weave the ancient mode of symbolic discourse together with the special languages of the parts of the psyche into a rich tapestry of ordinary language. This, above all, is ecological speaking.

CHAPTER 10

ECOLOGICAL DWELLING

(Faust opens a tomb and begins.)
It says: "In the beginning was the Word."
Already I am stopped. It seems absurd.
The *Word* does not deserve the highest prize,
I must translate it otherwise
If I am well inspired and not blind.
It says: In the beginning was the *Mind*.
Ponder that first line, wait and see,
Lest you should write too hastily.
Is mind the all-creating source?
It ought to say: In the beginning there was *Force*.
Yet something warns me as I grasp the pen
That my translation must be changed again.
The spirit helps me. Now it is exact.
I write: In the beginning was the *Act*.
(Goethe, *Faust,* 1224-1237)

For our culture, life is action. Life is doing, transforming, changing, growing, altering, creating. Very few of us can conceive of living the life of a Buddhist monk, in which actions are kept to a bare minimum and meditative activity of the mind is central. Concomitantly, excellence, whether it be moral, economic, political, social, or professional, is defined in terms of the performance of certain actions. We cannot be morally worthy unless we perform moral acts. We cannot achieve excellence in the world of business unless we do something to achieve greater profits. We cannot even attain religious excellence without performing some kind of religious acts, such as helping the destitute or spreading the word of God. For the West, action is the core of life.

Actions occur when agents deliberately transform their social or natural environments through linguistic or physical intervention. As living beings, we are constantly entering states of disequilibrium with our environments, states in which our needs are not being satisfied, and must transform the environment in order to fulfill our needs. Action that uses natural and social environments to satisfy one's needs is, by definition, exploitation. Exploitation is an ecological fact of life; no life exists without it. We are, by nature, plunderers and killers. As Whitehead said, "Life is robbery."

If we are to achieve ecological excellence and live in a way in which our needs are deeply satisfied, we must learn how to be successful exploiters. The key to successful exploitation was found by Aristotle long ago: the development of practical wisdom. Practical wisdom consists of having right desire and right reason. In our scheme of understanding, right desire involves wanting goods and activities that genuinely satisfy our needs without overemphasizing some needs to the significant detriment of others. The chief enemies of right desire are the psychological injuries of childhood that prevent us from wanting what is fulfilling to us. If we develop negative self-images, then we act in ways that frustrate ourselves. If we develop powerful ambivalences toward men, women, food, success, and so forth, then we will not be able to act in relation to these important parts of our environment in ways that can be fully satisfying. If we develop compulsive desires, then our needs cannot mature. We continue seeking infantile objects, even though these can no longer satisfy us as adults. Until either a felicitous set of experiences or a therapeutic working-through of the diseased desires cures us, we will have little chance of satisfying our basic needs, regardless of how well we can reason.

Right reason consists of (a) knowing what the basic human needs are and which ones are most important given the idiosyncratic strengths, weaknesses, alliances, and conflicts of needs within the individual, and her developmental stage and environmental conditions; (b) knowing how to appropriate materials and activities necessary to satisfy the needs; and (c) having a structure of values that can organize one's peculiar traits, talents, resources, needs, and conditions into a coherent life-picture and direct our actions with this vision in mind. The lack of any one of these aspects of right reason can result in our inability to satisfy our needs. The first two kinds of knowledge can be attained through various learning techniques, such as research, introspection, being counseled, and so on. However, the third aspect of right reason, namely, the construction of a coherent system of values, demands that one acquire the skill of seeing life with an eye for distant developments and underlying patterns of mutual enhancement. I know of no better study for the acquisition of this skill than philosophy, which, far from being the otherworldly and impractical discipline most people take it to be, is essential in practical life.

When we act with practical wisdom, we eliminate much of the senseless destruction that accompanies exploitation. Persons of practical wisdom remember that environments must satisfy all their needs, and they keep the full manifold of needs in mind, while unmindful persons transform the environment to meet one need or group of needs, but in so doing hinder their abilities to satisfy others. The environment is the source of the material goods necessary for survival. But it must also satisfy our aesthetic, religious, and epistemological needs. If our material appropriation desecrates the environment, then it reduces our abilities to satisfy these other needs. Likewise, if we act in our social environment only with the goal of attaining social recognition, we will probably not satisfy our needs for autonomy or intimacy. Our forgetfulness of certain needs while satisfying others is not an accident in our culture. It is the outcome of our most basic practice: specialization. With specialization we learn how to fragment and compartmentalize satisfactions so as to avoid conflicts. Thus, we can desecrate nature for secular purposes because we have moved sacredness into the confines of churches and moved aesthetic experiences to art galleries, museums, and natural parks. Adventure occurs on vacations. Knowledge is pursued in universities and businesses. Social recognition is situated in the realm of professional statuses, while intimacy occurs at home.

Although specialization of function has tended to fragment personal experience, it has been crucial for the development of modern society and is in large part responsible for important increases in productivity and freedom. Few of us, I think, would prefer to live in an Islamic world in which religion, law, politics, economics, and education are collapsed into a unity, nor do we need to if the primary syntheses of the self are strong enough to deal with the complexity that functional differentiation has created. But even if we have strong selves, functional differentiation has a tendency to produce a mirror differentiation in the self—to have parts of the self that function in certain spheres of activity while other parts get turned off. This kind of focused experience can be very stimulating and exciting, but because of its necessary limitations it can come to lack enough diversity and adventure to sustain vitality. Then experience in the context becomes repetitive and dull.

To act ecologically we must counter this trend toward social and personal specialization by attempting to be as fully human in our activities as is possible. Such action is dangerous and requires courage. How dare I bring my sexuality (but not seductiveness, which is a defense against sexuality), mortality, sense of beauty, need for autonomy, and feelings of sacredness into the classroom, where, as a good professional, I am to be present only as a philosopher? How dare I try to relate the professionally pure language of philosophy to ordinary language or demand that my students attend class not as minds but persons? Yet it is only to the extent we bring our full set of needs, emotions, and capacities to activities, and use them, that we feel a depth of human satisfaction and are able to prevent the environmental destruction that occurs through the presence of an unbalanced human nature acting in forgetfulness.

When we take the stance of exploitation, whether it be as full human beings acting with practical wisdom or something less than this, we experience the world as a mere extension of ourselves—it exists for our satisfaction. We need not worry about whether our life histories and psychological categories are distorting the world, for there is no world beyond the structuring given to it by our needs and cognitive frameworks. As such, the stance of exploitation captures a fundamental truth: we and the environment are so intricately inter-twined as to be inseparable. But this is not the whole truth, for not only are we seeking goods from the environment to satisfy our needs, but so are numerous other humans and other creatures. Often the satisfaction of one person means the dissatisfaction of some other living thing. Conflict brings us to the other side of the truth: the environment is not us; it is other. Conflict makes us see that the world is teeming with individuals who do not melt into a coherent coopera-tive network but stand opposed to us.

How are we, as ecologists, to respond to conflict? Insofar as we remain in the stance of exploitation, others, be they human or non-human, exist only for our use. The only needs that are legitimate are our own. Hence conflicts can be resolved only by appeal to force. Yet such a position is, as so many theorists have shown, self-defeating. If everyone takes the position that the only legitimate assertion of needs is his own, then the world becomes one of extreme hostility and aggression—in Hobbes's words, a war of all against all. Living in a world that we perceive as hostile and dangerous negates our possibilities for satisfaction by reducing the extent to which we can feel order, safety, and at home in world. A hostile world also evokes the emotions of fear, which poisons our bodies, and anger, which can so rivet us on our enemies that we become forgetful of all else.

Even if we were lucky enough to live in a world in which everyone but us respected the needs of others, it would still be against our interests to remain in the exploitative mode of existence. For one, we could not enter that activity that most invites us to be integrated human beings and that concomitantly satisfies more needs than any other activity: intimacy. Also, since we tend to project onto others how we view the world, we would see others as aggressively asserting their own needs and disenfranchising ours. The world is still experienced as hostile.

There are other reasons why we, as ecologists, cannot remain solely in the stance of egoistic expolitation. This stance sees the world as having only one center, "me," with everything else being a mere extension of the center. But in ecology, there are no centers: no centers of the universe, no centers of culture, no centers of biological eco-systems, no centers of the psyche. The universe is a vast intricate net-work of individuals, each of which is important in itself and for its relationships with others in the environment. Living in the absolutely centered world of egoistic exploitation prevents us from experiencing the richness and diversity of the environment. When we meet only ourselves or extensions of ourselves in the environment, life soon becomes unbearably boring.

Thus, we have a paradox: insofar as we remain beings seeking only our own satisfactions, we cannot achieve them. The only way to achieve the aims of egoistic exploitation is by transcending this point of view. While conflict annihilates our primordial world of egoistic striving, it is also the impetus to search for fuller, more satisfying ways to relate to others and our environments.

There are two paths out of egocentric exploitation: the first is the transformation of egoistic action into moral action, and the second is the overcoming of the sphere of action altogether.

Traditionally, morality has called us from our narcissistic plun-dering of the world to take into consideration the needs of others. We act morally when we empathically know how our actions affect the interests of others and place our actions under the constraint of universal principles, principles we would be willing for anyone to follow under any circumstances. Empathy connects us directly to the feelings and needs of others, such that we feel their wants and not just our own. However, by itself empathy tends to bias our actions toward those who are closest to us, and should be balanced by a process that attempts to find what is right from all perspectives and to formulate this into a principle that can govern our actions. Conversely, a morality that is nothing but principled action can be harsh and insensitive to the concrete and idiosyncratic wants and needs of the persons our actions most directly affect. Hence, principles need to be balanced by empathy. We become moral beings when we learn to live in the world as empathic and principled persons. Empathy brings love into the world; principles, justice.

Empathy is a capacity in which we gain knowledge of others by repeating in ourselves how they are feeling. What we empathize with can be what others are consciously or unconsciously experiencing. Empathic knowledge differs markedly from a cognitive knowledge of the feelings of another person, for such a knowledge need not reproduce the emotional tonality of the state known. That is, we can cognitively know that another person is angry without responding to the anger. But in empathy we must feel the anger of the other. Empathic knowledge, unlike cognitive knowledge, does not distance us from the world, but connects us in the most intimate way possible with the beings with whom we empathize. Empathy is the deepest form of sharing, for in empathic duplication we "become one" with the feelings of another person. This empathic sharing is the heart of all ethics of love, in which we are asked to be open to and join the joys and sufferings of other human beings.

Empathy is more than a knowledge-gathering event to prepare us for actions that involve others, it is itself an action. When we empathize with someone's feelings, we inherently affirm those feelings. This affirmation both mirrors the person back to herself, legitimating the feeling in the most profound of ways: by reproducing it. Other kinds of affirmation, such as the words *It is all right to feel what you're feeling,* are abstract, constructed by conventions, and received primarily by consciousness. But the mirroring affirmation of empathy is comprehended at the deepest levels of experience, levels at which our self-images are formed, nourished, or destroyed. This is why Heinz Kohut finds empathy to be the essential relation that therapists must have with their patients. Alfred Margulies[1] goes further in saying that empathy can not only cure devastated selves, but is also the key to creative self-development in all humans.

When we empathize with feelings in another person, we also must respond to our own feelings. If we have been repressing grief or anger, then experiencing these empathically in others is a stimulus for our experiencing our own anger and grief. Our fears of and defenses against our own emotions are the major blocks to empathy. How can we stand to "look" at other people to see what they are really feeling, if we cannot stand to look at ourselves to see what we are really feeling? The willingness to empathize with others demands that we be willing to empathize with parts of ourselves that have been cut off from conscious experience. Thus empathy, in affirming the feelings of others, is also a moment of profound self-affirmation.

In this process of empathizing we see the close relation between the ability to respond to the world morally and having a strong, vital self—the interrelation between morality and psychotherapy. If empathy is one of the two primary processes of taking the moral point of view, and having a strong enough self to encounter one's own emotions is a prerequisite for empathizing well, then having a strong self is a prerequisite for engaging in moral life. Since the overcoming of injuries to the self and building self-structures is a primary goal of psychotherapy,[2] I find its ends are congruent with those of morality. This view opposes those (I have mainly MacIntyre in mind) who confuse the methodology of therapy, which affirms all statements from the patient without ethical judgment, with the end of therapy, which is the production of a strong self able to act productively and morally in the world.

However, empathy is not without its dangers and problems. Perhaps the greatest danger in empathizing with others is over-identifying with them. That is, we can empathize so strongly with other people that we lose contact with who we are. We simply become them. When we lose the vital distinction between who we and others are, we both lose our power as independent agents, who might give other people some perspective and help with their conditions, and cease to mirror and affirm them. Worse, we threaten their very identities in our merger. As my daughter once said to her mother, who began to cry when she was crying, "Mommy, let me have my tears." Thus, while we need to empathize with the deepest needs and problems of other human beings to be moral, we cannot take this ability to the extent of overidentification.

The second problem with empathy is that it biases us toward those closest to us—biologically, socially, physically, and culturally. It is simply easier to empathize with those who are like us and close to us than with those who are foreign, whose ways and feelings we don't understand. Many Americans who shudder with horror when they empathically consider the effects of a nuclear war on themselves, their children, and their nation, contemplate with glee the annihilation of the Soviet Union.

To overcome these biases, moral agents must bring their actions under the guidance of moral principles. A moral principle is one that an agent is willing to assent to in all appropriate situations, regardless of who is using the principle. We determine whether we could assent to persons' following the principle under all conditions by going through a process philosophers call "universalization."[3] The process of universalization asks us to empathically imagine ourselves in a number of circumstances in which the principle under consideration is being used and be willing to assent to it in all cases, from all perspectives. Obviously, the test cases need to be difficult ones for the principle, ones in which conflicts with our other values occur, in order for the principle to receive a genuine test. For instance, to see whether we could consent to the principle "never lie," we imagine ourselves in a situation in which lying is the only way to save our child's life from malicious prosecutors (e.g., the position of the Jewish mother protecting her child from the Nazis). If we say that lying is right in this situation, then we cannot universalize the principle "never lie" and must either modify it (e.g., "never lie except in cases in which by lying one can prevent the suffering of an innocent person") or not accept it as a moral principle. After we have tested the maxim in question in a number of difficult cases and find we can assent to it in all those cases and are willing to act on the principle, then we have, for the set of actions covered by the principle (e.g., acts that have to do with truth telling), a moral principle.

By placing our actions under the constraints of universal principles, we transcend our normal exploitative self-centeredness and achieve a viewpoint in which we attempt to do what is right from all the perspectives of a situation, not just ours. The process of universalization is able to do this by freeing properties from individuals and evaluating their worth merely as properties rather than as properties belonging to a person we either favor or dislike.

The end product of the process of universalization is not a principle that any and every human being would agree to, for there are no such principles. There are no perfectly self-evident moral values nor any objective tests that can show us that we have found the absolutely correct normative maxims. What is important is that we go through the process of universalizing our maxims so that we can find what we accept as right and become moral beings. It is the process of thinking through what principles we can hold that removes us from our exploitative bias and makes us consider what other people need who are in different situations from ours.

The progeny of this principle-forming process is justice, for it is in the process of universalization that the concept of "treating all people equally" attains full meaning. It has been the principles and practice of justice that have limited the excessive use of power by those having political and social privilege. Here we must thank the poets, prophets, and philosophers for envisioning the possibility of a world of justice and convincing those in power that, even for them, the just life was more humanly fulfilling than the unbridled exercise of power. As Hesiod, the revolutionary peasant poet of the eighth century B.C. wrote, it is only through the practice of justice that we can transcend animal nature and experience the fullness of our human powers:

> The son of Kronos made this law for men:
> That animals and fish and winged birds
> Should eat each other, for they have no law.
> But mankind has the law of Right from him,
> Which is the better way. And if one knows
> The law of Justice and proclaims it, Zeus
> Far-seeing gives one great prosperity.[4]

Yet, despite its power to help us transcend our subjective biases, a morality of universal law has a number of problems. It tends to produce a harsh morality unsympathetic to the idiosyncrasies and nuances of individuals and situations. This is the morality of the stern father who puts rules and order above individual desires and demands obedience. It is also a moral position that can be formulated in such a way that reason becomes the only capacity involved in taking the moral stance, and this causes fragmentation of the psychic components. However, both these problems can be overcome when we combine universalization with the empathic aspect of the moral point of view. Empathy humanizes principles; principles overcome empathic prejudices.[5]

Obviously, the processes of love and justice can and do conflict. If they didn't, we wouldn't need both of them. Our logical, rational minds crave a methodology for resolving the conflicts, but I can offer none, for such a methodology would have to choose one of these values as being always higher (hierarchy) or find a still higher value that could rank them (hierarchy again). I do not think there is a higher value for moral action than empathy or justice, nor do I think one or the other of these values is clearly always superior. Moral life is not a matter of plugging in a methodology and finding an answer; it is an attempt—messy, intense, complex, intricate, tragic—to live in a world in which we and others accommodate our various needs and abilities to each other. If we develop the traits of being empathic and just, and attempt to apply these in all our affairs, then we are doing far better than many who cannot overcome the stance of egoistic exploitation.

For most Westerners, morality extends only as far as other human beings. Yet the range of morality need not be so limited. We can empathize with living creatures other than humans, and principles can extend over any range of objects, living or nonliving. Many cultures give trees, animals, rocks, mountains, and other objects the same kind of respect we reserve for people. One of the strongest movements in contemporary ethics has been the push to extend the range of the moral point of view to animals—particularly to the use of animals for food and scientific research.[6] This question of the proper range of morality is extremely important, for it determines the extent to which we can feel communally with others. When animals and inanimate objects are not included within the realm of moral action, they can be used as mere objects to be manipulated at will for human satisfaction. While the pragmatic benefits of such an attitude are clear, we lose feeling a bond with anything other than human beings. This results in the feeling of species isolation, of being thrown into a world with which we are completely unconnected. When we decide to extend our moral stance to creatures other than human beings, we become more profoundly connected to nature and feel less like lonely aliens on our own planet. But we are also more restricted in our relations to nature. No longer can we plunder other creatures for our own uses without a thought for their interests and without empathizing with their feelings. Connectedness has its costs, too, costs we must pay if we are to reclaim the earth as our home.

When we transform ourselves from narcissistic exploiters into moral actors, we find ourselves better able to satisfy some of our needs and to develop more fully our emotional and cognitive capacities. As moral beings we are capable of intimacy, friendship, and social interaction in ways that were simply unavailable to us as exploiters. With the reduction of conflict and the empathic unification with other humans and creatures, we feel more at home in the world. The ability to construct and act according to principles gives us a means to control our biases and unconscious prejudices and, hence, allows us to have more autonomous control of ourselves. This is crucial in satisfying all of the needs. As moral beings we can dwell in a world of peacefulness, personal dignity, and ecological connectedness. Our exploitative heritage has been overcome, and we can reap more fully the powers and possibilities of human existence.

Yet morality has its limitations also. Nietzsche wrote that we must attempt to live in a world "beyond good and evil," and Heidegger explored what such a life beyond morality might be. The problem with morality is that it reinforces action as our primary relation toward the world. When we adopt the life of moral action, we commit ourselves to a continual transformation of the world toward the good, a stance that will not allow us to accept the world the way it is and that constantly creates situations of destruction, tension, and conflict with others and the world that do not fit our ideal of the good. This non-acceptance of the world prevents it from being a home for us, and the nonacceptance of others we consider evil puts us in tension and con-flict with them. The urge to action, to creation, to transformation, thus brings in its wake a necessary alienation from the world, other persons, and cultural institutions. The Renaissance, which strongly encouraged individual action, and our age, which categorically demands it, are dynamic creative times, but ones that are restless and productive of anxiety.

The life of action also brings with it a profound underlying resentment against time. The past cannot be transformed by action—it is set like a great rock never to be moved. The present is the moment of finding the world unacceptable and preparing for the future, but the future by definition never comes, is never now. We also know that at some indeterminate moment in the future, the entire sum of our lives' actions will be brought to naught, for death will claim us and all we have done. Thus, for action, the past is intractable; the present, evanescent; the future, doom. We attempt to deal with this impossi-bility of time by mechanizing and regulating it with devices or being constantly forgetful of it. But time does not disappear; it lurks in the dark regions of our psyches and forever haunts us as the background of our experiences.

Life demands action and thus includes separation, alienation, restlessness, conflict, and resentment as underlying emotional tonalities. These cannot be eliminated, but they can be balanced by taking another stance toward the world, a stance that transcends the restless life of action and allows us to feel at peace. In this peaceful dwelling the earth becomes a home to us and our battle with time is overcome. Here there is no action, for there is no need for action. We feel complete; at rest. The burdens that personality has laid upon us—moral responsibility, individuation, proof of self-worth, death— vanish as we depart our realm of personal concerns and find ourselves in a realm of sacredness.

This peacefulness comes when we learn to dwell in acceptance, in the midst of the quiet joy of the sacred "Yes." Acceptance is not to be confused with resignation, which always has resentment within it; rather acceptance is a complete affirmation of all that is, has been, and will be. This affirmation is not a matter of speaking some abstraction such as "All is fine, I accept the world," but a total way of being on the earth. This way of being dawns on us when we engage in the two fundamental activities (not actions) of sacredness: meditation and mimesis. Meditation is the path of quietness; mimesis the path of ecstasy.

In meditation we attain quietness. It is a state in which our motionless bodies reflect our motionless minds, in which we do not act or think or desire, but just sit, at rest and at peace. Meditation does not try to transform anything, not even ourselves. We cannot even try to meditate or be quiet, for the very trying is an act antithetical to affirmation and peacefulness. Yoga can help the body stretch, so that it can more comfortably rest, and mantras can help clear the mind; but in the end we learn how to be quiet only by being quiet. In meditation we do nothing. Just sit. It appears so easy—to do nothing—and yet for us who are grounded in the world of action and dynamic personality, it is exasperatingly difficult, if not impossible.

The etymological root of *meditation* is the Greek *med*, which is found in *medomai*, "to be mindful of" and *Medusa*. It is also found in the Latin *mederi*, "to cure." How can meditation possibly be related to thinking, curing, and a serpent-haired goddess whose look turns one to stone?

The central myth concerning Medusa sees her as a horrible snake-haired monster who turns all who look at her into stone. But Medusa is really the primordial goddess of fertility whose serpent hair attests to her ancient wisdom and earthrootedness. She belongs to a time that predates individuation, political states, and a pragmatic striving that conceives of the future as different from the past. She comes from that ancient form of life that finds connection to the earth, not separation, to be primal and that locates the heart of life in ritual celebration of the earth's cycles. She has been transformed by a later culture into an evil sorceress who threatens to freeze the growth of ambitious young men, like Perseus, who wish to destroy the stifling old order and create a new Olympian world of individuation, commerce, and political states.

It is a myth that Medusa was killed by Perseus. In fact, she still lives and guards the portal into the land of meditation. Like Medusa, meditation threatens to turn all dynamic, achieving youths into regressive, unproductive children. In meditation we become stones and do nothing. And what if we liked this state so much that we became devoted to it? Meditation is not only difficult for Westerners, it is dangerous!

When we cease being afraid of the Medusa and her world of cycles, fertility, death, rebirth, nonindividuation, and connectedness—when we are willing to be turned into nonprogressive, nondynamic stones— then a kind of thought opens up to us that both cares and cures. Meditative thought—thought that thinks nothing, but is a thinking on thinking on thinking—is caring, for it takes care that it disturbs nothing, changes nothing. It leaves everything just as it finds it. It accepts and affirms the earth and all that dwell therein. Meditative thought also has the power to cure us of some of our deepest, most pervasive dis-eases: fear of death, anxiety concerning the future, and anxiety concerning our self-worth. While we are in meditative thought, we transcend the causes of these afflictions—time, action, and personality—to dwell in a kind of quietness and affirmative acceptance. The medicines with which our physicians so intensely seek to prolong life in the end always fail, for we always die. But the medicine of meditation allows us to overcome the world in which the life and death of personalities consumes all our desires and thoughts.

When we think nothing, the divinities appear. They are always present but remain hidden behind the objects and subjects, pasts and futures, desires and repulsions that constantly litter our experience. When this "ontic" world (as Heidegger calls it) disappears, then the gods have space to emerge. In meditation we find not our thought, but thought as a primordial irreducible process. We discover not our love, but a force of love that exists independently of our personal agencies and is given as a gift. We do not cause thought and love to be, they exist beyond us and call us into being. Like thought and love, all the emotions, needs, and capacities can be experienced in meditation as transcendent of personality, as fundamental powers of the world. When the concept of personality is merged with the forces, they become the pantheon of the gods—Zeus, Hera, Aphrodite, Hermes, and their siblings, parents, and children. But personality is a secondary structure, not primordial, and so these gods must disappear. The transcendent powers of the psyche that gave birth to the gods remain as ultimate sacred forces.

Meditation is a form of affirmation that transcends involvement with particulars. Mimesis, on the other hand, plunges into the world of particulars and affirms them in a ritual dance of reproduction. Mimesis occurs when we try to repeat in ourselves something we find outside ourselves. This ability to copy is one of the two great pillars on which learning is based (the other being reinforcement) and is exercised as naturally as our ability to eat. The genetically given ability to mimic explains why children grow up to resemble their parents even if they were not reinforced to do so or consciously attempted to avoid such repetition.

Mimesis stands at the center of ritual and, hence, at the center of primitive religion. In ritual the participants mimically reproduce an important structure or events such as the creation of the universe by the gods or the falling of rain, or the activity of such mana-filled beasts as birds, bears, and bulls.[7] Through mimesis people "become" what they are copying and hence gain the power of the gods, birds, bears, and bulls. We might say that meditation is a form of mimesis in which the meditator copies a stone and gains its power. It is no coincidence that stones are of primary importance in Zen gardens, as are still ponds, which in their reflection of the landscape teach us mimesis.

Mimesis is a sacred activity, for it attempts not to transform the world but to affirm it, or a portion of it, in the most profound sense of affirmation: mimetic reproduction. It is a process that says, "Yes, you are so worthy that I will to become you again and again and again." An object is sacred if it cannot be exchanged for anything else, and this is true of the mimetic object, which can only be mimetically reproduced. Conversely, the secular is defined by the market: anything can be given up if something better comes along. Ironically, the development of the secular was spurred by a process that mimics ritual mimesis: industrial mass production. Here the reproduction of countless objects from the same mold does not have the affirmative power of ritual mimesis, for the purpose of the reproduction is not the process of reproduction itself, but profit. Mechanical reproduction is only a means for producing objects and has no inherent value; ritual reproduction is its own end.

In its quest to break the bonds of a nonprogressive life of subsistence, Western culture has abandoned ritual mimesis as a grounding activity. This ancient form of sacred life cannot be regenerated through some kind of arbitrary construction, for rituals must grow out of the lived practices of a community, and our practices are inherently secular. Yet there are still ways we can engage in the affirmative power of mimetic activity. We have already discussed the most important of these ways: empathy. In empathy we do not seek to change another person but to know and accept them by reproducing their feelings and thoughts in ourselves. This is the bond that allows for communities to be formed. We can further extend this ability to empathize beyond the human realm to other living creatures. The extent to which we can empathize with other things is the extent to which we can feel the world as a home for ourselves. The world can become home only when we make it home—not by transforming it into objects for our consumption, but by reproducing it in ourselves.

We can also participate in mimesis through creating or appreciating the mimetic arts. Before Western art adopted the formalist stance of art for art's sake, it was grounded in the notion that art should mirror nature. This mirroring did not have to be a dull photographic imitation, for nature has hidden powers and forces that the artist can reveal. The mirroring of art was a way of affirming the natural, spiritual, and human worlds, of asserting worth through the act of reproduction. In shedding the notion that art must be mimetic, contemporary art has become fully free. All restrictive boundaries have been broken, and art can do anything it likes. But the cost has been high, for art has become so abstract and devoid of any meaning beyond itself and the affirmation of pure openness that it has become just one more secular process. Mimetic art, when it bursts with affirmative presence rather than mechanical reproduction, calls us into both the presence of what is being affirmed and the very act of affirmation itself. In the aesthetic experience, we mimic in ourselves the mimetic affirmation present in the dance or painting or sculpture and thereby become beings more capable of dwelling at peace with ourselves and the world. Dance performances, concerts, works of art, and architecture that mimetically responds to its environment may be impractical—they do not help us exploit the world, nor are they optimally efficient—but in calling us into moments of mimetic affirmation, they give us a connectedness that allows us to dwell on the earth as home.

Mimesis and meditation are, at first, practices that occur at particular times and places; but eventually they can come to characterize our way of being in the world. That is, we can develop the dispositions to be meditative and mimetically responsive in all of our actions and activities. When this development occurs, action ceases to have its restless, resentful backdrop and becomes fully free. Actions do not have to be done; the world is perfect just as it is. Nonetheless, I will to act. Why? Not because the world is unacceptable as it stands, but simply because I will to act. Life is change, creation, flux, movement. I affirm life; hence, I act.

There are a number of thinkers who would say that acceptance is the only way to dwell and have us all turn into Zen Buddhists or idealized American Indians. Others call us to the moral life as the life most fitting and noble for human beings; still others, the "realists," claim that life is egoistic exploitation and all else is illusion. These positions are all partial truths that capture a significant insight into what it means to dwell, but they have been captured by a hierarchical model which demands one way of life be best. Dwelling as full human beings means being exploitative, moral, and fully affirming. In the mature person, these ways of dwelling do not occur just in separate instances, but can come to be present in all activities. How can this be? Exploitation contradicts sacred acceptance; morality contradicts exploitation. Morality and exploitation demand action; sacredness demands inaction. These are contradictions, but human beings are not arguments in a logic text. We are concrete, complex creatures who can embody opposites as aspects of experiences and hold them in a dynamic tension. In this tension, this ecological balance, we learn how to dwell on the earth and make it our home. When the tension is broken and we become dominated by a single aspect, then some essential parts of our human nature become lost, and we exist as fragments, fragments that, by nature, feel isolated and alienated from the rest of existence. The crass exploiter, the person of unwavering moral standards, and the lonely monk attract us because they perfect a certain side of human nature, but in the end they are all distortions of human nature.

The etymology of the word *dwell* confirms this notion that dwelling involves the balancing of contradictory tendencies.[8] We now think of dwelling as inhabiting a place, but original meanings of 'dwell' included "to go astray," "to deceive or be deceived," "to tarry," "to hinder or be hindered," "to delay or be delayed," "to stun or be stunned." These original meanings point to a situational background for understanding dwelling, namely, the notion of being on a path trying to get somewhere. Dwelling happened when by one means or another someone was stopped, pulled off the path, and made to tarry at that place. Perhaps a sacred symbol halted us, or an epiphany occurred, or a landscape captured us with its beauty or symbolic power, or a people invited us to stay with them or forced us to. Whatever the reason, dwelling occurred when someone was pulled off the path and made to stop.

There seems to be reluctance, at least on the part of Westerners, to be pulled off paths. We want straight paths leading to definite goals. If we are to be exploitative, then let us do this fully without moral or religious restraints. If we are to be moral, then let us ceaselessly work for an ideal moral order, eschewing material goods and sneering at quiet contemplation. If we seek the sacred through meditation, then let us abandon the world. These paths arise naturally and claim us as the only ways to unify our lives or give ourselves direction.

Dwelling is what yanks us from our single-minded paths and stuns us into a momentary paralysis, a paralysis in which we can recall ourselves as full human beings. One thinks of Socrates' being stopped by his daimon, St. Paul on the road to Damascus, Odysseus awakening stunned in a mist on Ithaca, the Buddha's encounter with mendicants, Dante's being set upon by wild beasts. All were pulled from their paths and recalled to a part of life they had forgotten.

In dwelling, we live in three concentric worlds at once: the exploitative, the moral, and the sacred. Like most of us, dwellers are actively engaged in the world, attempting to satisfy their needs. They are concerned with food, shelter, social status, and friendships. They struggle with their sexuality and how to balance order and adventure. They strive for autonomy and try to create homes of beauty. Yet these pursuits are different for them than for others, for there is no stern set of the jaw, no fierce determination to win in the game of scarce resources. There is a twinkle in the eye and relaxed muscles in the face. The pursuits are not unbounded but have definite limits—limits within the realms of needs and morals. Limits give peace. But beyond the peace of limits is the peace of acceptance, the great "Yes" that tones each act of will with a quiet freedom from the will itself.

We in the West are not dwellers. Our modern world has been on a certain path now for several thousand years. Recent sages and events have tried to stun us and knock us off that path: Marx, Nietzsche, Freud, two world wars, the atrocities of the Nazis, the suffering of the Third World that the West has created. They have been partially successful, but we still push on, undaunted, alienated, restless, endlessly mobile, and toward what goal we do not know. We will learn to dwell only when we allow ourselves to be pulled off the path and are made to tarry. We tarry at a place when we allow ourselves to become contradictions. As contradictions we are always in the process of being stunned and knocked from our paths. Our moral natures stop our appropriative desires; our desires push us out of moral rectitude; acceptance takes us out of a world of moral import and the rage of desires, out of the worlds of justice and suffering, but soon our desirous self or moral self must overcome this static place. When we are able to live these contradictions simultaneously, then we will be full human beings and will once again be able to dwell on the earth.

Ecological dwelling is part of human excellence. As such, it is a paradox. As an ideal of human excellence, ecological dwelling demands that we transform ourselves and the world to be more able to dwell ecologically. But part of dwelling ecologically is to be free of ideals, to affirm the world and the self just as they are. Hence, part of the ideal of human excellence is not to be motivated by an ideal of human excellence. Also, the ideal of excellence posits that everything has a limit, and this includes limiting the ideal itself. Thus, in not having the ideal call us, in not trying to attain it, we attain it, at least in part.

This paradox stops us. We are stunned. We are urged to realize an ideal of excellence by relinquishing the ideal. We are asked to hold the ideal as the ultimate human good while renouncing the world of good and evil as a final reality. We are knocked off our path and caused to stay here, captured by this paradox. Now ecological dwelling begins.

CHAPTER 11

HEROINES AND HEROES
OF THE FUTURE

Today, in the West, we are unable to live ecologically. The ideal presented here is but a dim vision of life as it might become in the future. For ecological living to be a genuine possibility, there must be institutions to sustain it. But seemingly all of our present institutions are organized in terms of the two great enemies of ecological living: hierarchy and specialization. Governments, businesses, schools, professions, and even families are structured in hierarchical orders and demand specialized skills for carrying out particular functions. Since psyches tend to mirror the institutions that form them, we in the modern world seem for the most part doomed to have our thinking reduced to managerial analysis, our speech to pragmatic abstractions, and our dwelling to an alienated mobility.

Violent revolutions, the great vehicles of social change for most of our history, cannot generate the ecological future. For a revolution to succeed, it must have a hierarchical organization and a specialization of functions, characteristics that will be passed on to the postrevolutionary form of life. Revolutions also champion violence as a source of change and thereby reinforce the internal status quo of the fragmented psyche. Thus, revolutions can produce a change of governments and a redistribution of power and wealth, but for the psyche, they only produce more of the same.

How is the ecological future to be achieved? Mythology tells us that the most profound changes are catalyzed by heroes, persons who are able to break the limitations of past traditions and forge new worlds. Heroes always encounter and conquer obstacles that would destroy ordinary mortals. These obstacles usually represent important boundaries or limits to the structure of experience within a culture, a structure understood as so vital that anyone who challenges it is in danger of going insane or dying. The hero shows that life is possible beyond the boundaries.

Heroes first arose in the West to break the boundaries of a tribal, ritualistic, matristic, nature-oriented world. The obstacles they faced were monsters of nature (minotaurs, hydras, dragons, titans, boars, rivers, etc.), devouring female figures (Medusa, Amazons, Circe, Medea, etc.), or unconscious emotional forces (the underworld, Furies, etc.). The new world won by heroes such as Jason, Heracles, and Theseus was one in which humans could break from the stifling repetitive patterns of the tribe to individuate and have more conscious control over the fate of their worlds. The tribe is replaced by the political state.

The myths of this shift from nature-centered tribal life to political existence reveal dark ambiguities. While freedom and the possibility for a dynamic political and technological growth are gained, they come at the expense of subjugating that which had primary value in ritual society: women and nature, a subjugation which continues still. But the myths show that without a vital relation to nature and women, the male heroes cannot succeed. Jason cannot win the golden fleece without Medea, and when he attempts to leave her, he becomes a powerless fool. Theseus needs the earth goddess Ariadne to help him slay the minotaur and leave ritual Crete. But when he leaves her on Naxos to begin a new form of life at Athens, he falls into such a deep forgetfulness that he does not change the flag on his ship from black to white, and his father commits suicide. Heracles, the great civilizing force, becomes deranged and kills his family, must spend years as a woman (so forgetful is he of this form of life), and is killed when a centaur tricks his wife into putting the hydra's poison on his cloak. Fittingly, Heracles dies in a rage of burning skin. The myths hit the mark: if the founding of a male-dominated political system subjugates women and nature, then it will be plagued by fears of impotence, a competition so intense that males must kill their fathers, insanity, and desires which rage so strongly that they threaten to destroy any sense of wholeness we might be able to achieve.

The next generation of heroes, the Homeric warriors, are transitional figures. Like the earlier heroes, they are bent on individual glory and the destruction of the old female-centered world, as represented in Troy. But aside from Odysseus's postwar adventures and Achilles' battle with the river Scamandros, the obstacles these warriors face are not monsters of nature or devouring females, but other warriors. The boundaries crossed are not social taboos, but political borders, and the stakes are not the creation of a new organization of life, but the attempt of a certain form of life to attain political hegemony over all others. The old heroes destroyed the tribe to lay the ground for the creation of the state. The Homeric heroes are so closely identified with the state that their success and the state's success are equivalent. The struggle with nature and the heroes' connection to nature are forgotten.

In the *Iliad* we see what happens when the sacred woman (Helen) disappears and male heroes appear: a war of violent rage breaks out. The history of the patriarchal West is primarily a history of war, a history of who gains power over whom. But is this the history of women? Is their history to be written in terms of power?

The heroes from this time until the middle of the nineteenth century are political heroes. The boundaries broken are political, and the obstacles conquered are foreign peoples. From Alexander through the Caesars to Napoleon, the glory of the state and the hero are totally fused. The idea of a "proper boundary" for a state is lost; all states seek to control as much of the world as possible and use the hero as the primary vehicle for this extension of dominance. Boundlessness of power becomes the highest political value.

The realm of heroes and the breaking of boundaries shifts in the nineteenth century away from politics to economics. The revered heroes in the age of capitalism were the entrepreneurs who broke boundaries of personal wealth and amassed fortunes and power far beyond what earlier kings had dreamed of. No longer did young lads aspire only to be military heroes; their new models were Vanderbilt, Carnegie, and Mellon; their dreams were to establish economic empires, not political ones. Yet the goal of complete domination of a sphere of activity remained common to both politics and economics.

Indeed, capitalism calls for more than just a few heroes to break economic boundaries; it demands as a fundamental presupposition that there be no boundaries. What differentiates capitalism from all previous economics is its dynamism: profit is to be reinvested in production rather than used for the consumption of luxuries. This structure means that production must always be expanding, as must markets to absorb the increased production. If there were limits placed on production or on the exploitation of resources, markets, or profit, the system would be endangered, if not destroyed. Hence, capitalism itself is a type of hero, ceaselessly breaking boundaries and going beyond previous limits.

Capitalism also relies on the boundless as a breeding ground for invention and insatiable desire. Boundaries limit how we think and act; the boundless allows entrepreneurs to imagine and create new products without limit. Insatiable desires can never be fully satisfied because they admit no limits. No matter how much wealth we have, we always desire more. No matter how good our sexual lives are, we think we can have heightened excitement with a more glamorous part-ner. These limitless desires—for profit, wealth, food, adventure, sex, knowledge, individuation—are the fuel that keeps the expansionist furnaces of capitalism ever glowing.

Boundlessness is, of course, the conceptual equivalent of chaos, which, as the creation myths tell us, requires an opposite force to balance it, namely, the development of a structured society and per-sonal ego. Western society has balanced boundlessness by creating a complex hierarchical structure of specialized functions with clear boundaries, each of which can be boundless in the demands it makes on its practitioners. The psyche has responded to the boundless by creating hierarchical and analytical structures in the ego and by limiting its experiences to a small number of primary activities. The overly boundless requires the overly bounded.

So, while the loss of the category of "proper limitation" has helped produce the freest, most dynamic culture ever to exist, a culture in which life seems exhilaratingly open, offering fresh possibilities for thinking and living at every turn, this freedom is countered by the dark consequences of ego repression, the subjugation of women and nature, political totalitarianism, the limitation of specialized func-tions, and a struggle for power that threatens on the individual level to make life unbearably stressful and on the political level to annihi-late the world. In our boundless world everything—every psychological facet, institution, person, and nation—seeks to expand its power as far as market and legal forces will allow it. There are no natural boundaries to restrain anything. Nietzsche may not be correct, in a metaphysical sense, that everything is a will to power, but he is pro-foundly insightful in elucidating what has happened to the Western world and psyche. God had to die in the West because he was a boun-dary and a restraint.

A world without boundaries is also a world that cannot be a home. A place can be a home when it has a boundary and can be distin-guished from the foreign and dangerous. When the distinctions be-tween the familiar and the foreign, here and elsewhere, and the sacred and the profane get lost, then home makes little sense. Home is also a community where meaning is generated, a meaning that finds expression in the sacred language of the culture, be this religious or ideological. But in a world where the quest for power dominates all affairs, language loses meaning, for language becomes a tool by which we manipulate the world. Words are no longer to be trusted, and the community disintegrates. If the land and community can no longer be homes, neither can we be homes unto ourselves, for we can find no boundaries to our desires and have no power to fend off the demands of specialized functions. We become prisoners of forces beyond ourselves.

The final result of making the boundless a legitimate political ideal and an economic way of life has been the destruction of the possibility of heroism in the West. When the breaking of boundaries becomes commonplace, so do heroes. And a commonplace hero is hardly a hero. Hence, to a world that lives in the boundless, the astronauts' breaking of the great boundary of earth-boundedness is just another event, soon to be forgotten.

The hero has been replaced by the virtuoso. The virtuoso is a creation of specialization, a person who masters the skills of an occupation so well that she can play beyond the limits of the accepted norm at will. Nothing new is created, except new norms for the specialty. The obstacles that test the virtuoso's mettle are mere technical ones, the overcoming of them a mere matter of expertise and training. Unlike the old heroes, the virtuoso does not create new worlds but rather affirms the world of specialization and technological expertise.

How can there be heroes in a culture where breaking boundaries is the norm? Our new heroes will be paradoxes, for the boundary they must break is boundlessness. They must dare to declare the sanctity of limitation in a world that worships the unlimited and the boundless. They must give up the goal of heroes from the time of Homer to the present day: political and economic domination. In its place they seek to create an ecological world of mutual interaction in which the functions and limitations of all are honored.

While this new notion of heroism must be learned for men in our culture, it has been more or less present as a forced way of life for women, who in general have been confined within strict boundaries of marriage, certain tasks in the workplace, and certain functions in the community. They have not been allowed to experience the exhilaration and danger of boundlessness. For all humans, learning boundaries is an essential human task, but unless this learning is chosen freely, it will be resented. The courage and strength one feels in choosing self-limitation occurs only in situations where there is a real possibility for excess, for boundlessness.

Our new heroes and heroines will be the reverse images of the first heroes. The first heroes battled forces of nature, the tribe, and the unruly emotions to create civilization and the realm of the rational ego; our new heroes must battle the forces of civilization and the ego so that we once again can find our human nature and reestablish the earth as home. But this aim should not be interpreted as a regressive longing for tribal life. What our new heroes are seeking is the development of a new kind of living in which nature and culture are more symbiotically joined—in which reason, the needs, and the emotions work as partners in the common enterprise of human living, rather than as a set of domination–submission relationships. Like the old heroes, our new heroes and heroines will live in an ambiguous relation to nature and culture, not eschewing one for the other, but trying to achieve a precarious balance between them. Like those first heroic founders of Athens, Cecrops and Erichthonios, we must be humans with serpent tails.

The battle against an overly fragmenting, abstract, and repressive world is not fought with swords or guns, but with new ways of speaking, thinking, and dwelling. Our new heroes and heroines must risk having their hermeneutical thinking derided for lack of precision and analytical acumen, their symbolic speech laughed at as archaic and unprofessional, their balanced patterns of living inconsonant with the specialized lives of others. Indeed, the balanced life of the new hero and heroine (a direct opposition to the unbalanced life of the old) is an extraordinary accomplishment, but it will be scarcely noticeable by anyone in an age that demands ceaseless breaking of boundaries and ever larger accomplishments.

When the citadel of the hierarchical ego is smashed, and boundaries are placed on our various activities, needs, and capacities, then, paradoxically, we can begin to hear all the voices of the psyche and restore our fullness as human beings. The psyche will not be hierarchically structured into domination–submission relations—a class society writ small—but will be an ecosystem in which each need, emotion, capacity, and character trait has a legitimate place and voice. When each voice has a limit, then all can be heard.

How does one set psychic boundaries? How does one limit activities in an age when institutions are insatiable in their demands for time and allegiance? What gives unity to the psyche when the hierarchical self vanishes? The answer to all of these questions rests with the restoration of the Greek character trait *sophrosyne*. Usually translated as "moderation," "temperance," "balance," or "sobriety," the word *sophrosyne* literally means "safe-mindedness." For the Greeks, a mind was safe when each of its parts stayed within its own limits and the person as a whole did not try to go beyond human boundaries and become a god. *Sophrosyne* is honored not only by the ancient philosophers, but also by the dramatists and historians, as that habit of character that enables human beings to attain wholeness and avoid the tragic disasters that occur when we forget who we are.

However, the mind that must be kept safe is a foreign one to us, for the *phrēn* is the mind that resides in the diaphragm, not the mind located in the head (*noos*). The *phrēn*, or "chest-mind," is the place where emotions, thoughts, and needs intermix. These are not emotions, thoughts, and needs dulled, intellectualized, and civilized by a head-mind, but vital, powerful forces, each of which threatens through its immediate presence to dominate the psyche and make it forgetful of all else. *Sophrosyne* is what allows the *phrēn* to entertain these intense psychic productions without being overwhelmed. It does this by setting boundaries on every need, emotion, capacity, and psychic structure. With these boundaries in place, memory of what is most essential can remain intact and we can live full, balanced lives.

Without *sophrosyne* we do not have bad *phrēnes*, we have no *phrēnes* at all. For us who have lost *sophrosyne*, experience always occurs in the head, the place of the rational ego, and lacks the vitality and power that come when thought, emotion, need, and self intermingle in the more intense cauldron of the *phrēn*. Rather than balancing the competing psychic factors with *sophrosyne*, the rational ego uses repression to extirpate what does not fit its ego goals. *Sophrosyne*, by setting boundaries on every psychic component, keeps all of the psyche's constituents "safe"; repression raises some to seats of dominance and reduces others to servitude.

Aristotle says, "This is why we call 'self-control' sophrosyne: it 'preserves' our 'practical wisdom.' "[1] Here he connects *sophrosyne* to *sōizein*—"to save or preserve"—and *phronēsis*—"practical wisdom."[2] We preserve our practical wisdom when we are able to keep in mind a vision of what constitutes a worthy life in general and act so as to attain this vision. *Sophrosyne* can preserve our practical wisdom because it limits the desires and demands that press upon us, preventing them from overwhelming us with a rash impulse or a tyrannical, unbalanced way of life. Greek tragedy is rooted in heroes being in situations that unleash such powerful emotions and thoughts that *sophrosyne* is overcome and a rash irrevocable act committed. Living beyond tragic devastation is possible only when we retain our vision of a whole life and are able to control the pressures and impulses that would consume us.

Unlike the Greeks, the forces that knock us out of balance are not so much the emotions, but the ideals of excellence that are regnant in our society. The general pressure to develop the kind of psyche best able to excel in a technological world—a psyche ruled by an analytical, hierarchical ego—and the specific pressures to excel in whatever specific activities one chooses, especially one's dominant activity, make us forgetful of who we are as human beings and what constitutes our excellence as humans.

This value structure makes it almost impossible for us contemporary Westerners to develop the character trait of safe-mindedness. All character traits are habits and produced by reinforced habitual practice. That is, we learn how to set boundaries on desires and demands only by in fact setting such boundaries. Every time we say "no" to a desire or ego structure that threatens to dominate us, we become more *sophron* (safe-minded). This no cannot be the dominating no of ego control, for ego control itself must have a limit. Rather, the no emerges from the memory that keeps present the fullness of our human nature. That we can come to replace the dominating no with the no of memory is doubtful, for habits are developed in the context of childrearing, which in turn is set within the wider value structure of the culture, a value structure that in our culture emphasizes the domination of ego control, boundless desires, and specialization of activity.

Our new heroes and heroines will probably be older men and women who, while they have developed the character traits admired by the culture and lived out its values, have nonetheless been able to retain a memory of what we might be and admit a profound dissatisfaction with the culture. These persons will not, at the point of deepest unhappiness, attempt to drug themselves into oblivion or try even harder to meet the standards of excellence of the culture. They will still hear the voice of the psyche, which exists beyond that of the personality, calling out to the self—through disease, boredom, tension, mistakes, dreams, and visions—to overcome the imbalances that strangle the psyche and open up to rich multiplicity that we are.

The memories of these people will already have made them partially *sophron*, and they will build on this habit until the ego structures start to crumble and the emotions and needs emerge as vital forces. This process of self-overcoming is never without darkness and rage, for it is our very personalities we are destroying, with no firm knowledge that we will be able to emerge like the Phoenix from our own ashes. However diseased one's culture is, it is still the only home one knows; the path away from it is lonely and, for much of the trip, winds through a barren wasteland of destruction. We fill with self-doubt, for the end of the journey is dim and may only be a delusion rather than a vision. Courage is needed here: the courage of a hero or heroine.

With this courage we can develop the trait of *sophrosyne* and quit the domination structures of the totalitarian ego. We can then begin to create a balanced ecological psyche, a psyche that keeps at its center a memory of all that we are as human beings. The heart of this memory is not a remembrance of the past, but a vision of genuine human excellence and the ways of thinking, speaking, and dwelling necessary to achieve it. With *sophrosyne* and our vision of human excellence, we will once again be able to live as whole human beings and reap the full measure of happiness that is our due.

NOTES

Chapter 1. Introduction

1. Alasdair MacIntyre, in *After Virtue* (South Bend, IN: University of Notre Dame Press, 1981), locates the death of the Greek ideal in the Enlightenment, whereas I see the Enlightenment as a final permutation of this ideal. We differ because he emphasizes only one side of the ideal, namely virtues, leaving out what I take to be the core of the ideal: the psyche hierarchically organized by the power of reason.

2. See MacIntyre, *After Virtue*, chapters 10 and 11; and Adkins, *From the Many to the One* (Ithaca, NY: Cornell University Press, 1970).

3. See Martha Nussbaum, *The Fragility of Goodness* (Cambridge, MA: Cambridge University Press, 1986).

4. For Socrates, the universal (which, typically, was linguistically inexpressible) was found by dialectically working through definitions of moral terms, eliminating all forms that applied only to limited situations. On Plato's theory, universals are connected to forms, while for Aristotle the universal is embedded in a functional biology in which all the members of a species share a common end. For the Stoics, universals were the laws of nature with which one must be in harmony.

5. I use the Greek word *psyche* rather than 'mind' or 'soul' because 'mind' is too closely associated with consciousness and reason, while 'soul' is too closely associated with Christianity and the theory of personal immortality. 'Psyche' includes all the conscious and unconscious forces, structures, and capacities working within a person to produce activity; it will be further defined in chapter 3.

6. Plato, *The Republic*, in Hamilton and Cairns, *The Collected Dialogues of Plato* (New York: Pantheon Books, 1961), Book 4, 431a.

7. See MacIntyre, *After Virtue*, chapter 13.

8. Aristotle, *Nicomachean Ethics*, trans. Martin Ostwald (Indianapolis, IN: Bobbs-Merrill, 1962), Book 1, chapter 7, 1098a. It is odd that MacIntyre's analysis of Aristotle, in both *After Virtue* and *Whose Justice? Whose Rationality?* (South Bend, IN: Notre Dame University Press, 1988), fails to locate the biological telos of rationality at the center of Aristotle's ethical thought. Since MacIntyre places virtue in social practices and, thus, disconnects it from a biological function, it is understandable that he would want to read Aristotle as primarily a social philosopher rather than a biologist. But I think we must always see biology as the center of Aristotle's thought.

9. Aristotle, *Nicomachean Ethics*, bk. 10, chap. 8, 1178b.

10. The notion of a cooperative community living according to a common ideal is more a philosophic ideal than a statement of what existed in practice. While individual city states were undoubtedly more unified around religion and tradition than are our contemporary civil societies, they were still filled with factions. The concept of 'agon'—the contest—was as basic as that of community. Greeks fiercely competed against non-Greeks, against Greeks from other city states, and amongst themselves.

11. See *After Virtue*, chapter 5.

12. Three of the most important attempts to reestablish at least part of the Greek ideal are David Norton, *Personal Destinies* (Princeton, NJ: Princeton University Press, 1977); Alasdair MacIntyre, *After Virtue*; and Edmund Pincoffs, *Quandaries and Virtues* (Lawrence, KS: University of Kansas Press, 1986).

13. The distinction between pleasure and happiness and the relation of happiness to an ideal of human excellence will be discussed fully in chapter 2.

14. See chapter 10 for an explication of what is involved in moral reasoning.

15. E. O. Wilson, *On Human Nature* (Cambridge, MA: Harvard University Press, 1978), 7.

16. R. M. Hare, *Freedom and Reason* (Oxford: Oxford University Press, 1964).

17. See Robert Neville, *The Puritan Smile* (Albany, NY: State University of New York Press, 1987), chapter 1, for a discussion of why the proposal of any ethical system must be accompanied by irony. As he says, if ethics does not come with an ironic smile, it can quickly lead to totalitarianism.

18. See especially MacIntrye, *After Virtue*; James Wallace, *Virtues and Vices* (Ithaca, NY: Cornell University Press, 1978); and Pincoffs, *Quandaries and Virtues*.

19. Aristotle, *Nicomachean Ethics*, bk. 9, chap. 4 1166a. It strikes me that MacIntyre's love of Aristotle and hatred of psychotherapy do not cohere

exactly at this point. MacIntyre seems to think that psychotherapists are producing amoral narcissists, where what they are doing, according this theory, is making the patient's relation to himself nonnegating and positive. In so doing they are allowing a person who could not be moral before, due to ill relations in himself, to be moral. Not only is there not a conflict between psychotherapy well done and morals, as MacIntyre seems to hold, but rather they are mutually supporting.

20. This definition of virtue as a character trait that enables us to live well as a human being differs in some ways from the definitions given by contemporary virtue theorists. MacIntyre defines a virtue as "an acquired human quality the possession and exercise of which tends to enable us to achieve those goods which are internal to practices and the lack of which effectively prevents us from achieving any such goods." (*After Virtue*, 178). Since achieving goods in practices is essentially what constitutes living well for MacIntyre, we are in agreement about the definition of virtue, but not about what it means to live well. My definition is also in line with James Wallace's (*Virtues and Vices*) concept of a virtue as that which allows one to flourish. Our difference is that flourishing is left rather vague in his text, whereas I attempt to spell it out more fully. Edmund Pincoffs (*Quandaries and Virtues*) prefers lists of virtues to definitions, the closest thing to a definition being that a virtue is a trait that is likely to make us acceptable to others. While I think that virtues do do this, I do not think it is their essence to do so.

21. MacIntyre comes the closest of the virtue ethicists to developing a theory of human nature and a theory of living well. Living well is being engaged in practices within a tradition and in so doing developing a narrative center to the self. I do not think MacIntyre's narrative concept of the self is an adequate psychology of self—it certainly has no concept of the unconscious nor of how a narrative can solve the multifold issues in life that transcend one's story-line (see chapter 7). I also find that the key problem in ethics is a choice not between evil and good, but between competing goods. This being the case, it does not help us to know that living well means to be engaged in accomplishing the internal goods of practices; we need to know which practices are best for us.

22. Aristotle, *Nicomachean Ethics*, bk. 2, chap. 6.

23. A fuller explanation of the principles of ecology and their distinction from principles of hierarchy are found at the ends of chapters 4 and 7.

24. Gregory Bateson's *Steps to an Ecology of Mind* (New York: Balantine, 1972) appears from its title to be interested in an ecological structuring of the psyche, but it is concerned rather with how to develop an ecological consciousness of our environments.

25. In particular, I have been strongly influenced by Nancy Chodorow, *The Reproduction of Mothering* (Berkeley: University of California Press,

1978), Carol Gilligan, *In a Different Voice* (Cambridge, MA: Harvard University Press, 1982), and Jean Baker Miller, *Toward a New Psychology of Women* (Boston, Beacon Press, 1976). These authors are close to my own project of interweaving psychology with ethics. I am also indebted to my colleagues Judith Genova and Marcia Dobson for educating me in the many facets of sexism. I believe that gender discrimination is a pervasive structure that exists at all levels of social and psychological life. I am sure that despite my attempts to be aware of this discrimination and the help of a copyeditor with an acute eye for sexism, that the effects of such a structure are present in this text. Purity is not the issue; increasing our awareness and acts to correct this discrimination as it occurs in language and our socio/economic/political institutions is.

26. See Joel Kovel, *A Complete Guide to Therapy* (New York: Pantheon, 1976), 12; and Erwin Singer, *Key Concepts in Psychotherapy* (New York: Basic Books, 1965), chap. 3.

Chapter 2. Happiness

1. Herodotus, *The Histories*, trans. Aubrey de Selincourt (Baltimore: Penguin, 1972), 52.

2. Herodotus, *The Histories*, 53.

3. See Sophocles, *Oedipus at Colonus*, 1225.

4. Of the leading Greek heroes, Agamemnon is killed upon his return home by his wife, Aias (Ajax) commits suicide after losing a wrestling match to Odysseus for the armor of Achilles, who was killed while sacking Troy, and Diomedes refuses to return to an unfaithful wife and founds a Greek colony in Italy. The only hero besides Odysseus to return home is Menelaus, who must wander for years in Egypt and the East before returning to Sparta with Helen.

5. Aristotle, *Nicomachean Ethics*, book 1, chapter 7, 1098a.

6. Aristotle, *Nicomachean Ethics*, book 1, chapter 7, 1098a.

7. Oxford English Dictionary.

8. David Norton in *Personal Destinies* finds 'happiness' inadequate to express the Greek *eudaimonia* and uses that word in place of happiness. *Eudaimonia* literally means "the state of having a good *daimon*". As Jane Ellen Harrison points out in *Themis* (New York: Meridian Books, 1969) *daimons* are neither gods nor humans, but what humans become when they participate in a sacred ritual and take on the spirit of the tribe, especially the spirit of the tribal ancestors. Thus, a *daimon* is both a living particular mortal and a divine spirit. Socrates says in *The Symposium* that *eros* is a

daimon because it it neither human nor divine but an intermediary. He calls the voice which stops him from proceding with ordinary affairs his *daimon*. My analysis of happiness as the state in which the particularity of life is related to a held ideal captures the meaning of the *daimon* as a link between the mortal and immortal, and as a voice calling one to overcome momentary desires and to seek wholeness with the ideal. Since I think "happiness" can convey these meanings, I do not follow Norton in using *eudaimonia*, but I certainly follow him in holding that this is the highest human end.

9. Arthur Lovejoy, *The Great Chain of Being* (New York: Harper and Row, 1960).

10. Herodotus, *The Histories*, 76.

Chapter 3. Death of a Psyche

1. Aristotle, *De Anima*, book 2, chapter 1, 412b.

2. Heraclitus, *Fragments*, trans. Phillip Wheelwright, in *The Presocratics* (New York: Odyssey Press, 1966), 72.

3. *Hamartia* is what happens when one shoots the bow and misses the mark. It is commonly translated as "tragic flaw," or the character trait which brings about the downfall of a hero. However, this flaw is typically the strength of the hero, a strength which has gotten too large or out of proportion, a strength which misses the mark. Oedipus is destroyed because his reason pushes too far, Agamemnon is so kingly he forgets the wrath of a wife whose daughter he has killed.

4. Jean-Paul Sartre, *The Philosophy of Jean-Paul Sartre*, Robert Cummings, ed. (New York: Random House, 1965), 150.

5. Conrad Lorenz, *On Aggression*, trans. M. Wilson (New York: Harcourt, Brace & World, 1963), 264–5; quoted in Mary Midgley, *Beast and Man* (Ithaca, NY: Cornell University Press, 1978), 297.

6. Jane Ellen Harrison, *Themis* (New York: Meridian Books, 1969), 470.

7. The following thumbnail sketches of the various gods in no way do justice to their complexity, for each of them tends to take on a full complement of psychic powers. Yet, they all have certain defining characteristics that clearly distinguish one from another.

8. See Aeschylus, *Oresteia*, for an account of this transformation.

9. See A. W. H. Adkins, *From the Many to the One* (Ithaca, NY: Cornell University Press, 1970).

10. Thucydides, *Peloponnesian Wars*, trans. Crawley (New York: Modern Library, 1951), 191.

11. Plato, *Republic*, 370c. All quotations from Plato are from *The Collected Dialogues of Plato*, eds. Edith Hamilton and Hunnington Cairns (New York: Pantheon Books, 1961).

12. Plato, *Gorgias*, 493b.

13. Plato, *Phaedo*, 246.

14. Plato, *Republic*, 563d.

15. Plato, *Republic*, 423c.

16. Plato, *Republic*, 423d.

17. Plato, *Republic*, 351d.

18. Plato, *Philebus*, 20e.

19. Plato, *Apology*, 41d.

20. Plato, *Republic*, 441e.

21. Plato, *Republic*, 569c.

22. See Harrison, *Themis*.

23. The language I use here of "raping nature" is a mirror of language commonly found in the 17th and 18th centuries, which is poignantly detailed in Carolyn Merchant, *The Death of Nature* (New York: Harper and Row, 1983). I use this language not only to reveal a certain attitude toward nature but also to show how the female and nature were fused in this mentality which saw both as objects of exploitation. I am not advocating a return to the conceptual and symbolic fusion of sacred nature with the female, as some of "Goddess" and "Gaia" authors seem to want to do, for I believe that gendering of either the sacred or nature is dangerous, with significant social and political repurcussions. However, I am uneasy with leaving the sacred and nature merely neutered, for this leads to a decrease in eros and increase in objectification. Perhaps what is called for is an expansion of gender categories.

24. Francis Bacon, *Of the Proficience and Advancement of Learning, Divine and Humane: Works III*, 302, quoted in William Leiss, *The Domination of Nature* (Boston: Beacon Press, 1972), 56-7.

25. Descartes, *Meditations*, trans. E. Haldane (Chicago: *Great Books, Encyclopedia Britannia*, 1952), vol. 31, 98.

26. Descartes, *Meditations*, 98-99.

27. Max Horkheimer, *The Eclipse of Reason* (New York: Continuum Books, 1974), 97.

28. Friedrich Nietzsche, *Thus Spoke Zarathustra*, trans. Walter Kaufmann (New York: Penguin, 1978), 26.

29. Nietzsche, *Thus Spoke Zarathustra*, 26–27.

30. Nietzsche, *Thus Spoke Zarathustra*, 27.

31. Nietzsche, *Thus Spoke Zarathustra*, 27.

32. Nietzsche, *Thus Spoke Zarathustra*, 17.

Chapter 4. Ideals

1. See Karen Horney, *The Neurotic Personality of our Time* (New York: W. W. Norton, 1937) and *Feminine Psychology* (New York: W. W. Norton, 1973).

2. See R. M. Hare, *Freedom and Reason*, chapter 9.

3. More recently, Bernard Williams, *Ethics and the Limits of Philosophy* (Cambridge, MA: Harvard University Press, 1985) has attempted to show that no moral system can be finally justified or account for the vast multiplicity of ethical points of view in the world. Instead of bemoaning this state as a failure for philosophical ethics, he accepts it as the way things are and probably should be. He says that the only possible ground for having a universal ethic is if some structure of psychological or biological life could be determined as necessary for human well-being. Finding such a structure is the task of my work.

4. See Jacques Derrida, "Structure, Sign, and Play in the Discourse of the Human Sciences," in *The Structuralist Controversy*, eds. R. Macksey and E. Donato (Baltimore: John Hopkins University Press, 1970).

5. See chapter 7 for a full explication of the concept of personal identity.

6. Heinz Kohut, *Restoration of the Self* (New York: International Universities Press, 1977), chapter 4.

7. Erik Erikson, *Identity and the Life Cycle* (New York: W. W. Norton, 1980), 125.

8. H. Kohut and E. Wolf, "The Disorders of the Self and Their Treatment: An Outline," *International Journal of Psychoanalysis* (1978), 59: 413–25. Also, Erikson, *Identity and the Life Cycle*, 157–8.

9. See chapter 10 for a fuller exploration of this idea.

10. C. Fred Alford, *Narcissism* (New Haven, Yale University Press, 1988).

Chapter 5. Basic Needs

1. Garrett Thomson, *Needs* (New York: Routledge & Keegan Paul, 1987). In this fine little book Thomson argues persuasively for a theory of

fundamental needs, although he does not specify what the basic human needs might be. For him a fundamental need is that without which a person must suffer serious harm. Needs are an unimpeachable basis for value and always take priority in value decisions. They are inescapable in the sense that we do not choose whether or not to have them, and they do not depend either on our belief system or our current set of desires. Something can be a fundamental need for us without our knowing it or consciously desiring it. Although I read his book after I had written this chapter, I find it in agreement with the position I state here.

2. Carl Jung, *On the Nature of the Psyche*, trans. R. Hull (Princeton: Princeton University Press, 1969), 23.

3. See E. O. Wilson, *On Human Nature* (Cambridge, MA: Harvard University Press, 1978).

4. See Steven Jay Gould, *The Panda's Thumb*, (New York, W. W. Norton, 1980).

5. In relation to the need to come to terms with mortality, see Elisabeth Kubler-Ross, *On Death and Dying* (New York: MacMillan, 1970) and Ernest Becker, *The Denial of Death* (New York: MacMillan, 1973).

6. Shakespeare, *Titus Andronicus*, 2.1:80.

7. See Erikson, *Identity and the Life Cycle*, 57–67.

8. See Erikson, *Identity and the Life Cycle*, 100–105.

9. Leon Festinger, *Conflict, Decision, and Dissonance* (Palo Alto, CA: Stanford University Press, 1964).

10. Mircea Eliade, *The Sacred and the Profane*, trans. W. Trask (New York: Harper and Row, 1961), 33.

11. Charles Hartshorne, address given at Colorado College, Spring, 1978.

12. Gordon Taylor, *The Natural History of the Mind* (New York: Penguin, 1981), 14.

13. Heraclitus, *Fragments*, in Wheelwright, *The Presocratics*, 70.

14. Erich Fromm, *The Art of Loving* (New York, Harper and Bros., 1956), 8–9.

15. Thorstein Veblen, *Theory of the Leisure Class*, in *The Portable Veblen*, ed. Max Lerner (New York: Viking Press, 1958), 26.

16. Rom Harré, *Social Being*, (Totowa, NJ: Littlefield, Adams, 1980), 3.

17. See Irving Goffman, *The Presentation of Self in Everyday Life* (New York: Doubleday, 1959).

18. Veblen, *Theory of the Leisure Class*, 32.

19. Hannah Arendt, *Eichmann in Jerusalem* (New York: Penguin, 1976).

20. Erwin Singer, *Key Concepts in Psychotherapy* (New York: Basic Books, 1980), 118.

21. Erikson, *Identity and the Life Cycle*, 99.

22. Erikson, *Identity and the Life Cycle*, 122.

23. Nietzsche, *Thus Spoke Zarathustra*, 115.

24. Douglas Frame, *The Myth of Return in Early Greek Literature* (New Haven, CT: Yale University Press, 1978).

25. Martin Heidegger, *Poetry, Language, Thought* (New York: Harper and Row, 1971), 161.

26. Heidegger, *Poetry, Language, Thought*, 161.

27. Obviously, there is a long tradition of bargaining in religious history. Although religions may center on a relation to the sacred, they are concerned with many more needs than this one and hence are typically thoroughly immersed in the practical world. In short, there is much in religions that have little to do with the sacred.

28. Nietzsche, *Thus Spoke Zarathustra*, 217–8.

29. Rudolph Otto, *The Idea of the Holy*, in eds. John Lachs and Charles Scott, *The Human Condition* (New York: Oxford University Press, 1981).

30. Alfred North Whitehead, *Adventures of Ideas*, (New York: Free Press, 1967), 285.

31. The following discussion of beauty is deeply informed by John Dewey, *Art as Experience* (New York: Putnam Publishing Group, 1959) and Whitehead, *Adventures of Ideas*.

Chapter 6. Emotions, Capacities, Character

1. H. M. Gardiner, R. C. Metcalf, and J. G. Beebe-Center, *Feeling and Emotion: A History of Theories* (New York, American Books, 1937).

2. Robert Plutchik, "Emotion, Evolution, and Adaptive Processes," in ed. Magna Arnold, *Feelings and Emotions* (New York: Academic Press, 1980), 6.

3. Lazarus, Kanner, and Folkman, "Emotions: A Cognitive-Phenomenological Analysis," in eds. Henry Kellerman and Robert Plutchik, *Emotion: Theory, Research, and Experience* (New York: Academic Press, 1980), 200.

4. Carroll Izard, *Human Emotions* (New York: Plenum Books, 1977), finds ten basic emotions: interest, joy, distress/sadness, anger, disgust, surprise, contempt, fear, shame, and guilt. Sylvan Tomkins, "Affect as Amplification:

Some Modifications in Theory," in Kellerman and Plutchik, eds., *Emotion: Theory, Research, and Experience*, finds nine—Izard's ten minus guilt. Robert Plutchik, "A General Psychoevolutionary Theory of Emotion" in Kellerman and Plutchik, *Emotion: Theory, Research, and Experience*, finds eight basic emotions: anticipation, joy, sadness, anger, disgust, surprise, fear, and trust/acceptance. The analysis of emotions in this chapter closely follows the work of Plutchik and Izard.

5. Izard, *Human Emotions*, 86.

6. Izard, *Human Emotions*, 86.

7. Philosophical theories concerning the nature of intuition have, since Plato, been grounded in how intuition works in mathematics. I think this framework has distorted our understanding of intuition in everday life. In both cases thinking and connections are made beneath the level of consciousness and then a simple product is thrust into consciousness. In everyday life, intuition seems to concern itself with particulars, but in math and other intellectual fields, it works with connections of universals. I suspect there are at least several kinds of intuition which work in different ways (emotional intuition, intellectual intuition, practical intuition, etc.). I am most concerned here with emotional and practical life and gear the discussion of intuition to this realm.

8. Aristotle, *Nicomachean Ethics*, book 2, chapter 1, 1103a.

9. Ralph Waldo Emerson, *Emerson's Essays*, (New York: Harper & Row, 1926) 42.

10. Aristotle, *Nicomachean Ethics*, Book 2, chapter 6, 1107a.

Chapter 7. The Making of Psyche

1. Aristophanes, *The Birds*, trans. William Arrowsmith (New York: Mentor, 1961), 66–67.

2. The analysis of this archaic unification is taken from the works of Heinz Kohut. The best summary of his position is in his *Restoration of the Self.*

3. Kohut, *Restoration of the Self*, ch. 4.

4. Erikson, *Identity and the Life Cycle*, 57–67.

5. Kohut, *Restoration of the Self*, ch. 4.

6. See David Norton, *Personal Destinies*.

7. MacIntyre in *After Virtue* finds narrative unity to be the only sense of personal identity we need as human beings. I have a strong disagreement with this approach, for I think it fails to understand that the unconscious

early unification of the nuclear self is crucial for any adoption of a narrative, and fails to see that an ego identity is also needed to work through problems encountered in narrative pursuits. Not recognizing the archaic unity of the nuclear self is the major problem, for it is difficult to understand how psychoneurotic problems of self-indentity could occur if all we needed were a narrative unity. Many people with acceptable, even exciting, narratives have profound narcissistic personality and behavior disorders that cannot be explained in terms of failures in narrative structure. Hence, while I agree with MacIntyre that narrative unity is a crucial part of self-formation, I do not agree that it is the only or even the central part of the self.

8. Joseph Campbell, *Hero With a Thousand Faces* (Princeton, NJ: Princeton University Press, 1968).

9. The most thorough justification for how the concept of narrative is a necessary part of human experience is found in David Carr, *Time, Narrative, and History* (Bloomington, IN: Indiana University Press, 1986).

10. Erikson, *Identity and the Life Cycle,* 120.

11. See Rom Harré, *Social Being,* for how having a legitimate story is central both for the development of self and for having a place in the social world.

12. Note that these journeys all concern male development. However, the story I tell shortly concerning Eros and Psyche has most of the same elements present in Psyche's development—the loss of an untroubled early home, a descent into the underworld, the working through of impossible tasks, the coming to find a mature home in a love relationship.

13. Norton's *Personal Destinies* is an excellent example of how ethics and the concept of a psychological journey fit together.

14. See Erich Neumann, *Amor and Psyche* (Princeton, NJ: Princeton University Press, 1971) for a complete analysis of this myth.

15. See chapter 1, note 25.

16. Homer, *Iliad,* trans. Richard Lattimore (Chicago: University of Chicago Press, 1951), book 2, 204.

17. See Barry Schwartz, *The Battle for Human Nature* (New York: W. W. Norton, 1986).

18. Plato, *Republic,* 370c.

19. Sexuality that fragments from the rest of our human needs has become so common that it is the basis for a multi-billion dollar pornography business.

Chapter 8. Ecological Thinking

1. Martin Heidegger, *What is Called Thinking*, trans. J. Glenn Gray and Fred Wieck (New York: Harper and Row, 1968), 11.

2. *Mne* is a transformation of *men*, which is the root of *menos*—"mind."

3. Friedrich Nietzsche, *The Will to Power*, trans. Walter Kaufmann and R. J. Hollingdale (New York: Random House, 1968), section 918.

4. The mating of Zeus and Mnemosyne recalls the recent work of Nancy Chodorow, *The Reproduction of Mothering* and Nancy Gilligan, *In a Different Voice*. The qualities they associate with how women think and relate to the world are close to those I am associating with Mnemosyne, while Zeus represents their portrayal of male thinking and relating. The myth of the mating of Zeus and Mnemosyne and the theory I am proposing here resonate with Chodorow's and Gilligan's prescription that all of us need to integrate both ways of thinking and relating to be full human beings.

5. Harrison, *Themis*, 17, 453.

6. Harrison, *Themis*, 482.

7. See Carl Jung, "The Transcendent Function," in *The Portable Jung* (New York: Penguin, 1976), 273–300.

8. Nietzsche, *The Will to Power*, section 1850.

9. Heidegger, *What is Called Thinking*, 138–9, 144.

Chapter 9. Ecological Speaking

1. Jurgen Habermas, *Knowledge and Human Interests*, trans. J. Shapiro (Boston: Beacon Press, 1971), 217.

2. Shunryu Suzuki, *Zen Mind, Beginner's Mind* (New York: Weatherhill, 1970), 25.

3. Charles Scott, *Boundaries in Mind* (New York: Crossroad Publishing, 1982) gives a stimulating interpretation of how Hermes functions as a metaphor for psychic functioning. While different from the one offered here, I think the accounts can be taken as two aspects of this complex, many-sided symbol of Hermes.

4. "Hymn to Hermes," trans. Hugh G. Evelyn-White, in *Hesiod, The Homeric Hymns, and Homerica* (New York: G. P. Putnam's Sons, 1914) lines 260–268.

5. This historical material is taken from N. O. Brown, *Hermes the Thief* (New York: Random House, 1969).

6. Niklas Luhman, *Ecological Communication* (Chicago, University of Chicago Press, 1989) deals with the same problem. Luhman asks how any system which defines itself by a pattern of communication can recognize and deal with the environment of that system, which by definition, cannot be part of the communicative code. His answer of the environment's "irritating" the system and the system's "resonating" with the environment makes sense only if the environment can have some commonality with the communicative code of the system. A full analysis of what this commonality can be must lead, I think, to a discussion of symbolic language.

7. Sigmund Freud, *Introductory Lectures on Psychoanalysis*, trans. James Strachey (New York: W. W. Norton, 1966), 165–6.

8. Carl Jung, *Man and his Symbols*, (New York: Dell Publishing, 1964), 53.

9. Marija Gimbutas, *The Language of the Goddess* (San Franscisco: Harper & Row, 1989) shows that artifacts from the Neolithic era (7th millenium B.C.) reveal the presence of symbolic expression. I think her work is strong evidence for symbols being the foundation for meaning in language.

10. Paul Ricouer, *The Conflict of Interpretations* (Evanston, IL: Northwestern University Press, 1974), 298.

11. Aristotle, *Nicomachean Ethics*, book 9, chapter 4, 1166a.

Chapter 10. Ecological Dwelling

1. Alfred Margulies, *The Empathic Imagination* (New York: W. W. Norton, 1989).

2. Heinz Kohut, *How Does Analysis Cure* (Chicago: University of Chicago Press, 1984).

3. See R. M. Hare, *Freedom and Reason* for a justification for why universalization is a fundamental process of reasoning in ethical thought.

4. Hesiod, *Works and Days* in *Hesiod and Theognis*, trans. Dorothy Wender (New York: Penguin, 1973), 67.

5. My distinction between an ethics of empathy and an ethics of principles parallels Gilligan's distinction between the kind of ethics women tend to follow and the kind that men tend to follow in our culture. Gilligan and I agree that it is important for both genders to have value systems which incorporate the two types of ethics. See *In A Different Voice*, chapter 6.

6. There are a number of important books exploring the extension of moral categories to the non-human world. Two I recommend are Peter Singer, *Animal Liberation* (New York: Random House, 1977); and Tom Regan *All That Dwell Therein* (Berkeley, CA: University of California Press, 1982).

7. See Harrison, *Themis*, chapter 3.

8. This etymology of "dwell" differs from the one Heidegger offers in "Building, Dwelling, Thinking" (*Poetry, Language, and Thought*). Heidegger traces dwelling to the Old Saxon *wuon*, to stay in a place, and the Gothic, *wunian*, to be at peace, brought to peace, remain in peace. These terms fit with part of the concept of dwelling I am trying to elaborate, but do not have its paradoxical fullness. I am highly indebted to this article for offering the notion of dwelling as one which might take the place of action and for making me think about what human dwelling might be. Heidegger brings out the necessity for sacredness in dwelling, and shows how building can include this sacredness by gathering the fourfold (sky, earth, mortals, divinities).

Chapter 11. Heroines and Heroes of the Future

1. Aristotle, *Nicomachean Ethics*, book 6, chapter 5, 1140b.

2. Note by Martin Ostwald in Aristotle, *Nicomachean Ethics*, 153.

INDEX

Ideals, 2, 61–3; as contextual, 36, 61–2; and childrearing, 63; and self-worth, 63–4; critique of, 64–5; as necessary for development, 65–6. *See also* Excellence

Instincts, 40, 95

Interdisciplinary writing, 22–3

Interest/anticipation: as a basic emotion, 108

Interpretation, 151–2; and signs, 171–3; and symbols, 180–6; hermeneutical method of, 184–6

Intimacy: as a basic need: 86–9, 112, 193, 195; and ecological thinking, 164–5

Intuition, 115, 227n7

Is-ought problem, 15

Izard, Carroll, 111, 227n4

James, William, 82, 107, 117

Jason, 210

Jefferson, Thomas, 91

Johnson, Ben, 89

Journey, 25, 31, 32; as a central metaphor for the creation of psyche, 131, 136

Joy: as a basic emotion, 108

Joyce, James, 131

Jung, Carl, 159, 182, 183, 226n2, 230n7

Justice, 100; as part of moral action, 196–99

Kafka, Franz, 35, 82

Kant, Immanuel, 8, 11, 22, 23, 93, 139

Kierkegaard, Soren, 8

Knowledge: and the Greek ideal, 4; as a basic need, 94–97; capacities for gaining, 114–7; and thinking; 149

Kohut, Heinz, 24, 65, 125–6, 135–6, 196, 225nn6,8, 228nn2,3,5, 231n2

Kovel, Joel, 222n25

Kubler-Ross, Elisabeth, 226n5

LaBruyère, 89

Language: and the Greek ideal, 6; and the creation of psyche, 122; and signs, 171; as expressing different parts of the psyche, 173–4; ordinary language and the psyche, 175–77; as power of transformation, 179–80

Language, ecological: *See* Speaking, ecological

Leibniz, Gottfried, 54

Lewis, C. S., 133

Life: as different from personal order, 135

Limits, 207–8. *See also* Boundaries

Locke, John, 89, 91, 137

Lorenz, Konrad, 41

Love, 85, 92; as metaphor for creation of psyche, 100; as a reinforcer, 106; as part of morality, 133, 135. *See also* Intimacy

Luhman, Niklas, 231n6

MacIntyre, Alasdair, 7, 23, 197, 219nn1,2, 220nn7,8,12,18,19, 221nn20,21, 228n7

Making: metaphors of, 131–2

Malebranche, Nicolas, 89

Margulies, Alfred, 196

Marx, Carl, 11, 75, 134, 170

Marxism, 11, 207

Maslow, Abraham, 24

Maturity, 206

Meditation, 202–3

Medusa, 202–3

Melville, Herman, 39

Memory, 31, 167, 188, 215–7; and ecological thinking, 155–163; as stretching between the conscious and unconscious, 158; and thankfulness, 161–2

Merchant, Carolyn, 224n23

Metaphors. *See* Making, metaphors of

Mill, John Stuart, 11

Miller, Jean Baker, 134, 221n25

Mimesis: and empathy, 87; as a mode of knowledge, 114–5; and affirmation, 125; and sacredness, 202–5

Mind/body problem, 53

Morality, 195–201; and animals/plants, 200; problems with as a way of life, 201, as part of dwelling, 205

Moral psychology, 10, 14, 17–8, 19, 20; distinction of Riker's and Aristotle's moral psychologies, 118–9

Mnemosyne, 157–9, 188, 230n4

Multiplicity: as evil for Greeks, 4; and fragmentation, 19; and diversity, 20; and ecology, 20; in Plato, 43, 48; and basic needs, 75